Literary Criticism and Cultural Theory

Edited by
William E. Cain
Professor of English
Wellesley College

A Routledge Series

Literary Criticism and Cultural Theory
William E. Cain, *General Editor*

Museum Mediations
Reframing Ekphrasis in Contemporary American Poetry
Barbara K. Fischer

The Politics of Melancholy from Spenser to Milton
Adam H. Kitzes

Urban Revelations
Images of Ruin in the American City, 1790–1860
Donald J. McNutt

Postmodernism and Its Others
The Fiction of Ishmael Reed, Kathy Acker, and Don DeLillo
Jeffrey Ebbesen

Different Dispatches
Journalism in American Modernist Prose
David T. Humphries

Divergent Visions, Contested Spaces
The Early United States through the Lens of Travel
Jeffrey Hotz

"Like Parchment in the Fire"
Literature and Radicalism in the English Civil War
Prasanta Chakravarty

Between the Angle and the Curve
Mapping Gender, Race, Space, and Identity in Willa Cather and Toni Morrison
Danielle Russell

Rhizosphere
Gilles Deleuze and the "Minor" American Writings of William James, W.E.B. Du Bois, Gertrude Stein, Jean Toomer, and William Faulkner
Mary F. Zamberlin

The Spell Cast by Remains
The Myth of Wilderness in Modern American Literature
Patricia A. Ross

Strange Cases
The Medical Case History and the British Novel
Jason Daniel Tougaw

Revisiting Vietnam
Memoirs, Memorials, Museums
Julia Bleakney

Equity in English Renaissance Literature
Thomas More and Edmund Spenser
Andrew J. Majeske

"You Factory Folks Who Sing This Rhyme Will Surely Understand"
Culture, Ideology, and Action in the Gastonia Novels of Myra Page, Grace Lumpkin, and Olive Dargan
Wes Mantooth

"Visionary Dreariness"
Readings in Romanticism's Quotidian Sublime
Markus Poetzsch

"Visionary Dreariness"
Readings in Romanticism's Quotidian Sublime

Markus Poetzsch

Routledge
New York & London

Selections from Samuel Taylor Coleridge's *The Collected Works of Samuel Taylor Coleridge*, ed. J.C.C. Mays, Princeton University Press, 2002, are reprinted by permission of Princeton University Press.

Selections from William Wordsworth's *Home at Grasmere: Part First, Book First, of The Recluse*, ed. Beth Darlington, Cornell University Press, 1978, are reprinted by permission of the publisher, Cornell University Press.

Selections from John Clare's *Selected Poems and Prose*, eds. Eric Robinson and Geoffrey Summerfield, Oxford University Press, 1966, and from *Birds Nest*, ed. Anne Tibble, Mid Northumberland Arts Group, 1973, are reproduced with permission of Curtis Brown Group Ltd, London, on behalf of Eric Robinson, Copyright © Eric Robinson.

Routledge
Taylor & Francis Group
711 Third Avenue
New York, NY 10017

Routledge
Taylor & Francis Group
2 Park Square
Milton Park, Abingdon
Oxfordshire OX14 4RN

First issued in paperback 2014

Routledge is an imprint of the Taylor & Francis Group, an Informa business

© 2006 by Taylor & Francis Group, LLC

No part of this book may be reprinted, reproduced, transmitted, or utilized in any form by any electronic, mechanical, or other means, now known or hereafter invented, including photocopying, microfilming, and recording, or in any information storage or retrieval system, without written permission from the publishers.

Trademark Notice: Product or corporate names may be trademarks or registered trademarks, and are used only for identification and explanation without intent to infringe.

Library of Congress Cataloging-in-Publication Data

Poetzsch, Markus.
   Visionary dreariness : readings in Romanticism's quotidian sublime / Markus Poetzsch.
      p. cm. -- (Literary criticism and cultural theory)
   Includes bibliographical references and index.
   ISBN 978-0-415-97896-5 (hbk)
   ISBN 978-1-138-81359-5 (pbk)
   1. English literature--19th century--History and criticism. 2. English literature--18th century--History and criticism. 3. Romanticism--Great Britain. 4. Sublime, The, in literature. 5. Home in literature. 6. Country life in literature. 7. Nature in literature. 8. Setting (Literature) 9. Particularity (Aesthetics) I. Title. II. Series.

PR457.P64 2006
820.9'384--dc22
                                             2006018193

Visit the Taylor & Francis Web site at
http://www.taylorandfrancis.com

and the Routledge Web site at
http://www.routledge-ny.com

For Joachim and Hildegard

Contents

Acknowledgments — ix

Introduction
Placing the Sublime — 1

Chapter One
Sublime Descents: From Mountaintops to Home — 23

Chapter Two
Particularity and "Intimate Immensity" — 65

Chapter Three
Sublime Transport and the Making of Space — 111

Chapter Four
Simple Flowers and Familiar Soil: The Consolations of Everyday Life — 151

Conclusion
The Modern Remains of "Visionary Dreariness" — 187

Notes — 201

Bibliography — 209

Index — 217

Acknowledgments

All labours of this sort are necessarily the work of many hands and owe their conception to numberless conversations, both fleeting and enduring. For their insightful and incisive comments on early editions of the manuscript, their unswerving support, diligence and patience, I would like to thank Judith Thompson, Marjorie Stone, Ronald Tetreault, John Baxter and Anne Wallace. I am additionally grateful for all manner of assistance and encouragement from the Department of English at Dalhousie University and the Department of English and Film Studies at Wilfrid Laurier University. My work was generously supported by the Izaak Walton Killam Trust and the Social Sciences and Humanities Research Council of Canada. Additionally, I would like to thank the Faculty of Graduate Studies at Dalhousie University for their financial support of a research trip to the Lake District, Coventry and Northampton, as well as the Faculty of Graduate Studies and Research at Wilfrid Laurier University for a Book Preparation Grant. My greatest debts of love and gratitude are to my wife Jennifer, my son Samuel, my brothers Tobias and Friedemann, and to my parents, to whom this book is dedicated.

Introduction
Placing the Sublime

For literary critics and historians alike, the central place of the sublime in eighteenth- and nineteenth-century art, culture and aesthetics can neither be disputed nor overstated. Samuel Monk, for example, in a landmark treatise focused ostensibly on writers of the Enlightenment but almost from the outset disavowing the constraints of historical periodization, declares that "a study of the sublime in England comes very near being a study of English thought and arts" (3). More recent scholarship has tended to underwrite Monk's unbridled and indeed subsumptive enthusiasm for all things sublime. Jean-Luc Nancy, commenting on the enduring fashionableness of the sublime, offers the following retrospective prognostication about the genesis and impact of sublime analytics: "Beginning with Kant, the sublime will constitute the most proper, decisive moment in the thought of art. The sublime will comprise the heart of the thought of the arts" (50). Quibbling not so much with Nancy's sentiment as with his chronology (and surely his geography), Andrew Ashfield and Peter de Bolla remind their readers of the many *pre*-Kantian disquisitions on sublimity. Their elevation of the eighteenth-century tradition of the sublime to "the principal event" (1) in the history of aesthetics acknowledges the seminal contributions of such British writers as John Dennis, Joseph Addison, John Baillie and, above all, Edmund Burke. An obvious consequence of privileging a specific historical period as central to the tradition is the concomitant promotion of a select number of writers and works, thereby intensifying the debate over primacy. For what happens to Boileau, the niggling critic may ask, or more specifically, to Longinus, if Kant's work or Burke's is to be designated the benchmark of sublime analytics? Can one speak of a tradition of the sublime in England, or indeed elsewhere, without attending to Boileau's foundational translation of Longinus in 1674, through which the word 'sublime' first found its way into critical discourse? Well, as Angela Leighton points out, indeed, one can. Her turn

1

away from the rhetorical emphasis of *Peri Hupsous* to the naturally inspired theories of the Cambridge Platonists and to Thomas Burnet's *Sacred Theory of the Earth*, which, she suggests, "foreshadows many later descriptions of the workings of the sublime," specifically those of Wordsworth and Coleridge (Leighton 10),[1] marks yet another detour and reversal in the history of the sublime. My point in tracing the debate to this disputed juncture is simply to emphasize how distracting and ultimately unavailing ascriptions of chronology or disputes about textual primacy can be when the subject of study is as multi-faceted and polysemic as the sublime. In this much, then, we may concur with Samuel Monk, not in his blinkered claim that nearly all of English thought tends to the sublime, but rather in his recognition that sublimity—whether as sign or as signified—cannot be reliably pinched between a historian's fingers. The fact that the present study is centered on a specific regional literature and historical period—English Romanticism—is therefore not a reflection of a belief in the uniqueness of the sublime to that period, or still less, of an attempt to elevate Romantic sublimity to a position of theoretical preeminence in the history of aesthetics; what the focus on the Romantic period reflects, rather, is an acknowledgment of the variations and redirections that sublime experiences and expressions underwent in late-eighteenth- and early-nineteenth-century literature and life, and the consequent insufficiency of a single overarching analytical framework for an aesthetic of sublimity.

The sublime is, after all, concerned with excess, with that which transcends conventional modes and categories of representation. It attests to what cannot be properly contained or reconciled—what, in effect, cannot be thought at all. Attempts to 'think' it have, as the following passage by Michel Deguy so ably demonstrates, typically brought one to the very extremities of language from which one hangs over an abyss of meaninglessness:

> The sublime is the ephemeral immortality of the point gained, adverse speech snatched from death where the totality of becoming-and-passing-away concentrates itself. Sublimity at once belongs to the mortal curve and surmounts it, overhangs it tangentially like a remarkable 'turning point,' a pineal apex where the body is united with and suspends itself in the soul, a utopia of infinitesimal weightlessness as at the labile peak of the highest leap. Nothing remains 'in the air,' and the fall away from the sublime is fatal. (9–10)

Deguy's focus on the rhetorical or Longinian sublime represents, of course, only one strand in a still more convoluted and tangled body of analysis. As

Stephen Land points out, what makes the sublime such an elusive concept is that it "cannot be confined to either the word or the mind or the world but [. . .] is somehow realized in the meeting of all three" (38). Studies of sublimity, consequently, must be flexible in charting their domain; they must attend not only to theoretical constants and commonplaces but also to what is discursively liminal, what tends to disrupt and even break down the very forms and bounds that have, over hundreds of years of scholarship, endeavoured to give shape to an idea that is by definition formless and boundless.

The present study concerns itself precisely with this discursive and conceptual excess, with a sphere of experience central to and indeed inextricable from Romantic life and writing, but one that has hitherto been excluded from theorizations of the sublime. That sphere, as I would like to suggest, is what we loosely term the everyday, the ordinary, the familiar. By shifting the analytical focus from a sublime of magnitude and vastness, power and fear, to a sublime of small familiar spaces and common natural objects, a sublime of quotidian experiences and consolations drawn from meanest flowers, I propose to place the sublime not merely at "the heart of the thought of the arts" but at the heart of everyday life. Such a radical extension of the boundaries of transcendent experience, an extension, paradoxically, by means of contraction—what in William Blake's poetics is so aptly described as "see[ing] a World in a Grain of Sand / And a Heaven in a Wild Flower" (1–2)[2]—has a clarifying or distilling effect on our understanding not only of Romantic aesthetics but also, I would argue, of Romantic ideology. Indeed, an expansive revisioning of the sublime on the level described by Blake calls into question one of the most fundamental and persistent critical assumptions about the Romantic period, namely, that its "artistic output," as Roger Cardinal reiterates in a recent essay on the aesthetics of Romantic travel, "was governed by an urge to transcend the familiar and commonplace" (135). Insofar as this assumption, which Jerome McGann attributes to our "uncritical absorption [of] Romanticism's own self-representations" (1), has shaped our understanding of what is not sublime as well as what is, I shall offer it here (in its various expressions) as a context, a contradistinctive backdrop if you will, against which to elucidate an alternate, quotidian experience of sublimity.

Where the ideology of Romantic sublimity is concerned, a governing assumption is that writers of the period were in fact interested in transcending not only the lows of everyday life—what Wordsworth glosses as the "dialogues of business, love and strife" (98)[3]—but the terrifying heights of nature as well, all in the service of freeing the self from corporeal and cultural corruptions, a process culminating in a kind of self-apotheosis. To what extent this ideological framework is in fact a Romantic self-representation or a modern exegetical paradigm applied to Romantic texts remains a point of some debate and one which the present study will undertake to clarify; for now, let us simply say that its influence on our understanding of the period is profound. Indeed, for most of the twentieth century, an emphasis on conquest and self-aggrandizement has characterized the critical discourse of Romantic sublimity. A cursory survey of three seminal book-length studies of the subject suggests as much. In M.H. Abrams's *Natural Supernaturalism*, a work in which, to borrow Hazlitt's canny assessment of Coleridge, "[t]here is no subject on which [the author] has not touched, none on which he has rested" (62–63), encounters between the Romantic subject and nature's terrifying sublimity are presented as analogical reworkings of the Book of Revelation. As Abrams contends, "the Scriptural Apocalypse is assimilated to an apocalypse of nature; its written characters are natural objects, which are read as types and symbols of permanence in change" (107). Significantly, the role of the poetic imagination in these interchanges with supernature is elevated to that of a messianic "Redeemer" (119), which, by thwarting the threats and dangers of a sublime landscape, restores to the mind its lost paradise of sovereignty. John Jones's *The Egotistical Sublime*, essentially a reinterpretation of Keats's criticism of Wordsworth, likewise makes claims for the "larger landscape" (95) of the poet's mind—a topographic imagination—that somehow comprehends and contains the splendour of nature's mightiest prospects. For Jones, as for Abrams, the sublime is conceived as an assertion of the powers of imagination over those of nature, a subsumption, in effect, of the objective by the egotistical. Thomas Weiskel, finally, also considers the interrelated powers of the poetic imagination and the self in *The Romantic Sublime*. While his nuanced treatment of the Wordsworthian sublime does not confine itself solely to the Gondo Ravine and Mount Snowdon passages of *The Prelude*, his reading of these conventionally transcendent encounters borrows from both Abrams and Jones by foregrounding the role of a subsumptive or sublimating ego which "melts the formal otherness of things and reduces them to material or to substance" (59). It is only through the incorporation of natural grandeur, Weiskel argues, that "the Romantic ego approaches godhead" (62).

Clearly encoded in these three readings of the Romantic sublime is the language of Burkean and Kantian aesthetics and the concomitant assumption that the Romantics in large part simply adopted their formulations of transcendent experience, centered as they are on encounters with objects or phenomena that by their magnitude and vastness exceed the subject's capacity to represent them internally, thereby inducing a sense of awe or admiration. Although inspired ostensibly by the sublime object, this awe or admiration is ultimately reflected back upon the subject, given her/his capacity to withstand, despite fear, the surpassing might of supernature. In *A Philosophical Enquiry into the Origins of Our Ideas of the Sublime and the Beautiful*, Burke describes this moment of sublime self-exaltation as

> a sort of swelling and triumph, that is extremely grateful to the human mind; and this swelling is never more perceived, nor operates with more force, than when without danger we are conversant with terrible objects; the mind always claiming to itself some part of the dignity and importance of the things which it contemplates. (74–75)

Given that Burke throughout the *Enquiry* links the sublime to the divine, to the ultimate source of infinity (Brooks 17), the sublime encounter may be understood as enabling the subject to establish an affinity not only with the sublime object but also with the perceived presence behind it. What begins as fear, then, culminates in a subjective "triumph," a sensible participation in the power behind all "terrible objects."

For Kant, that power is associated not vicariously but directly with the subject. Indeed, his conception of sublime pleasure in the *Critique of Aesthetic Judgement* is reducible to a kind of egoistic satisfaction brought about by the mind's—specifically, the imagination's—capacity in the face of unlimited magnitude (mathematical sublime) and power (dynamic sublime) to assert its independence of these forces. Where Burke distills the sublime to a communion with divine otherness, Kant characterizes it as a recognition of transcendent power within:

> The astonishment amounting almost to terror, the awe and thrill of devout feeling, that takes hold of one when gazing upon the prospect of mountains ascending to heaven, deep ravines and torrents raging there, deep-shadowed solitudes that invite to brooding melancholy, and the like—all this, when we are assured of our own safety, is not actual fear. Rather it is an attempt to gain access to it through imagination, *for the purpose of feeling the might of this faculty in combining the movement of the mind thereby aroused with its serenity, and of thus being superior to internal and, therefore, to external, nature*, so far as the latter can have any bearing upon our feeling of well-being. (121, emphasis added)

In this interaction between natural and mental "might," the imagination, though unable to represent external vastness internally, nonetheless refuses subjection to the influences of nature and thus "locate[s] the absolutely great only in the proper estate of the Subject" (Kant 121). This idea of a subjective triumph over objective nature, intimated by Burke's analysis and more fully elaborated by Kant, lies at the heart of our critical conceptions of Romantic sublimity.

I will call this the mountaintop paradigm of the sublime, given its dual focus on the grandest aspects of nature and the aggrandizement of the Romantic subject. The effect of this paradigm on the direction of Romantic studies has been to designate a select number of writers and texts as essential to the canon, with the sublime becoming, as Theresa M. Kelley observes, "the arbiter of greatness in Romantic poems" (135). For the better part of the twentieth century, that has meant foregrounding the 'big six'—Wordsworth, Blake, Coleridge, Byron, Shelley and Keats—and tracing the essence of sublimity in their works. The aforementioned studies by Abrams, Jones and Weiskel draw their examples almost exclusively from this list and in fact even pare it down somewhat. Neither Abrams nor Jones, for instance, includes Byron, Shelley or Keats in his discussion of the sublime, and Weiskel entirely excises Blake from his thesis, given the poet's "perverse [. . .] insistence that only when vision is determinate, minute, and particular does it conduct to or contain infinity" (67). "[Blake's] sublime," Weiskel contends, "is not the Romantic sublime" (67). Notwithstanding such individual discriminations, the main thrust of our modern speculations on Romantic sublimity has tended, at least until recently, to distill the concept to a few salient examples or literary moments. A typical list might include Wordsworth's mountain-top rambles in France, Italy and Wales, the mythic scope and energy of Blake's post-lapsarian cosmology, Coleridge's opiate visions of stately pleasure-domes, the Byronic pre-occupation with transcendent solitude, Shelley's titanic depictions of suffering, rebellion and redemption, and Keats's poetic encounters with idealized or sublimated otherness. Not surprisingly, what these examples reveal about the Romantic subject has tended to the formation of yet another stereotype: that of the lone wanderer, usually male, who, exhausted by the grind of his diurnal round, seeks solace, refreshment or inspiration in the primeval purity of nature, and there discovers some trace of transcendent otherness, often gendered female, with which he communes and by which he is transformed, even if only for a moment. Until recently, this was the governing narrative of self and sublimity in Romantic poetics. Writers whose conceptions of subjectivity and the sublime fall somewhat outside the parameters of this theoretical framework, have, as Vincent de Luca notes in his study of Blake, been largely neglected by critics (3).

With the recent burgeoning scholarly interest in the works of lesser-known and hitherto marginalized Romantic writers, particularly working-class and women poets,[4] the focus and direction of sublimity theorists has begun to change. Feminist critics in particular have challenged the ascendancy of a sublime aesthetic built predominantly on, and continuing exclusively to foreground, the works of male writers. Their responses may be distilled into two general exegetical strategies: a rejection of the supremacy, relevance and efficacy of a sublime aesthetic or, conversely, the establishment of a specifically feminine sublime. Elizabeth Fay's *A Feminist Introduction to Romanticism* is clearly built upon the former strategy. In attempting to account for the absence of a sublime poetics among Romantic women writers, Fay argues that women were precluded from contributing meaningfully to the discourse of sublimity on the basis of direct discriminatory practice by their male peers.[5] Not only was it "usual for a woman writer claiming to have experienced the sublime to be mocked by her male contemporaries," but

> [w]omen were generally held to be biologically unfit for the sublime even when some did practice it, because men writers continued to portray women as incapable of real thought or imagination, and particularly incapable of vision. (14)

Significantly, when characterizing the sublime of the High Romantics, Fay does not associate it with either real thought, imagination or vision; on the contrary, its attempted leaps of transcendent thought end, in her estimation, in heaps of "silly emotion" (14). Thus, although the sublime, as a specifically "male achievement gained *through* women as female objects, [. . .] is closed off to women writers" (14), Fay offers little cause for bemoaning that loss. If anything, her argument intimates that female readers may likewise wish to close themselves off from the sublime.

In opposition to this view, critics like Barbara Freeman and Anne K. Mellor reassert the centrality of the sublime to an understanding of Romantic (and modern) aesthetics by positing a category of transcendent experience to which women not only had access but which they shaped exclusively. In *The Feminine Sublime* Freeman charts a middle course between Wordsworthian sublimity, which she claims "consume[s] the very otherness it appears to bespeak," and the Keatsean sublime, which "depends upon the self's awareness of its own absence" (8). Drawing on the work of Luce Irigaray, Freeman ascribes to female Romantics an incipient capacity for numinous encounter "in which the self neither possesses nor merges with the other but attests to a relation with it" (9). Particularly in the works of late-eighteenth- and early-nineteenth-century novelists like Fanny Burney, Ann Radcliffe and Jane Austen, Freeman notes a tendency "to employ agency in precisely the way that the Kantian sublime defends against" (76). Notwithstanding their emergent resistance to an inherited discourse of transcendent experience in which alterity is assimilated, female writers in the Romantic era were not, according to Freeman, uniformly successful in establishing a revisionist or transgressive aesthetic. Their use of feminine agency, she argues, is "almost exclusively reactive" (77) and their handling of the sublime verges rather on a parody than an outright rejection of the Burkean and Kantian models (79). For Freeman, the feminine sublime may begin at the turn of the nineteenth century but its full flowering awaits a thorough "disrupt[ion] [of] the oppositional structure male/female" (10), a breakdown, in other words, of the very categories that make otherness calculable and containable.

Where Freeman's study distinguishes only traces of resistance to the prevailing norms of aesthetic experience in women's literary Romanticism, Anne K. Mellor's groundbreaking *Romanticism and Gender* posits an outright rejection of those norms and the concomitant establishment of a new category of sublimity inflected by an "ethic of care" (3). Following Arthur Lovejoy's lead in pluralizing the period, Mellor introduces a binary of masculine and feminine Romanticisms, each associated with a distinct version or vision of the sublime. The masculine sublime is essentially the model I have already described, that of the solitary male subject incorporating or assimilating nature as the female other. As an experience it entails "isolation, a struggle for domination, exaltation, and the absorption of the other into the transcendent self" (Mellor 101)—a sequence corresponding precisely to the Burkean and Kantian movement from fear to self-aggrandizement. In opposition to this model of masculine empowerment Mellor propounds a reactionary feminine sublime, which in some instances adopts the traditional machinery of terror but equates it with patriarchal authority, and in others disavows the terms of Burke's and Kant's analyses altogether and instead locates the sublime in the bonds of family and community, and in a co-participatory relationship with the natural other specifically gendered as female. In support of this latter model of sublimity Mellor marshals as evidence the novels of Sydney Owenson and Susan Ferrier, and Helen Maria Williams's commentaries on Wordsworth's "Ode"—a selection which clearly reflects her commitment to a more expansive, inclusive, gender-balanced canon. Yet more than merely attending to previously unknown or marginalized female writers, Mellor's binary of masculine and feminine Romanticisms foregrounds a comprehensive vision of *all* the literature produced in the period. Her models of sublimity in like manner represent an attempt to account for all expressions of transcendent experience, to contain all its variations and permutations, all its inherent excesses, under the rubric of gender. Rather than disrupting the oppositional structure of masculinity and femininity, Mellor makes it the

Placing the Sublime

basis for her exegesis. Rather than questioning the degree to which the masculine sublime or mountaintop model in fact accounts for the various male expressions of sublimity, Mellor assumes its validity and establishes a countervailing model—the other half of sublime experience—on the basis of that assumption. I would like to suggest that such a totalizing and consequently reductive framework cannot but prove unsuitable to a study of transcendent excess. Indeed, even as Mellor attempts to open the field to include the works of previously marginalized writers, she excludes many others, both male and female, canonical and non-canonical.

Let me offer three examples of a kind of sublimity that falls clearly outside the bounds of Mellor's proposed binary. The first passage, so central to the Romantic poetics of self, needs perhaps no contextualization:

> At a time
> When scarcely (I was then not six years old)
> My hand could hold a bridle, with proud hopes
> I mounted, and we rode toward the hills:
> We were a pair of horsemen; honest James
> Was with me, my encourager and guide:
> We had not travelled long, ere some mischance
> Disjoined me from my comrade; and, through fear
> Dismounting, down the rough and stony moor
> I led my horse, and, stumbling on, at length
> Came to a bottom, where in former times
> A murderer had been hung in iron chains.
> The gibbet-mast was mouldered down, the bones
> And iron case were gone; but on the turf,
> Hard by, soon after that fell deed was wrought,
> Some unknown hand had carved the murderer's name.
> The monumental writing was engraven
> In times long past; and still, from year to year,
> By superstition of the neighbourhood,
> The grass is cleared away, and to this hour
> The letters are all fresh and visible.
> Faltering, and ignorant where I was, at length
> I chanced to espy those characters inscribed
> On the green sod: forthwith I left the spot
> And, reascending the bare common, saw
> A naked pool that lay beneath the hills,
> The beacon on the summit, and, more near,

> A girl who bore a pitcher on her head,
> And seemed with difficult steps to force her way
> Against the blowing wind. It was, in truth,
> An ordinary sight; but I should need
> Colours and words that are unknown to man,
> To paint the visionary dreariness
> Which, while I looked all round for my lost guide,
> Did at that time invest the naked pool,
> The beacon on the lonely eminence,
> The woman and her garments vexed and tossed
> By the strong wind. . . . (279–316)⁶

I have begun with Wordsworth because he, perhaps more than any other writer of the Romantic era, has been associated with a sublime of mountaintops and grandeur, a self-empowering aesthetic that Keats dubbed "egotistical." In Mellor's binary, Wordsworth is the poster-boy for masculinist transcendence, insatiably consuming nature's mightiest prospects and in the process annihilating the female other. The poet's noted tendency to "unite[] irreconcilable opposites" (de Man 142) is attributed by Mellor to his "arduous repression of the Other in all its forms" (149). Freeman, in like manner, distills the Wordsworthian sublime to a celebration of "the self's triumph over anything that would undermine its autonomy" (21). Whether or not one subscribes to these readings—and, clearly, they have gained currency in scholarly circles—their true exegetical scope has yet to be determined. When applied, for example, to the "spots of time" (XI.258), the first of which is excerpted above, they fail to explain either the inspiration of the sublime moment or its effects on the poet. Centered on common objects, settings and activities, and distinguished rather for their consolatory than self-aggrandizing effects, Wordsworth's "spots" or localized memories owe their sublimity to a perceived effusion of the numinous on the surface of everyday life. Thus a collection of ordinary sights—a pool, a beacon, and a woman bearing a pitcher on her head—is transformed into a scene of "visionary dreariness," a scene no longer amenable to the faculties of representation. Neither the boy nor the adult poet is capable of assimilating the otherness he encounters; still faltering and ignorant long after the moment has passed, Wordsworth can only claim a dim awareness of its power, its effect on "[t]he workings of [his] spirit" (XI.389), and the consequent urge to return to it and "drink, / As at a fountain" (XI.384–5). Significantly, the passage's emotive effect is derived in part from Wordsworth's tendency to evoke and then overturn our expectations of a more traditionally sublime moment. The narrative of recollection begins with separation, fear, and a symbolic encounter with death, yet none of these constituent elements moves the poet beyond words. The characters inscribed in the earth, the very emblems of supernatural presence, frighten the boy but do not transfix him; it is only on his reascent of the common, when the crisis of fear has abated, that he is truly arrested in his motion. And the source of arrest is not vastness, magnitude, or even death itself, but dreariness, dreariness and life—a lone woman struggling against the wind. In effect, what Wordsworth presents is an unfulfilled, unconsummated gesture to the Burkean machinery of sublime terror, which in turn is supplanted by a moment of quotidian sublimity centered on the things of everyday life. Wordsworth's attention to the everyday, to the wonders clothed in dreariness that are plainly scattered around us, forms a thematic thread running through *The Prelude,* from the raven's nest episode in Book I to the poet's ascent of Snowdon in Book XIII. Indeed, even this latter passage, so often read as a conventional representation of "circumstances awful and sublime" (XIII.76), is marked by a distinctly quotidian sensibility. What the limitless vistas from Snowdon's heights evoke in Wordsworth, almost as an afterthought to "[t]he perfect image of a mighty mind, / [. . .] that feeds upon infinity" (XIII.69–70), is a renewed appreciation for the imagination's capacity to "build up greatest things / *From least suggestions*" (XIII.98–99, emphasis added). Active, robust minds, he concludes, "need not extraordinary calls / To rouse them; in a world of life they live" (XIII.101–102). This aesthetic preoccupation with "least suggestions," with an immediacy of wondrousness, finds perhaps clearest expression in Wordsworth's Prospectus to 'The Recluse,' where commonness—or more specifically, a mind "wedded" to its varied manifestations—is invested with the most sublime potential:

> Paradise and groves
> Elysian, Fortunate Fields—like those of old
> Sought in the Atlantic Main—why should they be
> A history only of departed things,
> Or a mere fiction of what never was?
> For the discerning intellect of Man,
> When wedded to this goodly universe
> In love and holy passion, shall find these
> A simple produce of the common day. (47–55)[7]

This Wordsworthian capacity to trace the fabulous—"Paradise and groves / Elysian"—in "the common day" is also of course juxtaposed in the Romantic period by examples of a more concrete engagement with the "produce" of commonness. One need, in fact, look no further than to the work of William's sister Dorothy. Reflecting an extraordinarily intimate, precise and lively engagement with sensible reality, her journals and poetry speak to the operation of "a pragmatic domestic imagination" (Levin 169). Dorothy must not, however, be understood as a mere chronicler of daily tedium. Indeed, her recognition of the aesthetic richness of everyday life is as pronounced as William's, even though that richness, as in the following poem entitled "Floating Island at Hawkshead" (c.1820), manifests itself not as islands in the Atlantic but instead as a simple "slip of earth":

> Harmonious powers with nature work
> On sky, earth, river, lake and sea;
> Sunshine and storm, whirlwind and breeze,
> All in one duteous task agree.
>
> Once did I see a slip of earth
> By throbbing waves long undermined,
> Loosed from its hold—*how* no one knew,
> But all might see it float, obedient to the wind;
>
> Might see it from the verdant shore
> Dissevered float upon the lake,
> Float with its crest of trees adorned
> On which the warbling birds their pastime take.
>
> Food, shelter, safety, there they find;
> There berries ripen, flowerets bloom;
> There insects live their lives and die—
> A peopled *world* it is, in size a tiny room.
>
> And thus through many seasons' space
> This little island may survive,
> But nature (though we mark her not)
> Will take away, may cease to give.
>
> Perchance when you are wandering forth
> Upon some vacant sunny day
> Without an object, hope, or fear,
> Thither your eyes may turn—the isle is passed away.

> Buried beneath the glittering lake,
> Its place no longer to be found,
> Yet the lost fragments shall remain
> To fertilize some other ground.[8]

Bearing in mind William's subversion of the conventional machinery of sublime encounter in the first spot of time, we may say that Dorothy here effects an even more radical transgression of traditional aesthetic categories. Despite adorning her textual landscape with a verdant shore, blooming flowerets and a glittering lake and thereby gesturing to a poetics of beauty, she proceeds to make a dissevered lump of earth—the epitome of dreariness—the especial object of attention and the locus, ultimately, of sublime wonder. What makes dreariness so wondrous in this case is its apparent *un*commonness, its rare and brief appearance on the surface of everyday life. Indeed, Dorothy's description of the island is informed almost from the outset by an understanding of the transience of this "peopled world"—it will, as she relates, pass away. In accepting the island's passing as inevitable reality, Dorothy does not, however, diminish the sublime mystery of the event. Nature's reasons for engulfing this tiny world are not elaborated; the island is simply taken away, ceased to be given, not capriciously but according to some inscrutable rhythm or round (like that in which William's Lucy is rolled with her rocks and stones and trees). What brings this seemingly insignificant and unspectacular phenomenon into the realm of the sublime is Dorothy's perception of those "Harmonious powers" in nature that establish balances between passing and renewal, compensations, if you will, for apparent loss. For Dorothy, nature's compensatory economy expresses itself in the fact that, though the island's fragments are lost from view, they "remain to fertilize some other ground." What is lost remains: a fitting paradox of sublime excess just below the surface of this "world of life."

Like Dorothy Wordsworth, John Clare reveals in his work an uncommon fascination with common things. His prose fragments, journals and even his poems read at times like the field notes of a pioneer botanist or ornithologist, so rigorous are they in their commitment to particularization and detail. As Edward Strickland suggests, Clare is "the most purely empirical of the Romantic poets" (142). His is not, however, simply a mimetic aesthetic. Indeed, as the following excerpt, entitled 'Dewdrops,' from Clare's Northampton Asylum Notebooks illustrates, his empirical depth of focus is counterbalanced by a sense of childlike awe and wonder, a sense (if I may tweak a modern label) of realism's magic:

> The dewdrops on every blade of grass are so much like silver drops that I am obliged to stoop down as I walk to see if they are pearls, and those sprinkled on the ivy-woven beds of primroses underneath the hazel, whitethorns & maples are so like gold beads that I stooped down to feel if they were hard, but they melted from my finger. And where the dew lies on the primrose, the violet & whitethorn leaves they are emerald and beryl, yet nothing more than the dews of the morning on the budding leaves; nay, the road grasses are covered with gold and silver beads, and the further we go the brighter they seem to shine, like solid gold and silver. It is nothing more than the sun's light and shade upon them in the dewy morning; every thorn-point and bramble-spear has its trembling ornament: till the wind gets a little brisker, and then all is shaken off, and all the shining jewellery passes away into a common spring morning full of budding leaves, Primroses, Violets, Vernal Speedwell, Bluebell and Orchis, and commonplace objects.[9]

In 'Dewdrops,' depth of focus seems in fact to contribute to the semiotic shift experienced by the poet. And I say *experienced* because it is not he who summarily imposes an admittedly conventional metaphoric association on the landscape; the landscape, rather, appears to impose it on him. As he suggests, he is "obliged" to stoop down and touch the drops that appear to him as pearls and gold beads. Clare is, for a moment at least, genuinely confused by what he sees or thinks he sees. He twice, in fact, reminds himself that the spectacle before him is merely a trick of dew and sunlight, so powerful is its perceptual sway. Even though the moment of sublime defamiliarization is ultimately dispelled by a reassertion of reason, the catalogue of flora and so-called "commonplace objects" with which Clare ends his account has somehow lost its commonness. Primroses, vernal speedwell, bluebell and orchis are not always what they appear to be, or rather, do not always appear to be what they are; as signifieds they may carry multiple meanings and in that semantic excess, that moment of apparent otherness, they partake of the sublime. Given that "Clare's equation of the simple and normal—the commonplace in fact—with the sublime runs counter to the whole tradition" (Strickland 154), it is little wonder that he has been generally removed from discussions of Romantic transcendence and, as Juliet Sychrava notes, associated almost exclusively with a transcriptive aesthetic (82). As I would like to suggest, however, it is precisely the poet's commitment to a meticulous transcription of his surroundings that enables him to reveal the sublime within the folds of everyday reality.

Significantly, the three foregoing examples of what I mean by quotidian sublimity are by no means isolated responses to eighteenth-century aestheticizations of magnitude and terror. Whether by directing their gaze to the world immediately around them, to cottages and gardens, scenes of domestic labour and leisure, or else by turning with scrupulous care to the unregarded wonders of the natural world, to nests and solitary flowers, slips of earth and dewdrops, local and loco-descriptive Romantic writers evoke the sublime in the experience of everyday life. Alternately transfixing and being transfixed by quotidian reality, writers as various as William and Dorothy Wordsworth, John Clare, Robert Burns, Joanna Baillie, Samuel Taylor Coleridge, John Thelwall, Anna Letitia Barbauld, Mary Russell Mitford, William Hazlitt, Thomas De Quincey, Leigh Hunt, Anne Grant and Felicia Hemans evince a Blakean capacity to see a world in a grain of sand. Given that this simultaneously microscopic and telescopic perspective revitalizes a connection with an inherently broad and variegated sphere—that of everyday life—it yields a range of responses from "gentle shock[s] of mild surprise" (*Prelude* V.407) to moments of "visionary dreariness." Indeed, what I have termed an 'expansive revisioning' of the sublime accommodates experiences and expressions of simple wonderment, reverent awe, as well as those visionary soarings of imagination that, in Wordsworth's aesthetic, defy "[c]olours and words." Yet, as I will suggest, what these experiences have in common is their tendency to make the sublime productive of a sense of consolation, comfort, even community. Where Burke's aesthetic emphasizes the excitation of ideas of pain and danger, the Romantic quotidian sublime, distilled to temporal spots and the miniature worlds of everyday life, retains what Wordsworth calls in the 1850 *Prelude* a "renovating virtue" (XII.210)—a potential, that is, to nourish and repair the mind. Notwithstanding the current fashion of sublimity, there is to date no comprehensive theorization of the quotidian as a possible realm or vehicle of the sublime. Accordingly, the present study will offer a re-reading of the Romantic sublime as both a psychological event and a theoretical framework by widening its purview to include not only mountaintops but grains of sand.

By expanding the range of sublime encounters to encompass the everyday, the present study will also offer a theoretical position from which to collapse the gendered divisions of aesthetic experience promulgated by Burke's association of sublimity with masculinity and beauty with femininity, and by Mellor's no less polarizing distinction between masculine and feminine sublimity. Where Burke's classifications of taste established and maintained a hierarchy of aesthetic experience in which (male) transcendence not only eclipses (female) pleasure and love but is indeed more closely aligned with divinity itself, Mellor's paradigm assigns a reactionary aesthetics to women alone, and thus makes no attempt to account for the sublime experiences of writers like Robert Burns, Samuel Taylor Coleridge and John Clare, which differ sharply from her criteria of masculine transcendence. While Mellor does attempt to de-essentialize her gendered 'Romanticisms' by conceding that some writers were "ideological cross-dressers" (171)—she includes Keats and Emily Brontë in this camp—the label is itself connotative of a sort of marginalized literary perversion, an idiosyncratic excess bent merely on flaunting its difference. What I hope the present study might elucidate is a sphere of experience and writing that cuts across the boundaries of gender, a sphere predicated simply on a sensitivity to the wonders of everyday life.

This category of everyday life is one which contemporary criticism has assiduously excluded from its theoretical and ideological reflections on the Romantic period. Karina Williamson attributes this blindness to the prevalence of a "debased Romanticism, which rules that there is a category of experience and expression which is poetic and all the rest is ordinary and inadmissible" (187). Although Williamson does not make the connection directly, clearly the "poetic" category of experience and expression here implicated is the sublime, specifically as it is based on the Burkean and Kantian models of grandeur and self-aggrandizement. It would indeed not be unreasonable to suggest that the sheer weight of critical analysis devoted to a single version of transcendent encounter—that of the self feeding on mountaintop infinity—is one of the main reasons why, as Stuart Curran notes, "[q]uotidian values [. . .] have been largely submerged from our comprehension of Romanticism" (189). By neglecting the experiences of what is arguably the majority of Romantic writers, the "[m]ale labouring-class poets, as well as women of all classes [who] made everyday life and mundane fact their province" (Williamson 187), our conception of the period risks continued debasement and distortion. And as I have already indicated, such distortion also affects our understanding of major figures like Wordsworth and Coleridge whose poetic preoccupations are not reducible to a mountaintop aesthetic. What remains then is not only "[a] whole corpus of ignored work [waiting] to be mapped" (Shiner and Haefner 5) but an entire category of unelaborated experience. As the present study will suggest, this "*terra incognita* beneath our very feet" (Curran 189) consists at its most basic level of grains of sand.

The actual process of elaborating everyday experience and sublimity is of course rather more complicated than simply thrusting a spade in the ground or, in Keatsean fashion, "pick[ing] about the gravel."[10] As Laurie

Langbauer points out, "'The everyday' is a foundational category [. . .] so taken for granted [. . .] that it is almost never defined" (47).[11] Langbauer's imputation is obviously broad in scope, pertaining as readily to our habits of scholarship and criticism as to the way we live. The Hegelian epigraph, "Was ist bekannt ist nicht erkannt,"[12] makes the point still more trenchantly by distinguishing professed familiarity ('Bekenntnis') from true knowledge ('Erkenntnis'). In the more recent language of Pierre Bourdieu, the difference is one of practice and theory. A practice, for Bourdieu, is an "activity" or "relation" (*Outline* 1) in a broader social system by which that system manages to perpetuate itself. As Randal Johnson notes in his introduction to Bourdieu's *The Field of Cultural Production*, practices are typically "directed toward the maximising of material or symbolic profit" (8). A good example is Bourdieu's case study of parallel-cousin marriage in *Outline of a Theory of Practice*. The movement from practice to theory entails a recognition of the underlying strategies and rules that govern the deployment and efficacy of social practices. Yet notwithstanding the influence of Bourdieu's theories on the foundations of sociology, anthropology, and cultural studies, his elucidation of everyday life on the level suggested by the present study is somewhat limited. Indeed, the examples I have furnished from the Romantic period suggest a kind of quotidian experience and interaction that is far more elementary than the machinery of spousal selection. Wordsworth's perception of "visionary dreariness," for example, is centered on everyday activities (riding, walking) and common objects or settings (a hill, a beacon, a pool, a girl, a pitcher). Dorothy's sense of the wonders of natural regeneration in "Floating Island at Hawkshead" is likewise grounded in a local and familiar setting, a pool near the lake of Esthwaite, and centered on an unspectacular disappearance, a sinking "slip of earth." Clare's 'Dewdrops,' finally, recalls such basic activities as walking and natural observation, and weaves its sublimity from the threads of local flora and other unnamed "commonplace objects." In order to theorize these rudiments of everyday life—what is in effect the quotidian half of quotidian sublimity—I will turn to the work of Henri Lefebvre and Michel de Certeau, devoted as it is to an interpretation of the social, political and creative significance of the most common human behaviours and activities.

Lefebvre's *Critique of Everyday Life*, written in response to a perceived "deterioration of the conditions of existence" of the French rural working class in the mid-twentieth century, locates in the realm of everyday life "the sum total of relations which make the human—and every human being—a whole" (97). For Lefebvre, the everyday is inextricably bound up with our common humanity. By extension, theorizations of the everyday involve a reduction or distillation, by degrees, to an irreducible plane of universal existence and experience, a downward movement to roots and growth:

> There is a cliché which with a certain degree of justification compares creative moments to mountain tops and everyday time to the plain, or to the marshes. The image the reader will find in this book differs from this generally accepted metaphor. Here everyday life is compared to fertile soil. A landscape without flowers or magnificent woods may be depressing for the passer-by; but flowers and trees should not make us forget the earth beneath, which has a secret life and a richness of its own. (Lefebvre 87)

Even more dramatically than Curran's evocation of the "terra incognita," this passage invests the soil of everyday life with creative potential, with "secrets" and "richness"; the everyday, in other words, is not simply unknown because it is unregarded but also because it may exceed our faculties of knowledge. Like Curran, Lefebvre associates the cultural disregard and denigration of quotidian experience with a nineteenth-century aesthetic weaned on what he characterizes as "the marvelous" (105). Its Romantic manifestations, he argues, consist of "a mediocre compendium of witches, ghosts and vampires, of moonlight and ruined castles" (106)—an obvious imputation of the gothic sublime which, rooted in Burke's *Enquiry*, is associated principally with the novels of Ann Radcliffe and Matthew Lewis but may be traced back to Horace Walpole's *Castle of Otranto*, published only seven years after Burke's groundbreaking treatise. Where the marvelous seals its mysteries by varieties of imposture and illusion, the familiar, Lefebvre argues, is what is truly "unknown [and] . . . still beyond our empty, darkling consciousness" (132). Ironically, by thus pushing the everyday beyond the horizon of immediate comprehension while still acknowledging that it "besieg[es] us on all sides" (132), Lefebvre's analysis to some extent foregrounds its own theoretical and definitional limitations. Ably insisting on what the everyday is not, Lefebvre is far less precise in telling us what it is. His *Critique*, accordingly, intended as but the first of three volumes on the subject,[13] must be understood as a propaedeutic of sorts, a manifesto of intent, a wakening call to arms or, rather, to spades.

Michel de Certeau's *The Practice of Everyday Life*, written almost twenty years after Lefebvre's *Critique*, more directly elucidates the spaces of quotidian life through the behaviours that shape those spaces. By examining the basic function of routine movements and activities like walking, cooking, reading, even dwelling, especially where they take place within an urban grid of streets and buildings, de Certeau theorizes them as "tactics" or ways of "reappropriat[ing] the space organized by techniques of sociocultural production" (xiv). The everyday, in other words, becomes a sphere of political and social empowerment. Movement within and against the grid is not reducible merely to escape or resistance (Ross 69) but includes creative renegotiations of space. In de Certeau's paradigm, where one chooses to live and how one arranges domestic space become ways of defining and claiming that space, of defining and claiming the self.

Clearly, this ethos is reflected in the Romantic focus on the quotidian, which serves in part to counter the increasing marginalization and occlusion of rural domestic spaces and values by the accelerations of nineteenth-century industry and urbanization. The return to the mundane, familiar and immediate is a return to foundations, to stability. Yet by writing about everyday life and making its scenes the locus of poetic inspiration, Romantic writers were not simply shoring up fragments against the ruins of loftier expectations. Their work, as Williamson suggests, must not be construed as a defensive or reactive posture, shaped solely by what threatens rather than inspires it (188–189). More than merely encouraging a reconnection with local, domestic space, Romantic writers in a sense *create* the spaces they inhabit; for much as the act of sitting or walking or cooking is, according to de Certeau, "a spatial acting-out of [a] place" (98), so the recollection and transcription of such movements in writing serve to construct and compose the space itself.

The present study, in like manner, may be conceived as the spatial acting-out of an idea, namely that of quotidian sublimity. In order to define its scope and reveal its constituent materials and experiences—that is, to sketch spatially what I wish to expound theoretically—I have divided my analysis into a four-fold explication of everyday settings or spaces, everyday objects, everyday activities and experiences, and everyday consolations. Chapters One and Two (settings and objects) offer a material illustration of quotidian sublimity, moving telescopically from the broader spaces of home and domesticity to the individual objects that fill those spaces, while Chapters Three and Four (activities and consolations) elucidate the cognitive and experiential dimensions of quotidian sublimity, again refining and internalizing the focus from an elaboration of outward behaviours and activities to a reading of inward states and experiences.

Chapter One delineates the Romantic turn from mountaintops to home and the concomitant shift in perspective from limitless vistas to what Coleridge distinguishes as "[o]ne spot with which the heart associates."[14] From the many Romantic writers in both verse and prose who directly engage local and particularly rural life, I have drawn principally on the works of William Wordsworth, Robert Burns, and Joanna Baillie, whose evocations of cottage life and domesticity juxtapose the mundane and the marvelous, the familiar and the unexpected, thereby creating not only passive scenes of shelter but vital spaces of creativity and regeneration. The descriptions of everyday objects in Chapter Two are centered on selections from John Clare, Mary Russell Mitford, Anne Letitia Barbauld, Dorothy Wordsworth, William Wordsworth and Robert Burns, with especial attention given to the emergent nineteenth-century aesthetic of smallness and particularization. Adopting Gaston Bachelard's focus on "felicitous space" (xxxv), I explore Romantic engagements with the "intimate immensity" (Bachelard 183) of interior domestic space and the adjoining world of flowers, birds, nests and even insects. Chapter Three draws on the writings of John Thelwall, Anna Letitia Barbauld, William and Dorothy Wordsworth, William Hazlitt, Leigh Hunt, Thomas de Quincey and Samuel Taylor Coleridge in order to elaborate such everyday "tactics" as digging, washing, walking, skating, traveling by coach and reading, and to explore their relationship to "everyday creativity" (de Certeau xiv), under which rubric is included the simultaneous creation of space and literary text. Chapter Four, finally, elucidates the consolations of quotidian life as represented, on one hand, by what Keats terms the "simple flowers of childhood" and, on the other, by the familiar soil of home described in the verse of Dorothy Wordsworth, Anne Grant and Felicia Hemans. Familiar soil, as I will suggest, transcends the merely physical space of home, the enclosure, that is, of roof and walls, and corresponds more readily to recollected or dreamt space.

While the present study does not undertake to dispute the predominance of the Burkean and Kantian formulations of sublime experience in the late-eighteenth- and early-nineteenth century, it does question their exclusive hold on literary practice. Even though some writers like Coleridge and Wordsworth tended, at least theoretically, to support the general premises of Kant's, if not Burke's, transcendentalist aesthetics (Modiano, "Kantian Seduction" 18), their own verse, like that of so many Romantic poets, evinces a continual return to and concern with the spaces, the "tactics," the marvels of everyday life. In *Biographia Literaria*, Coleridge in fact distills the notion of poetic genius to this capacity to reinvest the quotidian with the freshness of first sight:

> to combine the child's sense of wonder and novelty with the appearances which every day for perhaps forty years had rendered familiar: [. . .] this is the character and privilege of genius, and one of the marks which distinguish genius from talents. And therefore it is the prime merit of

genius, and its most unequivocal mode of manifestation, so to represent familiar objects as to awaken in the minds of others a kindred feeling concerning them, and that freshness of sensation which is the constant accompaniment of mental no less than bodily convalescence. (49)

What this passage affirms, aside from the richness, constancy and restorative potential of the everyday, is the degree to which age and maturity may enervate our connection to the life of "familiar objects." Indeed, for Coleridge it is familiarity itself—a sort of habituated blindness—which inures us to the wonders of our daily surroundings and corrupts all "freshness of sensation." More seriously, the consequences of prolonged and uninterrupted "familiarity" entail a detachment from two vital sources of healing: the childhood self and the "kindred feeling" of humanity—what corresponds in effect to the bond between self and other. Familiarity, thus, is not associated with connection or community but with isolation. The work of poetic genius, conversely, because it is rooted in the everyday, effects a revitalized relationship with the spaces of home, with the self and the other.

If we, as modern readers and critics, have any incentive or advantage in embarking on a study of Romanticism's quotidian literature, it is surely our collective *un*familiarity with the terrain. Indeed, only wonder and a sense of novelty should characterize our engagement with a body of work so little theorized. The chief aim of the present study is to initiate that engagement and consequently to widen the traditionally narrow scope of sublime analytics. A less obvious but perhaps no less vital motivation has grown out of the research itself, specifically out of an examination of the ideological frameworks presented by critics to justify the exclusion of quotidian experience from their discussions of Romantic sublimity. Thomas Weiskel, perhaps most conspicuously of all, illustrates the prevailing critical ambivalence about a quotidian poetics in his discussion of Wordsworth's "leveling muse" (21). Despite conceding that for Wordsworth the most fructifying encounters between self and natural other "culminate in an imaginative community with nature at her simplest and humblest," Weiskel undercuts this "revolutionary" idea by claiming that "certainly *we* are no longer plunged into bathos by daffodils" and proceeds on that assumption to propose "a structure [of] the sublime that *transcends its local determinants*" (21, emphasis added). In other words, because "we" as modern readers no longer relate to or value an affective and imaginative community with natural simplicity, our theoretical models must transcend such "local"—that is, contextually particular and hence limited—preoccupations and instead frame history in our own image. It is precisely this kind of criticism, as McGann suggests, which, by "abolish[ing] the distance between its own (present) setting and its (removed) subject matter . . . [and establishing] an unhistorical symmetry between the practicing critic and the descending work[,] will be to that extent undermined as criticism" (30). What begins as criticism, in other words, becomes ideology. As an ideological stance, then, Weiskel's claim that we are no longer plunged into bathos by daffodils clearly compromises our understanding of the Romantic period and the role of the quotidian in its literature. No less troubling is what such a statement suggests about us as modern readers. For if we strip away the obvious and by now time-worn insinuation of Romantic histrionics, we are left with the rather humbling conclusion that we are growing not only increasingly insensitive to the wonders of everyday life, but that we flaunt an apparent indifference to that insensitivity as a sign of having grown up. My conviction, of course, is that this ideology of familiarity serves to misrepresent the present much as it has been used to misrepresent our understanding of the past. Whatever our contemporary relationship to the everyday may be, it is yet amenable to experiences of wonder and novelty. Familiarity, even if defiantly borne, is not terminal. Indeed, I would suggest that a reevaluation of the quotidian in our own day hinges on our willingness to engage it in the past.

Chapter One
Sublime Descents: From Mountaintops to Home

The history of English Romanticism does not yield a defining moment of reversal in the upward trajectory of sublime analytics, an irremediable turn, that is, from the ether of transcendent heights to the familiar embrace of home. Indeed, as I have already suggested, experiences of mountaintop and quotidian sublimity exist side by side in the literature of the period. Nevertheless, there are intimations, as early as the 1790s, of a longing to move both physically and imaginatively into those spaces or spots, as Coleridge notes, "with which the heart associates." According to Linda Marie Brooks, the reason for this retreat from natural magnitude and grandeur may have to do with the deleterious effects of such sublime encounters on the integrity of the Romantic self. Distinguishing between the positive or teleological sublime of Burke, which in a sense rescues the overawed subject by establishing a participatory relationship between it and the divine presence that underlies all supernature, and the negative sublime of Kant, which posits an outright failure of the imagination to conceptualize the transcendent object, Brooks claims that Romantic accounts of sublimity are typically negative in nature, tending rather to undermine than gird the self by threatening it with an unfathomable excess of meaning (2). While acknowledging that Kant does in the end restore power and efficacy to the subject through the intervention of reason, a faculty "which can contain the sky, indeed the universe, as a grain of sand" (22), Brooks nevertheless emphasizes the failure of the imagination to body forth this contained infinitude as a sensible image or concept. Weiskel's reading of Kantian aesthetics likewise maintains that "there can be no sublime moment without the implicit, dialectical endorsement of human limitations" (44). While this discursive shift to human finitude and the frustration of the Romantic imagination appears to yield a plausible explanation for the emergence of an alternate sublime aesthetic, the relationship between mountaintop and quotidian sublimity is, as I will suggest, rather more vexed.

For if the paradoxical recognition of inner boundaries in the contemplation of outer boundlessness contributed to the Romantics' longing for home and familiarity, for a sublime at their feet rather than above their heads, the domestically-oriented poems by Coleridge, William Wordsworth, Robert Burns and Joanna Baillie that I will be discussing in this chapter suggest that the numinous moments of everyday life are neither more coherent nor intelligible than those experienced in the face of natural immensity. Moreover, the notion that one version of sublime encounter grows out of the menaces and frustrations of another implies a mutual incompatibility between these experiences which the literature of the period does not support. Indeed, if we return to the example of Coleridge, we see evidence of an openness and susceptibility to transcendence at both the supernatural and mundane levels.

Coleridge's "Lines Written in the Album at Elbingerode, in the Hartz Forest," composed in Germany in 1799 as an entry in an innkeeper's guestbook, foregrounds the interplay between natural grandeur and domestic longing, between Kantian aesthetics and the poet's heart for home:

> I stood on Brocken's sovran height, and saw
> Woods crowding upon woods, hills over hills,
> A *surging* scene, and only limited
> By the blue distance. Heavily my way
> Homeward I dragged through fir-groves evermore,
> Where bright green moss heaves in sepulchral forms,
> Speckled with sunshine; and, but seldom heard,
> The sweet bird's song became an hollow sound;
> And the breeze murmuring indivisibly
> Preserved its solemn murmur most distinct
> From many a note of many a waterfall,
> And the brook's chatter, mid whose islet stones
> The dingy kidling with its tinkling bell
> Leapt frolicsome, or old romantic goat
> Sat, his white beard slow-waving. I moved on
> In low and languid mood, for I had found
> That grandest scenes have but imperfect charms,
> Where the sight vainly wanders, nor beholds
> One spot with which the heart associates
> Holy remembrances of friend or child,
> Or gentle maid, our first and early love,
> Or father, or the venerable name
> Of our adored country! (1–23)[1]

These opening lines, recalling the all-encompassing perspective of Johnson's *Vanity of Human Wishes*, introduce the poet at the moment of sublime apotheosis, when all of animated nature is before and below him. Albeit visually striking, the moment is also strikingly brief. In the space of three-and-a-half lines, the human usurpation of nature's "sovran height" is supplanted by a heavy, homeward dragging of feet. For reasons not immediately apparent, the poet's physical elevation has induced an inverse plunge in spirits. There is, notably, nothing in the moment of transcendence suggestive of a negative encounter, of an imagination overborne by conceptual excess and a consequent breakdown of the self's representational faculties. On the contrary, the poet is able to represent or define the limits of the "surging scene" below him by the "blue distance" of the sky above. He himself, moreover, remains distinct, differentiated, subsumed neither by the rolling waves of hill and wood nor by the vastness of the sky. The causes of his "low and languid mood," as he subsequently explains, have nothing to do with his own limitations but rather with those of nature: "grandest scenes have but imperfect charms." Specifically, he cites Brocken's distance from and unrelatedness to the spaces and affective associations of home as the source of its imperfections. The power of nature, in other words, is here quite dramatically circumscribed by the poet's own relational longings. Because Brocken is unrelated to "home," to the "Holy remembrances" that have shaped and sustained the poetic self, its "charms" are not able to transfix Coleridge for more than a moment.

Home, in this dialectic, signifies of course much more than the poet's "adored country" of England. As Duncan Wu (527) notes in his edition of the poem, Coleridge's evocation of home is drawn from Robert Southey's nostalgic *Hymn to the Penates* (1796) in which the latter pays homage to the Roman "Household Gods" (16)[2] or numina of domestic life. Claiming that these everyday muses "gave mysterious pleasure, made me know / Mine inmost heart, its weakness and its strength" (26–7), Southey, still in the heat of his pantisocratic fever, envisions a place "[w]here by the evening hearth Contentment sits / And hears the cricket chirp" (128–30). More significantly, he offers an exact template for Coleridge's own displacement and homesickness:

> Often as I gazed
> From some high eminence on goodly vales
> And cots and villages embower'd below,
> The thought would rise that all to me was strange
> Amid the scene so fair, nor one small spot
> Where my tired mind might rest, and call it *Home*.

> There is magic in that little word:
> It is a mystic circle that surrounds
> Comforts and virtues never known beyond
> The hallowed limit. (251–260)

While Southey's elevated perspective is not necessarily connotative of mountaintop sublimity, his textual attentiveness to the rich and varied life below his feet—a life in which he cannot participate, given his physical and emotional distance from it—clearly prefigures Coleridge's disenchanted view from Brocken. The fact that physical elevation need not necessarily inspire infinite perspective but instead may refine one's vision and redirect one's focus to the small, circumscribed spaces of home—embowered cots and villages—implies the operation of an alternate aesthetic. As Southey's characterization of home as a "mystic circle" suggests, he is evoking the enigma of a space which, though defined and measured, still exceeds the observer's grasp. Sublime excess, in other words, is produced by the juxtaposition or intersection of measurable and immeasurable limits. One may trace and thus determine the empirical boundaries of a home but its "magic" has to do precisely with what is "*never known*"—those "Comforts and virtues" which only have existence within the circle and cannot be translated beyond, comforts and virtues so unique and individuated that they cannot even be generalized from one home to another. Home for Southey is "hallowed ground" because only within its bounds is the secret language and experience of home understood; only within is the displaced self re-placed and centered; only within is the longing for home itself stilled.

Thus Coleridge is still disconsolate when he drags his way "homeward" because the home here implied is no more than a rented lodging, an inn at Elbingerode, a space almost as far removed from the poet's hallowed ground as Brocken itself. I say *almost* because the text does offer some evidence of an adjustment in the poet's ostensibly disconnected relationship to nature the moment he begins his descent. Indeed, the poet's attention to his surroundings, suggested by the level of descriptive detail, appears to increase even though his mood remains low. From Brocken's height he characterizes the world as a "surging scene," with indistinct woods "crowding" one upon another, unnamed hills rolling wave-like in a sea of uniform green; yet the moment he wends his way back to the inn, he distinguishes "fir-groves" and "bright green moss" speckled with sunshine. This visual specificity is accompanied by a heightening of other senses, particularly hearing. In the course of seven lines the poet perceives a "bird's song," "the breeze murmuring," "many a note of many a waterfall," "the brook's chatter" and a goat's "tinkling bell"—each one, as he notes, "*most distinct*" (emphasis added). Whereas the poet's sight from Brocken's summit "vainly wanders," his hearing, upon descent, is keenly attentive to the sounds of the natural world, seizing upon minute variations in pitch and tone. In effect, what Coleridge manages to evoke is nature's richness, complexity, even its dissonances—its seemingly infinite variety. Breeze and waterfall and brook have each a sound, a life, entirely their own. To subsume them all within a surging scene is to annihilate their individual essences—what Gerard Manley Hopkins many years later would characterize as *inscape*.

It may of course be objected that Coleridge's delineation of individual essence, begun, as it were, on second sight (and sound) when he turns homeward from Brocken, is irreconcilable with his theories of an "esemplastic" (*Biographia* 91) or unifying imagination. The emphasis on particularity indeed appears to imply a reversal or retrogression of the imaginative processes outlined in *Biographia Literaria*. Speaking, for example, of the 'secondary' imagination, which is likened to an echo of "the eternal act of creation" (167), Coleridge suggests that

> [i]t dissolves, diffuses, dissipates, in order to re-create; or where this process is rendered impossible, yet still, at all events, *it struggles to idealize and to unify*. It is essentially vital, even as all objects (as objects) are essentially fixed and dead. (167, emphasis added)

While the poet's reconstitution of woods and hills into a "surging scene" clearly indicates an idealizing and unifying impulse, the particularization of sight and sound in the poet's descent from Brocken seems at best a preliminary process in the imagination's re-creative teleology. The characterization of objects, moreover, as "fixed and dead" seems to undermine the value, indeed, the very notion, of individual essence. One must of course always be mindful, as Brooks (128) notes, that Coleridge's theories of the imagination do not lend themselves quite so readily to summary conclusions. Indeed, his long-anticipated disquisition on the mind's creative faculties—Chapter XIII of the *Biographia*—is celebrated as much for its tactical evasiveness as for its theoretical influence. Supplying a bogus letter from a friend instead of the promised '*tertium aliquid*,' the link, that is, between the physical universe and the universe of ideas and mental constructs, Coleridge distills his theory in a single paragraph outlining the aforementioned categories of primary and secondary imagination. No doubt recognizing the insufficiency of this expedient, he promises at chapter's end a "critical essay on the uses of the supernatural in poetry and the principles that regulate its introduction" (167)—an essay that was never in fact written. When he at last and unavoidably returns to the imagination in his characterization of Wordsworth's poetic genius, Coleridge offers a decidedly more measured account of its subsumptive tendencies:

> This power [. . .] reveals itself in the balance or reconciliation of opposite or discordant qualities: of sameness, with difference; of the general, with the concrete; the idea, with the image; the individual, with the representative; the sense of novelty and freshness, with old and familiar objects, [. . .] and while it blends and harmonizes the natural and the artificial, still subordinates art to nature; the manner to the matter. . . . (174)

In effect, what Coleridge asserts here is the integrality of the particular and individual to the evocation of the general and representative. Surging scenes of woods and hills must be grounded in a perceptual machinery precise enough to distinguish fir-groves and mounds of moss; the rush of waterfalls, likewise, must be measured in individual "notes." Such precision, moreover, ensures that the objects of external nature are redeemed from their fixity and lifelessness, that art continues to be subordinated to nature, and manner, to matter.

With these ideas in mind, one may theorize the homeward descent from mountaintops as a poetic attempt to return to the particular and familiar details of everyday life, the constituent elements of sublime experience. For Coleridge, notably, this return to the everyday is accompanied by a kind of sublime encounter that is distinct from the unifying visions inspired by Brocken. Indeed, he does not simply descend from mountaintops in order to return to them with a clearer perspective: he finds inspiration in the very act of descent. The poet's notebook account of his peregrinations in the mountains of Cumbria in the summer of 1802, for example, contains a telling episode of his scramble down Scafell along a steep ridge called Broad Crag. Having completed what he suspects is "the first Letter ever written from the Top of Sca' Fell,"[3] Coleridge begins his descent with reckless confidence:

> the first place I came to, that was not direct Rock, I slipped down, and went on for a while with tolerable ease—but now I came (it was midway down) to a smooth perpendicular Rock about 7 feet high—this was nothing—I put my hands on the Ledge, and dropped down. In a few yards came just such another. I *dropped* that too. And yet another, seemed not higher—I would not stand for a trifle, so I dropped that too. . . . (*Inquiring Spirit* 234–5)

The exhilaration of the poet's initial descent does not, however, occlude the very real and immediate effects of such 'drops' on his body. As he notes, "the stretching of the muscle of my hands and arms, and the jolt of the Fall on my Feet, put my whole Limbs in a *Tremble*. . . . I shook all over" (235). This textual attentiveness to the physical is particularly important to an understanding of the experience that follows. Being arrested in his downward progress by a drop "twice [his] own height" (235), Coleridge relates a striking sequence of events:

> My limbs were all in a tremble. I lay upon my Back to rest myself, and was beginning according to my Custom to laugh at myself for a Madman, when the sight of the Crags above me on each side, and the impetuous Clouds just over me, posting so luridly and so rapidly northward, overawed me. I lay in a state of almost prophetic Trance and Delight and blessed God aloud for the powers of Reason and Will, which remaining no Danger can overpower us! O God, I exclaimed aloud, how calm, how blessed am I now. I know not how to proceed, how to return, but I am calm and fearless and confident. If this Reality were a Dream, if I were asleep, what agonies had I suffered! What screams! When the Reason and Will are away, what remain to us but Darkness and Dimness and a bewildering Shame, and Pain that is utterly Lord over us, or fantastic Pleasure that draws the Soul swimming through the air in many shapes, even as a Flight of Starlings in the Wind. (235–6)

Not unlike Wordsworth's apostrophe to the imagination in Book VI of *The Prelude*, Coleridge's sublime reverie derives its rhetorical effect largely from what has preceded it. Having quite literally dropped from Scafell's summit, collapsed physically in the process of an arduous descent, and skirted the edges of a no less profound psychological lapse—the laughing descent into madness—Coleridge is suddenly upraised in mind and spirit by an apperception of those inner faculties, reason and will, which preserve the self from annihilation by outer excess.

This moment of sublime self-apotheosis is, as I will suggest, predicated on the act of descent, on the retreat from the heights of natural grandeur. Indeed, there is nothing in the poet's mountaintop letter to his wife that rivals the experience of his descent. Though obviously impressed by the views from Scafell's summit, Coleridge is neither cast into a spell nor beset by visions of infinity; on the contrary, he enumerates in some detail the scene before and below him, the "eleven ridges and three parallel Vales with their three Rivers [. . .] falling into the Sea" (233). This is clearly not what Kant classifies as '*das Erhabene.*' However, when the poet finds himself suddenly prostrate on a rocky ledge and sees above him the enormous crags he has just left behind, a sense of the sublime is vividly awakened. This latter moment, notably, depends on the poet's experience of the former, the experience of having conquered the summit. For what is so distinctive about Coleridge's epiphany—namely, the absence both of fear and of a breakdown of his imaginative faculties (what Neil Hertz terms the moment of "sublime blockage")—seems to stem directly from the poet's previous engagement with the sublimity of Scafell. Having already reached the summit, essentially measured its dimensions by the exertion of his hands and feet, and thus incorporated this phenomenon into his experience of natural immensity, he has already triumphed over the dynamically sublime. Consequently, the trance-like state he enters upon beholding the towering crags and clouds in descent is suggestive not of a suspension but of an assertion of his representational faculties; it is, as he relates, a "prophetic" state of "Delight" given his direct and unmediated recognition of the supremacy of reason and will over nature. He is, in other words, "overawed" by himself, by his capacity to overcome the threats of supernature—all without fear and that "momentary check of the vital forces" which Kant (91) deems essential to experiences of the sublime.

Not only is this moment of Coleridgean sublimity dependent on descent, but it seems to hinge more precisely on the poet's physical collapse. Indeed, one may suggest that the trance he falls into is partially induced from within, that is, by utter exhaustion, even as it appears to the poet to be entirely prompted by the lurid prospects of supernature. His body, in other words, his most familiar and immediate surroundings, may be at the root of his perceived transcendence. Certainly the fact that he looks up at all while climbing down is owing to the physical exertions that bring him to the point of collapse. His mind, accordingly, is wrought upon as much by the infirmity of his constitution as by the powers of nature, for it is only in the realization of the obvious disparities between flesh and rock that the redemptive workings of reason and will become apparent. When Coleridge at last recovers his energies and completes his descent, he again attends with fascinating detail to the corporeal evidence of his sublime encounter:

> I felt an odd sensation across my whole Breast—not pain nor itching—and putting my hand on it I found it all bumpy—and on looking saw the whole of my Breast from my Neck—to my Navel, exactly all that my Kamell-hair Breast-shield covers, filled with great red heat-bumps, so thick that no hair could lie between them. They still remain but are evidently less and I have no doubt will wholly disappear in a few Days.

> It was however a startling proof to me of the violent exertions which I had made. (236)

This "startling proof" of the body's participatory role in the experience of mountaintop sublimity serves to distinguish Coleridge's relation to natural immensity from that of most other writers and theorists of the period. He is clearly not some disembodied mind feeding on infinity. His attention to the "heat-bumps" on his chest while surrounded by cliffs and crags is suggestive of a simultaneously contractive and expansive perspective. Indeed, as Raimonda Modiano notes, Coleridge's belief in supernature as the only source of wondrous or numinous experiences began already to wane by the turn of the nineteenth century. His poetry, consequently, tends increasingly to "emphasize the 'finer influence from the Life within' and resist the influence of 'outward forms'" (Modiano, *Concept of Nature* 88).

An illuminating example of this retreat from natural grandeur is "Apologia Pro Vita Sua,"[4] written two years before the poet's sublime descent from Scafell:

> The poet in his lone yet genial hour
> Gives to his eyes a magnifying power:
> Or rather he emancipates his eyes
> From the black shapeless accidents of size—
> In unctuous cones of kindling coal,
> Or smoke upwreathing from the pipe's trim bole,
>   His gifted ken can see
>   Phantoms of sublimity.[5]

Clearly evident here is an incipient distrust of those "accidents of size" that distract the eye and raise it above the wonders of everyday life. Like Blake, who in *The Marriage of Heaven and Hell* predicates apperceptions of infinity on a thorough cleansing of "the doors of perception,"[6] Coleridge associates poetic genius with emancipated vision—a renunciation, in other words, of those grand objects or vistas typically associated with transcendence. Truly "gifted ken," he suggests, will discern sublimity in the most familiar and ordinary spectacles—a smouldering piece of coal, a smoking pipe, perhaps a fluttering 'stranger' on a grate. As these examples imply, poetic vision is for Coleridge dependent on magnification and particularization: it is, in short, true *in*sight. Interestingly, an analogue for this poetic insight is what Coleridge identifies in *Biographia Literaria* as "self-intuition," which he defines, in an appropriately microscopic metaphor, as the capacity to "interpret and understand the symbol that the wings of the air-sylph are forming within the skin of the caterpillar" (139).

The theoretical implications of this magnifying and particularizing insight extend, of course, far beyond the sensory or self-reflective; in effect, what Coleridge propounds is an emancipation not simply from the lure of immensity but from prevailing aesthetic conventions, including both the Burkean machinery of sublime terror and, as I will suggest, the Kantian model of transcendence. The physical turn from mountaintops to home is thus also a philosophical turn, and a radical one at that. Indeed, an overview of the aesthetic tradition inherited by Coleridge yields no theoretical basis for establishing a category of sublime experience on the details of everyday life. Beginning with Longinus, the everyday is in fact designated the antithesis of all that evokes sublimity. The opening chapters of *Peri Hupsous* draw unequivocal distinctions between what degrades and what elevates the poetic mind:

> [I]n our ordinary life nothing is great[,] which it is a mark of greatness to despise. . . . That is really great, which gives much food for fresh reflection; which it is hard, nay impossible, to resist; of which the memory is strong and indelible. (Longinus 11–12)

According to this aesthetic paradigm, "ordinary life" is only useful in the production of "great" or sublime thoughts insofar it awakens in the beholder a suitably virulent contempt of the ordinary. Conversely, that which is "really great" or inherently sublime, impresses itself on the mind irresistibly and indelibly; it possesses by its freshness or novelty and continues, when once considered, to generate thoughts of preoccupying unfamiliarity. As Longinus explains, the only natural objects capable of thus dominating the mind are those of physical or spatial immensity:

> as by some physical law, we admire, not surely the little streams, transparent though they be, and useful too, but Nile, or Tiber, or Rhine, and far more than all, Ocean; nor are we awed by this little flame of our kindling, because it keeps its light clear, more than those heavenly bodies, often obscured though they be, nor think it more marvellous than the craters of Etna, whose eruptions bear up stones and entire masses, and sometimes pour forth rivers of that Titanic and unalloyed fire. Regarding all such things we may say this, that what is serviceable or perhaps necessary to man, man can procure; what passes his thought wins his wonder. (65–66)

Longinus's seemingly intuitive association of smallness with transparency and immensity with obscurity leads him to establish a hierarchy of aesthetic experience that persists in large part to the present day. Because smallness and familiarity are transparent or *seen through*, they are immediately known and made "serviceable," that is, put under the dominion of human thought and action; immensity, on the other hand, because it is neither immediately nor completely amenable to sensory experience, "passes thought" and becomes an object of perpetual wonder and desire. What results is the effective sundering of everyday life from the realms of wonder, and this indeed may be Longinus's most significant contribution to the history of aesthetics.

For theorists of the English Enlightenment, notably, Longinus's work offered ample scope for critique, revision and elaboration—not because of its evident disdain for ordinary life, but rather for its failure to establish or even speculate on the "physical law" that enables the cognitive leaps from smallness to clarity, and immensity to wonder. As Ashfield and de Bolla suggest, for Augustan writers, aesthetics was "not primarily about art [or rhetorical criticism] but about how we are formed as subjects, and how as subjects we go about making sense of our experience" (2). The experience they were most interested in clarifying—namely the sublime—was nevertheless deemed, in clear accordance with the Longinian paradigm, to have no relation to everyday life. Thus, in attempting to answer the central question, 'What is it that moves me?' theorists like Joseph Addison lifted their gaze unvaryingly above and beyond the particular scenes and spaces of quotidian existence to manifestations of natural grandeur. The reason for this visual adjustment, as Addison explains in *The Spectator* (No. 412), is that

> [t]he Mind of Man naturally hates every thing that looks like a Restraint upon it, and is apt to fancy itself under a sort of Confinement, when the Sight is pent up in a narrow Compass. . . . On the contrary, a spacious Horison is an Image of Liberty, where the eye has Room to range abroad, to expatiate at large on the Immensity of its Views, and to lose itself amidst the Variety of Objects that offer themselves to its Observation. (336)

Like Longinus, Addison is here making an implicit claim for the transparency or intelligibility of all that falls readily within the scope of (visual) perception. The small scenes of home and hearth, no matter how variegated, represent a "confinement" to the roving eye because it cannot "lose itself" in them; simply put, it cannot exceed their known (i.e. perceived) limits. This somewhat paradoxical desire for a perceptual freedom that enables the loss of representational control is only satisfied, according to Addison, by intercourse with unfamiliarity:

> Every thing that is *new* or *uncommon* raises a Pleasure in the Imagination, because it fills the Soul with an agreeable Surprise, gratifies its Curiosity, and gives it an Idea of which it was not possessed before. We are, indeed, so often conversant with one Set of Objects, and tired out with so many repeated Shows of the same Things, that whatever is *new* or *uncommon* contributes a little to vary Human Life, and to divert our Minds, for a while with the Strangeness of its Appearance: It serves us for a kind of Refreshment, and takes off from that Satiety we are apt to complain of in our usual and ordinary Entertainments. (336)

Here again everyday life is relegated to a sphere of established, or rather, exhausted knowledge, its objects serving only to tire and depress the imagination. The acquisition of such knowledge, moreover, is dependent not on any formal method of study or inquiry but simply on a state of familiarity with the objects and scenes in question; as Addison suggests, to be "conversant" with everyday life is enough to know it fully, enough apparently to induce boredom. Ironically, the effects of this degradation of commonness redound also upon the sublime itself, which, in Addison's terms, becomes little more than a physical stimulant, an antidote to listlessness, a momentary bump in the everyday rut of sensory torpidity.

Reacting to the predominantly corporeal focus of Addison's sublime aesthetic, John Baillie in *An essay on the sublime* (1747) transforms the experience into a state of psychical and moral exaltation. Thus what begins as an inundation of the senses serves ultimately (and universally) to buoy the soul:

> every Person upon seeing a grand Object is affected with something which as it were extends his own Being, and expands it to a kind of Immensity. Thus in viewing the Heavens, how is the Soul elevated; and stretching itself to larger Scenes and more extended Prospects, in a noble Enthusiasm of Grandeur quits the narrow Earth, darts from Planet to Planet, and takes in Worlds at one View! (4)

Baillie's proposal of an expansive movement of the soul analogous to that of the eye, an unfettered ranging, that is, over the object of immensity, is a mainstay in almost all subsequent discourses on the sublime. Unlike the eye, of course, the movement of the soul is not delimited by the object itself; on the contrary, the soul takes on the duality of sense and imagination, combining the rigours of thorough perceptual exploration with the transcendent leaps from perceptible reality to unbounded ideation. More importantly, by taking in "worlds at one view," the soul not only exercises its experiential and creative faculties but also effects a moral elevation of the subject. As Baillie points out, natural sublimity inspires "a *noble* enthusiasm of grandeur" (emphasis added). In explaining the source of this nobleness, Baillie offers another and perhaps still more influential analogy: "We often confess the sublime as we do the deity; it fills and dilates our soul without [us] being able to penetrate into its nature, and define its essence" (5). The direct experience and subsequent contemplation of sublimity, in other words, represent forms of spiritual devotion in which the subject participates, even if only partially and momentarily, in an existence greater than itself. For Baillie, as for Longinus and Addison, this greater existence is associated exclusively with natural immensity:

> We know by Experience, that nothing produces this Elevation equal to large Prospects, vast extended Views, Mountains, the Heavens, and an immense Ocean—but what in these Objects affects us? for we can view, without being the least exalted, a little Brook, although as smooth a Surface, nay, clearer Stream than the Nile or Danube; but can we behold these vast Rivers, or rather, the vaster Ocean, without feeling an elevated Pleasure? A flowery Vale, or the Verdure of a Hill, may charm; but to fill the Soul, and raise it to sublime Sensations, the Earth must rise into an Alp, or Pyrrhenean, and Mountains piled upon Mountains, reach to the very Heavens. . . . Is it not, therefore, the Vastness of these Objects which elevates us, and shall we not by looking a little narrowly into the Mind be convinced that large Objects only are fitted to raise this Exaltedness? (5–6)

Holding to the notion of a direct, literal correspondence between physical (objective) and soulful (subjective) elevation, Baillie dismisses the lesser prospects of everyday life as merely transparent charms. Flowery vales and hillside verdure have, as he suggests, only superficial effects on the subject, their pleasures neither "elevating" nor penetrating deeply enough to "fill the soul." In moral terms, these essentially perceptual diversions fail to ennoble the subject, to exalt her/him through a communion with transcendent greatness. Although Baillie does not trace this argumentative thread to its logical conclusion by positing a link between the contemplation of commonness or littleness and the subject's *de*moralization, he does in fact characterize the things and spaces of everyday life as encumbrances to the achievement of our highest moral potential:

> The Soul naturally supposes herself present to all the Objects she perceives, and has lower or higher Conceptions of her own Excellency, as this Extensiveness of her Being is more or less limited. An universal Presence is one of the sublime Attributes of the Deity; then how much greater an Existence must the Soul imagine herself, when contemplating the Heavens she takes in the mighty Orbs of the Planets, and is present to a Universe, than when shrunk into the narrow Space of a Room, and how much nearer advancing to the Perfections of the universal Presence? (6)

The suggestion that intercourse with natural immensity facilitates one's advance to "the perfections of the universe" shifts Baillie's discussion finally and definitively beyond the realms of taste and sensory experience to that of ethical conduct. What in Longinus's and Addison's work was merely intimated—the link, namely, between good taste and moral rectitude—is here given direct expression. This tendency to theoretical heterogeneity, notably, is not unique to Baillie's work; on the contrary, it represents a defining marker of Enlightenment aesthetics, particularly of its engagement with the excesses of sublimity. As Ashfield and de Bolla suggest, "the boundaries between distinct discourses begin to lose their definition as the sublime transforms both itself and its neighbouring discursive forms" (6). Where the discourse of the everyday is concerned, however, this transformation is in effect a crystallization, a hardening of boundaries, a complete disseverance from the spaces, experiences and influences of sublime encounter. To be "shrunk into the narrow space of a room" is for Baillie tantamount to physical imprisonment, sensory deprivation and moral debilitation—a comprehensive withering of life and self.

Whereas Baillie's analytic tends to remove the everyday not only from theorizations of sublimity but from aesthetic experience altogether, Burke offers the most comprehensive and integrative Enlightenment theory of taste, attending as readily to nature's small as to its mighty objects and prospects. "Taste," as he suggests in the *Enquiry*'s introductory discourse, "is not a simple idea, but is partly made up of a perception of the primary pleasures of sense, of the secondary pleasures of the imagination, and of the conclusions of the reasoning faculty, concerning the various relations of these, and concerning the human passions, manners, and actions" (58). From the pleasures of sense and imagination to the minutiae of human action, Burke's theoretical aspirations compass the sum of human experience. His work is not, however, presented as an overthrow or abandonment of earlier paradigms but rather as a distillation, clarification and expansion of their analytical scope.

The *Enquiry* indeed in large measure adopts the founding assumptions of Longinian aesthetics as well as the theoretical preoccupations of Burke's contemporaries. Sublimity, for example, is cast in immediately recognizable terms as a state of "astonishment [in which] . . . the mind is so entirely filled with its object, that it cannot entertain any other, nor by consequence reason on that object which employs it" (Burke 78). Given that astonishment for Burke is rooted in fear, the most powerful in his catalogue of passions, the physical qualities capable of inducing such a response are those that suggest a threat to the subject: terror, obscurity, power, vastness, infinity, uniformity, magnitude, difficulty, loudness, etc. Although Burke makes occasional allowance for such relatively small objects as serpents and fireworks in his textual examples, he, like the theorists before him, grounds his understanding of sublimity in physical immensity and boundlessness:

> hardly anything can strike the mind with its greatness, which does not make some sort of approach towards infinity; which nothing can do whilst we are able to perceive its bounds; but to see an object distinctly, and to perceive its bounds, is one and the same thing. A clear idea is therefore another name for a little idea. (Burke 82)

This is not merely a regurgitation of Longinus's assumed link between smallness and transparency, but a further extension of its interpretive scope, moving from objects to ideas, from the physically quantifiable to the subjectively valued. Leaving aside for a moment the troubling implications for Burke's own rhetorical clarity, there is little doubt that his train of thought threatens here to run most roughly over the world of everyday objects. Not only is a comprehensive view of physical boundaries equated with seeing an object "distinctly" and thus in effect understanding it completely, but the distinct or "clear" mental representation of such an object is dismissed as a "little idea," a cognitive trifle utterly incapable of inspiring sublime astonishment.

It is worth noting that, despite its extensive Longinian roots, Burke's analysis does not in the end relegate all small objects to little ideas. Indeed, one exception to the rule seems to be microscopic materiality, a brief discussion of which Burke appends to his chapter on vastness:

> [I]t may not be amiss to add to these remarks upon magnitude, that as the great extreme of dimension is sublime, so the last extreme of littleness is in some measure sublime likewise; when we attend to the infinite divisibility of matter, when we pursue animal life into these excessively small, and yet organized beings, that escape the nicest inquisition of the

> sense, when we push our discoveries yet downward, and consider those creatures so many degrees yet smaller, and the still diminishing scale of existence, in tracing which the imagination is lost as well as the sense, we become amazed and confounded at the wonders of minuteness; nor can we distinguish in its effect this extreme of littleness from the vast itself. For division must be infinite as well as addition; because the idea of a perfect unity can no more be arrived at, than that of a complete whole, to which nothing may be added. (88)

Although this call to "push our discoveries yet downward" is not, as I will suggest, answered with any seriousness until the Romantic age, Burke's avowal of the "wonders of minuteness" serves to redeem at least pockets of everyday life from the aesthetic void into which Baillie had plunged the entire realm. It bears reiterating, of course, that this is not a conclusive but only a speculative redemption. Given that minute sublimity is unrelated to the ideas of pain and danger, it clearly cannot be accommodated within Burke's larger theoretical framework. His evident hesitation to elaborate on the posited links between infinite division and infinite addition or to clarify in what precise "measure" extreme smallness is sublime leaves the discursive boundaries between transcendence and the everyday largely intact.

If Burke is reluctant to associate smallness with the aesthetics of sublimity, he is clearly willing to assign it to the domain of beauty, which he characterizes as "that quality, or those qualities in bodies, by which they cause love, or some passion similar to it" (99). Smallness is for Burke in fact the most definitive of beauty's marks, pervading both the rhetoric of love, in what he calls "diminutive epithets" (114), and the physical world of love objects. Commenting on the differences between admiration and love, Burke suggests that

> [t]he sublime, which is the cause of the former, always dwells on great objects, and terrible; the latter on small ones, and pleasing; we submit to what we admire, but we love what submits to us; in one case we are forced, in the other we are flattered, into compliance. In short, the ideas of the sublime and the beautiful stand on foundations so different, that it is hard, I had almost said impossible, to think of reconciling them in the same object, without considerably lessening the effect of the one or the other upon the passions. So that, attending to their quantity, beautiful objects are comparatively small. (115)

Here the lines between sublimity and the world of small and everyday objects are sharply re-inscribed. The sublime, simply put, cannot be small because a relative decrease in its physical dimensions would eventually put it under the subject's control—a term that implies full perceptual knowledge (i.e. a sense of boundaries) and a consequent freedom from fear. The relationship between the subject and the aesthetic object is thus framed as a power struggle culminating in the submission of one to the other. Where there is no clear victor in the contest, as happens when a small object partakes of the sublime or a large one of the beautiful, the aesthetic experience itself is compromised, with the subject feeling neither unalloyed love nor admiration. Even in such instances, however, Burke suggests that

> the sublime suffers less by being united to some of the qualities of beauty, than beauty does by being joined to greatness of quantity, or any other properties of the sublime. There is something so over-ruling in whatever inspires us with awe, in all things which belong ever so remotely to terror, that nothing else can stand in their presence. There lie the qualities of beauty either dead or unoperative. . . . (142)

A mountain flecked with wildflowers, in other words, retains its sublimity because of overwhelming size; an idyllic pond overhung by storm clouds, conversely, preserves neither its beauty nor assumes the character of the sublime, presumably because of its limited dimensions. Thus, where sublimity is concerned, size or "greatness of quantity" indeed matters most. Though Burke concedes that lesser objects and humbler prospects—what I have associated with the everyday—may arouse an aesthetic response insofar as they manage by their physical proportions to "flatter" the subject into a sense of mastery or control, he clearly subordinates that response to the intensity of sublime admiration. Love and the related responses of pity and compassion are in Burke's taxonomy the "lesser" or "domestic" virtues (143).

Although Burke's work was contested on moral grounds, most vigorously by Mary Wollstonecraft who in *A Vindication of the Rights of Men* (1790) objected to its implicit sexual politics, its tendency, as she notes, to "convince [women] that *littleness* and *weakness* are the very essence of beauty" (112), the *Enquiry*'s aesthetic foundations remained largely unchallenged throughout the eighteenth and early nineteenth century. The deluge of sublime speculations inspired by Burke's success tended in fact, particularly in Britain, only to elevate and extend his theoretical influence and, consequently, to widen the aesthetic gap between supernature and everyday life. Alexander Gerard's *An Essay on Taste* (1759), for example, reiterates the necessary relation between physical magnitude and experiences of sublimity, going so far as to suggest that littleness or "meanness," by comparison, "renders any object, to which it adheres, disagreeable and distasteful" (11). Henry Home's *Elements of Criticism* (1765) argues that we are by nature attached to things "great and elevated" (109) but remain aesthetically indifferent to their physical opposites; "[l]ittleness, and lowness of place," he claims, "neither give pleasure nor pain" (113). In the influential *Lectures on Rhetoric and Belles Letters* (1783) Hugh Blair likewise asserts that "amplitude or greatness of extent, in one dimension or other, is necessary to Grandeur" and that to "[r]emove all bounds from any object [is to] . . . render it sublime" (47). In the regularity of our everyday surroundings, Blair laments, "[w]e see the limits on every side; we feel ourselves confined; there is no room for the mind's exerting any great effort" (51). As these examples suggest, the divisions between the quotidian and the sublime were not simply maintained but in fact amplified by the adherents of Burke's aesthetic philosophy.

With Kant's publication of the *Critique of Aesthetic Judgement*, the seminal discourse on taste for writers and theorists of the Romantic age, the tide of critical consensus was turned not so much against Burke as away from him. Dismissing Burke's study as "merely empirical," Kant characterizes his own work as a "transcendental exposition of aesthetic judgements" (130)—the distinction being expressed in a shift of analytic focus from the object to the subject, that is, from the sublime stimulus to the actual cognitive experience or event. An object is for Kant only relevant to the transcendent encounter insofar as it "lends itself to the presentation of *a sublimity discoverable in the mind*" (92, emphasis added). The Burkean emphasis on irresistible feelings of terror and awe in the face of natural grandeur is thus replaced by an interior and ultimately subjective criterion of what constitutes or facilitates sublimity. Kant's *Critique*, simply put, liberates the mind from the prepossessing effects of form and dimension; as he suggests, "the sublime is to be found in an object even devoid of form" (90). This disseverance of sublimity from any particular physical manifestation, including grandeur, clearly indicates a levelling of the aesthetic playing field, an openness or susceptibility to the experience of wonder in any environment, even the everyday. Yet if Kant's aesthetic invites such a paradigm shift in theory, it also militates against it in practice by grounding ostensibly subjective determinations of taste in the principles of common sense (*sensus communis*) which confer on all judgements a "universal validity" (82). "Cognitions and judgements must," according to Kant, "together with their attendant conviction, admit of being universally communicated; for otherwise a correspondence with the Object would not be due to them" (83). Even the sublime, in other words, must be communicated in terms that allow for general comprehension and consent, for a correspondence with a recognizably sublime object.

To reduce the sublime to a series of idiosyncratic discourses or expressions would, in Kant's terms, effect the dissolution of the aesthetic itself.

Holding to the position that "Judgment [. . .] is the faculty of thinking the particular as contained under the universal" (18), Kant therefore proceeds to explore the sublime through the conventional rhetoric of grandeur and might even as he strives to maintain the idea of objective formlessness:

> But in what we are wont to call sublime in nature there is such an absence of anything leading to particular objective principles and corresponding forms of nature, that it is rather in its chaos, or in its wildest and most irregular disorder and desolation, *provided it gives signs of magnitude and power*, that nature chiefly excites the ideas of the sublime. (92, emphasis added)

The evident theoretical tension between the simultaneous invocation and disavowal of form pervades Kant's discussion of both the mathematical and dynamic sublime. The former category of transcendence is in fact defined not as a cognitive event at all but as an objective quality: "that is sublime in comparison with which all else is small" (97). By adopting an absolute standard of magnitude Kant appears on one hand to be removing sublimity entirely from the realm and governance of the senses while on the other invoking a physical property (i.e. size or dimension) that only has meaning as it relates to perception. The physical and perceptual indeed consistently threaten to undermine Kant's ostensibly transcendental theory. His discussion of the mathematically sublime object offers a telling example of theory falling headlong over matter:

> Here, now, it is of note that, although we have no interest whatever in the Object, i.e. its real existence may be a matter of no concern to us, *still its mere greatness, regarded even as devoid of form, is able to convey a universally communicable delight* and so involve the consciousness of a subjective finality in the employment of our cognitive faculties, but not, be it remembered, a delight in the Object, for the latter may be formless. . . . (96, emphasis added)

Notwithstanding Kant's insistence that an object's "real existence" or "form" is irrelevant to the experience of sublimity and that our "delight" inheres ultimately in the self, in our "cognitive faculties," he acknowledges with evident chagrin that an object's "mere greatness"—a direct concession to the physical—*is* in fact conducive to a sense of the sublime. By suggesting, moreover, that objective greatness *conveys* rather than merely elicits sublimity, Kant is on the verge of shifting the locus of aesthetic control from the subject back to the object. Here, as elsewhere in the *Critique*, the analytic lines between sensible and supersensible sublimity are drawn so exceedingly fine as to be practically indiscernible.

No less problematic is Kant's tendency to succumb to the rhetorical sway of Longinus and Burke even as he struggles to resist their theoretical influence. He reiterates for example, without objection, the conventional association of "magnitude" with "a kind of respect," and the "absolutely small" with "a kind of contempt" (96). Perhaps most unmistakable of all, however, is the catalogue of objects and phenomena by which he exemplifies the sublime in nature:

> Bold, overhanging, and, as it were, threatening rocks, thunderclouds piled up the vault of heaven, borne along with flashes and peals, volcanoes in all their violence of destruction, hurricanes leaving desolation in their track, the boundless ocean rising with rebellious force, the high waterfall of some mighty river, and the like, make our power of resistance of trifling moment in comparison with their might. But, provided our own position is secure, their aspect is all the more attractive for its fearfulness; and we readily call these objects sublime, because they raise the forces of the soul above the height of vulgar commonplace, and discover within us a power of resistance of quite another kind, which gives us courage to be able to measure ourselves against the seeming omnipotence of nature. (110–111)

These visions of dynamic sublimity, so charged with terror and violence, recall not only Burkean grandiloquence but an entire century of aesthetic discourse. The rhetorical emphasis on external manifestations of grandeur, boundlessness and might, succeeded by a series of far less dynamic internal compensations, clearly underscores the power of the sublime object. Indeed, it is the object that here "raises the forces of the soul" and thus initiates the sublime encounter. The subject, conversely, can only react to the external stimulus and rouse itself in exact proportion to that threat: as Kant suggests, it measures itself against supernature. The only clear casualty in the struggle between subject and object, mind and might, is "vulgar commonplace"—the things and spaces, in other words, associated with everyday life. Thus Kant reinscribes here the discursive and experiential boundaries between the quotidian and the sublime. Not only are these realms unrelated and irreconcilable, but each transcendent encounter serves to reinforce their difference by elevating the subject above the mundane and enabling, from that exalted position, a comprehensive view of the relations between the self, the supernatural and the sublunary. As Kant suggests, the sublime moment consists in a

> power (one not of nature) to regard as small those things of which we are wont to be solicitous (worldly goods, health and life), and hence to regard [supernatural] might (to which in these matters we are no doubt subject) as exercising over us and our personality no such rude dominion that we should bow down before it, once the question becomes one of our highest principles and of our asserting or forsaking them. (111)

The sublime experience, in other words, facilitates an understanding not only of absolute greatness but of a scale of greatness by which to assess the everyday. Compared to the mind (specifically to reason), and to the might of supernature, such things as worldly goods, health and life are "small." It is only by maintaining this perspective, by rising above the material and corporeal limitations of immediate surroundings, that the subject can contend with supernature and resist its "rude dominion." In effect, Kant is here arguing for the aesthetic and moral value of ascent, for elevated and expansive views that enable a clearer conception of the scale of greatness and the subject's pre-eminent place within that scale, for a removal from the entrammelling spaces of home, for that "*isolation from all society* [which] is looked upon as something sublime" (129)—precisely those physical and imaginative postures, in other words, which critics have always associated with Romantic transcendence.

What the earlier example of Coleridge, himself a student of Kantian aesthetics, makes so strikingly clear, however, is that these postures of conquest and self-exaltation do not elucidate the gamut of transcendent experience in nineteenth-century life and art. Many Romantic writers, as Modiano suggests, were searching for "a different kind of sublime experience that did not involve a dramatic crisis or any form of therapy by fear and shock" (*Concept of Nature* 108).[7] The "crisis" of sublimity that is here implicated includes not only the initial encounter with natural excess and the imagination's desperate attempt to represent apparent formlessness—what Modiano glosses as "the competitive measuring of power between man and nature" (108)—but also, and perhaps more importantly, the subject's separation from the spaces and affections of home. Certainly for Coleridge it is the keen sense of distance and displacement from home that initiates his descent from mountaintops and serves to shift his "gifted ken" from supernatural immensity to quotidian sublimity. Although the poet's longing for home represents a longing for very specific, personalized spaces and embraces, for "holy remembrances" of a distinct self and other, it is also more broadly speaking a longing for the everyday, for familiarity, community, security and shelter. These ostensibly physical and psychological consolations—the self enclosed by discernible boundaries and surrounded by familiar objects—contribute in turn to one's perceptual welfare. Indeed, freedom from the lure of immensity enables a detailed scrutiny of objects, a precise sketching of edges and reading of surfaces, an engagement with objective reality that is based on direct sensory experience rather than intuited transparency, on seeing *true* rather than seeing through.

Some writers like Anna Letitia Barbauld in fact favoured the perceptual solidity of everyday reality over the rarefied visions of sublime metaphysics. Her "To Mr. [S.T.] C[olerid]ge," published in 1799 while the titular poet was himself beginning to question the premises of Kantian aesthetics, warns of the deleterious effects of the "high progress to eternal truth" (27).[8] Although Barbauld's criticism comprehends all spheres of intellectual endeavour that estrange the subject from everyday life, her especial target is revealed in the poem's setting:

> Midway the hill of science, after steep
> And rugged paths that tire the unpractised feet,
> A grove extends; in tangled mazes wrought,
> And filled with strange enchantment:—dubious shapes
> Flit through dim glades, and lure the eager foot
> Of youthful ardour to eternal chase.
> Dreams hang on every leaf: unearthly forms
> Glide through the gloom; and mystic visions swim
> Before the cheated sense. Athwart the mists,
> Far into vacant space, huge shadows stretch
> And seem realities; while things of life,
> Obvious to sight and touch, all glowing round,
> Fade to the hue of shadows. (1–13)

The "hill of science," an amalgam of Burkean empiricism and Kantian transcendentalism, is presented as a physical object of sublimity that enchants the imagination but cheats the senses. Those who brave its steeps in quest of "mystic visions," who pursue the obscurity of "dubious shapes," the boundlessness of "vacant space" and the magnitude of "huge shadows," enter an "eternal chase"—an interminable, visionless peregrination whose only approach to infinity is represented by its own inexhaustible futility. The effort of ascent brings no insight or clarity; on the contrary, it forces upon the subject an exchange of substance for shadow, "obvious" perceptual reality for "seeming realities," "glowing" life for sempiternal darkness. A diet of such "unsubstantial food" (30), Barbauld warns, may induce one to "[l]ook[]down indignant on the grosser world, / And matter's cumbrous shapings" (31–2). This disdain for the ordinary, so reminiscent of Longinus, is centered specifically on objects amenable to "sight and touch"; although large and "cumbrous," they are neither awesome nor sublime; on the contrary, their boundaries or "shapings" are so well defined as to entrammel the flitting gaze of a dream-fed imagination. For Barbauld, those who practice such disdain in the name of a supersensible aesthetic are on "dangerous ground" (36) both literally and theoretically because they have forsaken the substantive realities of everyday life that "brace [the] mind" (39). In response to these shifting and shadowy metaphysics, her closing wish for Coleridge—"Now heaven conduct thee with a parent's love" (43)—enshrines the values and consolations of home, making earthly parental care the model for divine guidance.

This call to return home, whether from metaphysics, mountains or cities, resonates throughout the literature of the period. Related but certainly not reducible to the "sentimental primitivism" (Noyes xxiv) typically associated with Romanticism, the textual emphasis on home and domesticity represents a search for roots, stability and the substantive truths of origin on one hand, but also for healing, regeneration, growth, and even political resistance, on the other. These, in any event, are the values that literary and social critics have most frequently ascribed to the domestic sphere. While most theorizations of home in the Romantic period are drawn specifically from the experiences and written texts of women, their conclusions also shed needed light on the experiences of male writers, including labouring-class poets and canonical authors, who made the spaces, objects and consolations of home the locus of their work. As much as the domestic realm has tended both theoretically and practically to accentuate differences in gender role and identity, it also serves at a fundamental level to collapse these distinctions by foregrounding essentially human needs and experiences such as shelter, security and society. Shirley Ardener, for example, in a cross-cultural study of different social 'maps,' concludes that "[c]ommunities often regard the space closest to that occupied by the family as a relatively secure and predictable inner world in contrast to the potentially hostile and untrustworthy space outside" (10). While one may dispute the assertion that familial space is always strictly an "inner world"—in the nineteenth century it comprised the garden, the neighborhood, at times even the countryside—Ardener's emphasis on safety and predictability certainly re-entrenches the most basic and commonly held ideas about home. Susan J. Wolfson, attending specifically to Romantic constructions of home, describes it as "a refuge from the world, a place of spiritual and emotional restoration, or even foundation of patriotic love" (140). For male writers, she suggests, it satisfies a "regressive longing . . . [for] maternal nurture" (140). Although Wolfson reiterates the primary role of home as sanctuary, she also highlights the propinquity of private and public spheres and the degree to which the former in fact braces and sustains the latter. Susan Levin goes so far as to associate the depictions of home and family particularly in women's literary Romanticism with a political and aesthetic radicalism that "refus[es] to appropriate the world" (173) and invests value in relationships rather than in the self. Karina Williamson in like manner argues for the "oppositional" character of the literature of home, for its tendency to "call into question the values encoded in [established genres], above all the assumption that domestic experience is irredeemably 'low'" (189).

This spectrum of domestic associations, ranging from predictability and safety to opposition and radicalism, and comprising both the physical and literary "texts" of home, is, for all its apparent breadth and variety, notable for the absence of any sense of wonder, any trace of the magic and mysticism which Southey explores in the *Hymn to the Penates*, and which, as I have suggested, intimates the quotidian sublime. The reasons for this absence have most obviously to do with the long-standing and critically enforced distinction between the discourses of sublimity and the everyday, the transcendent and the mundane—what eighteenth-century scholars classified as the "high" and the "low." Some modern critics, notably, have also endeavoured to preserve this distinction, that is, to separate the experiences of supernature and domesticity, though not with the aim of maintaining the Burkean hierarchy of aesthetic experience. Instead, they have sought to distill from domestically-situated writing a distinctly feminine voice or discourse, one grounded at all times in the material and emotional realities of home. Carol Shiner Wilson, for example, in an essay centered on Romantic women writers' reappropriation of the icon of the Good Mother, draws an explicit boundary between the domestic literature of women and men. The former, she suggests, is based on "actual" experience (171), whether that includes stitching, cooking, or reading to children; the latter, conversely, is marked by a desire to move beyond the perceived limitations of the real. Wilson argues for instance that "Coleridge's domestic scenes in 'Frost at Midnight' and 'The Eolian Harp' are merely starting points for transcendental visions" (187)—a statement which not only calls into question the verisimilitude of those scenes but also maintains the discursive divisions between the domestic and the sublime. According to Wilson, domestic ideology cannot accommodate the transcendent flights of an imagination expressly "privileged as male" (187). Susan Levin draws a similar conclusion from her analysis of the "romanticisms" of Dorothy Wordsworth and her contemporaries:

> Texts by romantic women writers explore the powers of domestic, passive, natural continuities in the context of the powerful, assertive male revolutionary consciousness that we characterize as the High Romantic Vision. In word and deed, men are spinning off in all directions, not fully taking into account the structures offered by a more pragmatic domestic imagination. (169)

By thus distinguishing the domestic imagination from the unruly sublimating impulses of male poets, Levin, like Wilson, in effect perpetuates the aesthetic divide between sensible and supersensible reality. Home in this paradigm is a "pragmatic" sphere, ensuring both physical and emotional continuity; it is a refuge from the dizzying quest for sublimity, a secure and passive wonderlessness. Although Levin concludes her analysis by characterizing women's romanticism as "a writing of the domestic that deals with the *grandeurs* and griefs of women as care givers and keepers of community" (173, emphasis added), the exact nature of those "grandeurs" or their relation to sublimity is never elucidated. Given the attendant sexual hegemony of traditional models of sublimity, feminist critics not surprisingly evince a reluctance to reconcile such theories with the discourse of domesticity. In the literature of the Romantic period, however, the expressions and experiences of home are frequently and variously blended with the language of transcendence. For many writers, male and female, home was not a refuge from sublimity but an alternate site for experiencing and representing it. Southey's *Hymn*, as I will suggest, is but one of many texts which evoke the numinous character of home without occluding its significance as a space of security and stability, growth and empowerment.

William Wordsworth's *Home at Grasmere*, for example, expresses the same emotional and creative longings that turned Coleridge's gaze from mountaintops to the everyday but also translates that longing into a direct engagement with the spaces of home. Begun in 1800, completed in 1806, published in part as the Prospectus to *The Recluse*, periodically revised, and finally republished in its in entirety after Wordsworth's death in 1888, the poem represents a literally life-long struggle to distill the boundless impressions of the bounded universe of Grasmere. From the opening perspective atop Loughrigg Terrace to the descent (through memory) into Grasmere vale itself, the poem juxtaposes a sense of physical enclosure and embowerment with a description of teeming life and plenitude that seems to surge up to the rim of the valley's bowl and spill over into the sky itself:

> The place from which I looked was soft and green,
> Not giddy yet aerial, with a depth
> Of Vale below, a height of Hills above.
> Long did I halt; I could have made it even
> My business and my errand so to halt.
> For rest of body 'twas a perfect place;
> All that luxurious nature could desire,
> But tempting to the Spirit. Who could look
> And not feel motions there? I thought of clouds
> That sail on winds; of breezes that delight
> To play on water, or in endless chase
> Pursue each other through the liquid depths
> Of grass or corn, over and through and through,
> In billows after billows evermore;
> Of Sunbeams, Shadows, Butterflies, and Birds,
> Angels, and winged Creatures that are Lords
> Without restraint of all which they behold.
> I sate, and stirred in Spirit as I looked,
> I seemed to feel such liberty was mine,
> Such power and joy; but only for this end:
> To flit from field to rock, from rock to field,
> From shore to island, and from isle to shore,
> From open place to covert, from a bed
> Of meadow-flowers into a tuft of wood,
> From high to low, from low to high, yet still
> Within the bounds of this huge Concave; here
> Should be my home, this Valley be my World. (17–43)[9]

What is essentially a recollection of the boy poet's first impressions of Grasmere foregrounds precisely those values that for Wordsworth transform mere space into a home: the security of enclosure, natural abundance and a sense of spiritual liberty. One might also include in this list an immediacy of inspiration, for the moment the boy stops to rest, he is seduced again into a vicarious experience of movement, feeling, as he says, the lure of "motions" all around him.

These motions, notably, transect boundless and bounded space, beginning above Wordsworth's head in a vast expanse of sky and scudding clouds, and shifting to the ground below where breezes play upon the water, grass and corn. Paradoxically, as this force of wind veers from sky to vale, from endless space to enclosure, and animates objects of increasingly substantive reality (clouds to water to grass to corn), Wordsworth characterizes its effects with progressively transcendent rhetoric: the movement of wind is an "endless chase," "over and through and through, / In billows after billows evermore." This blurring of lines between sublimity and everyday life also extends to the catalogue of living things that Wordsworth claims are "Lords / Without restraint of all which they behold." He includes in this exalted body not only birds, butterflies and all flying insects ("winged Creatures") but even ethereal beings such as "Angels," setting them all on the same level of existence and attributing to them an equal governance of the kingdom that is Grasmere. As Bruce Clarke notes, Wordsworth's Grasmere is a "gathering place where transcendence and immanence meet each other in rhetoric" (360). The poet himself participates in this confluence of sensible and supersensible power as he imagines the flight of his own spirit across the worlds below, above and around him. Flitting to and fro like a fly in an enormous bowl, he passes freely from vast fields to solitary rocks, from openness to minute enclosures, from transcendent heights to earthly hollows, and back again—always, as he notes, "Within the bounds of this huge Concave" but never, seemingly, confined. Although the valley is a finite space with discernible limits, it is also for Wordsworth a vast "World," given his attention to, and participation in, life of even the smallest dimension. An insect, a bed of meadow flowers, a tuft of wood, the sky itself—each of these entities, the 'low' and 'high,' preoccupy the poet in equal measure, perceptually and textually. Their vastness has nothing to do with size or power. Part of Wordsworth's poetic aim in exploring the spaces and memories of home is clearly to defend everyday life from the taint of lowliness and aesthetic inconsequence. He offers, in dispute of such conventional associations, his own experience of the inspirations of familiarity:

> Yes, the Realities of Life—so cold,
> So cowardly, so ready to betray,
> So stinted in the measure of their grace,
> As we report them, doing them much wrong—
> Have been to me more bountiful than hope,
> Less timid than desire. (54–59)

The bounteousness and boldness he associates with the "Realities of Life"—a phrase that comprehends quotidian objects, phenomena and spaces, everything, in short, that falls within "the common range of visible things" (*Prelude* II.182)—refers to their influence not only on the senses but also, and more importantly, on the poetic heart and mind. For Wordsworth, the things of everyday life are integral to both affective and creative well-being; their "grace" is such that they root the self in familiarity while also emboldening it to grow, to reach beyond itself for "wisdom" (63).

Wordsworth's own poetic boldness in *Home at Grasmere* consists, as I have suggested, in a repeated obfuscation of the discursive lines between high and low nature. The sidereal and earthly hemispheres are not simply brought into direct propinquity but are at times reflections of one another, as though the poet were examining them through a speculum. Commenting, for example, on the signs of human habitation in Grasmere, Wordsworth offers the following description:

> Thy Church and Cottages of mountain stone—
> Clustered like stars, some few, but single most,
> And lurking dimly in their shy retreats,
> Or glancing at each other cheerful looks,
> Like separated stars with clouds between. (140–144)

Albeit distinctly bounded, the valley is a lower heaven; its stars, though composed of less radiant material than their celestial counterparts, twinkle with light and "cheerful looks," conveying not only wonder but also warmth and invitation. Grasmere is quite literally a heaven in which to wander and make a home. As Wordsworth points out, however, the vale's contained, benignant and immanent sublimity is also awe-inspiring—indeed, no less so than natural grandeur which threatens with excess and boundlessness. After all, what draws the poet to Grasmere is not the fact that it mirrors the vastness and power of the universe but rather that this "small abiding-place of many men" (165) *is* a universe in itself,

> A termination and a last retreat,
> A Centre, come from wheresoe'er you will,
> A Whole without dependence or defect,
> Made for itself and happy in itself,
> Perfect Contentment, Unity entire. (166–170)

Wordsworth's micro-cosmology ascribes to Grasmere the perfect completeness and integrity usually associated with entire solar systems. Like a gravitational axis, the valley floor represents a center around which various constellations of life swirl in orbit. Wordsworth's description of the birds above Grasmere Lake offers a vivid example of such bounded and perpetual movement:

> Behold them, how they shape,
> Orb after orb, their course, still round and round,
> Above the area of the Lake, their own
> Adopted region, girding it about
> In wanton repetition, yet therewith—
> With that large circle evermore renewed—
> Hundreds of curves and circlets, high and low,
> Backwards and forwards, progress intricate,
> As if one spirit was in all and swayed
> Their indefatigable flight. (292–301)

Rendered with the avidity of an astronomer, this image of bird flight "evermore renewed" recalls the "endless chase" of breezes, each in a sense serving to maintain or "gird" the very integrity of the space they occupy. Indeed, while each curve, each circlet, traces the flight of individual birds, it also and more importantly perpetuates the center itself. "Wanton repetition," a habit of movement, defines the space that is home. For Wordsworth, Grasmere is of course not an arbitrary center, "adopted" as it were on a whim or by chance. On the contrary, it is a fixed and predetermined focus, a center, as the poet reminds us, "*come from wheresoe'er you will*" (emphasis added).

For Wordsworth, the value of such a center is inestimable not only as a physical space but also as an internal representation. Commenting in *The Prelude* on the place and function of home in his mental landscape, he returns to the image of the microcosm. Amid the tumult of thought and the storms of human passion—"things," as he observes, "[l]east understood" (VIII.591–92)—the fixed center of home exerts on the poetic mind a calming and balancing influence:

> Yet in the midst
> Of these vagaries, with an eye so rich
> As mine was through the chance on me not wasted
> Of having been brought up in such a grand
> And lovely region, I had forms distinct
> To steady me: these thoughts did oft revolve
> About some centre palpable, which at once
> Incited them to motion, and controlled,
> And whatsoever shape the fit might take,
> And whencesoever it might come, I still
> At all times had a real solid world
> Of images about me. . . . (VIII.594–605)

For Wordsworth, the wavering human mind needs a "palpable" or, as he writes in the 1850 edition, a "substantial" center around which to organize itself. Ideas need to be grounded in the everyday, in a "real solid world"; like physical bodies, they need a home, a stable, originating center, if they are to grow, to move, to have weight in the world. Thus the physical microcosm of Grasmere in which Wordsworth establishes an orbit, a home, is also a mental microcosm, perfect in itself, capable of centering thought and grounding the poet at all times in a world of solid images and dependable truths. As Wordsworth makes clear, however, not any home can serve as such a center. Of urban life he is particularly wary, associating it with "endless dreams / Of sickliness" (VIII.608–609) rather than solidity and well-being. Grasmere is an ideal home, a "sublime retirement" (723), because human habitation is kept in balance with natural life, the former occupying a sphere, an orbit, that is no more essential than that of birds or breezes. Grasmere's abundance in fact depends on the maintenance of balance and order, on an equal gift of space and life to all. To this extent, the vale represents not only a spatial but also a moral ideal. As Wordsworth suggests, Grasmere

> Can give us inward help, can purify
> And elevate and harmonize and soothe,
> And steal away and for a while deceive
> And lap in pleasing rest, and bear us on
> Without desire in full complacency,
> Contemplating perfection absolute
> And entertained as in a placid sleep. (391–397)

In spite of Wordsworth's attempt to generalize the beneficent effects of Grasmere vale, the fullness of its influence—its "perfection absolute"—is clearly limited to those who have made their home and found "pleasing rest" in its midst. Home is still, even in the public domain of the written text, an ultimately private experience. Indeed, one may go so far as to suggest that Wordsworth only adumbrates "sublime retirement" in *Home at Grasmere*, moving slowly from the valley's rim in a wide peripheral orbit around a center that is never precisely elaborated. Home, as he himself acknowledges, has a yet narrower compass than Grasmere vale: home is also Dove Cottage. In a brief passage recalling his arrival with Dorothy, Wordsworth brings the reader to the cottage door but no further:

> Bright and solemn was the sky
> That faced us with a passionate welcoming

> And led us to our threshold, to a home
> Within a home, what was to be, and soon,
> Our love within a love. Then darkness came,
> Composing darkness, with its quiet load
> Of full contentment. . . . (259–265)

The transition from daylit arrival to "Composing darkness" is so swift that the cottage, Wordsworth's "home / Within a home," is occluded, its spaces unexplored, its wonders wrapped in quietness.

Notwithstanding Wordsworth's reluctance to usher the reader inside, a crossing of the cottage threshold—the culmination of the homeward descent from mountaintops—is essential to an elucidation of quotidian sublimity. Indeed, one may argue that this inner universe of home is as important to Romantic aesthetics as supernature itself. There is clearly no shortage of domestically-situated writing in the period, most of it, though not all, produced by women and male working-class poets. Their particular emphasis on the space of home, moreover, is often independent of any previous encounters with mountaintop sublimity. Poets like Robert Burns and Joanna Baillie, for example, recognized the unique wonders of home without any preparatory tutelage in and struggle against an aesthetic of grandeur. Their work, like much descriptive verse of the mid and later eighteenth century, tends to the details of everyday life, the scenes of home and hearth that, set amidst but also against the forces of nature, promote domestic felicity—what William Cowper describes in *The Task* as "[the] only bliss / Of Paradise that has survived the fall" (III.41–42).[10] The domestic poetry of Burns and Baillie also, however, anticipates Southey's notion of home as a "mystic circle" by adumbrating spaces and moments that transcend the merely commonplace or simply felicitous. Moving beyond the prevailing eighteenth-century conception of home as a physical and emotional compensation for the costs of labour (Goodridge 71–72), these early Romantic works in effect open domestic space to sublime possibilities.

Burns's "The Cotter's Saturday Night," composed during the winter of 1785–6, offers an inner glimpse of "life's sequester'd scene" (6)[11]—the cottage home of a family of Scotland's labouring poor. Despite being alternately dismissed by modern critics for its patriarchal sentimentalism (Bold 221) and attacked for the "unseemly incongruity" (Snyder 171) that results from Burns's yoking together of vernacular Scots and English in the borrowed framework of Spenserian stanzas, the poem does convey, as John Wilson notes in an 1819 commentary in *Blackwood's Magazine*, "an intensity of the feeling of home" (qtd. in Bold 218). This "feeling" is clearly much more than mere sentimentalism; it comprises not only emotions but also the physical space of home. In effect, one may suggest that what Burns evokes is a *sense* of home, the intensity of which is related to the intensity or depth of his descriptive focus. The image of the "toil-worn Cotter" (14) stooping to gather his "spades, his mattocks, and his hoes" (16) before plodding wearily homeward already conveys the sharpness and clarity of Burns's poetic vision, his attention to the details of everyday life. The Cotter's arrival is rendered with equal precision:

> At length his lonely cot appears in view,
> Beneath the shelter of an agèd tree;
> Th'expectant wee-things, toddlin, stacher through
> To meet their dad, wi' flichterin' noise and glee.
> His wee bit ingle, blinkin bonilie,
> His clean hearth-stane, his thrifty wifie's smile,
> The lisping infant, prattling on his knee,
> Does a' his weary kiaugh and care beguile,
> And makes him quite forget his labour and his toil. (19–27)

The emotions of return do not distract the poetic eye and thereby occlude the "lesser" manifestations and spaces of home. From small children ("wee-things") to a small fire ("wee bit ingle") to the Cotter's "thrifty" wife, Burns is primarily concerned with the comforts of littleness. It is indeed littleness that makes the Cotter "quite forget" about the only excess his meagre life boasts—the unending round of toil and worry. In effect, he loses himself in the details of home, in his eldest daughter's "braw new gown" (34), his wife's "needle and her sheers" (43) and, above all, in the small tales of everyday life, the trivial chatter and recollections through which "[t]he social hours, swift-wing'd, unnotic'd fleet" (39). These stories, notably, also include the "uncos" (40)—the uncommon or extraordinary—that each family member has heard or seen throughout the day.

The image of the family bound together by stories is repeated in Burns's description of the evening devotions. Yet where the "uncos" was formerly but a part of familial conversation, here it becomes the narrative focus:

> The chearfu' supper done, wi' serious face
> They, round the ingle, form a circle wide;
> The sire turns o'er, wi' patriarchal grace,
> The big ha'-Bible, ance his father's pride:
> His bonnet rev'rently is laid aside,

> His lyart haffets wearing thin and bare;
> Those strains that once did sweet in Zion glide,
> He wales a portion with judicious care,
> And 'Let us worship God!' he says, with solemn air. (100–108)

Recalling Southey's evocation of home as a "mystic circle," this tableau of a family concentred around a fire in worship refines and contracts the boundaries of that mystic space. This home within a home, this circle within a circle, is quite literally a sanctuary. The family's "serious" looks, the Cotter's reverent attention to appearance, his "judicious care" in selecting a reading, his "solemn" incitement to praise—all contribute to a sense of imminent encounter with sublime presence. Humble everyday surroundings and simple manners do not diminish the sanctity of the occasion but in fact enhance it. As Burns notes, the family's "artless notes in simple guise" (109) far outstrip the more majestic "Italian trills" (114) in their capacity to raise "heart-felt raptures" (115). It is only "in some cottage far apart" (151) that one hears "the language of the soul" (152). The family's small and mystic circle of household devotions also, notably, anticipates a circle of truly prophetic dimensions. As Burns suggests,

> thus they all shall meet in future days,
> There, ever bask in uncreated rays,
> No more to sigh or shed the bitter tear,
> Together hymning their Creator's praise,
> In such society, yet still more dear;
> While circling Time moves round in an eternal sphere. (139–144)

The familial circle of home represents the culmination, the focal point, of human fellowship with the divine; within its bounds the human mingles with the heavenly, the temporal with the eternal. The precise nature of that communion, albeit inspired and prefigured by the Cotter's family devotions, is such that it overawes the poet's powers of description, leaving him only to hint at what he cannot conceive: "In such society, *yet still more dear*" (emphasis added). What he evokes with clarity, however, is the solidity, the inviolability, of the "eternal sphere." Transposed from earthly to celestial realms, the familial space of home continues to gird those within much as it is girded from without by "circling Time." In Burns's domestic cosmology, all circles, those of work, worry and life itself ("this weary mortal round" [75]), are ultimately transcended by the mystic circle of home, the source of emotional and spiritual welfare.

Joanna Baillie's "A Winter's Day" in like manner expounds the benefits of a solid, well-girded domestic sphere. Published anonymously in 1790 as part of her *Fugitive Verses* and praised by William Enfield in the *Monthly Review* in November 1791 for its "true unsophisticated representations of nature" (qtd. in Lonsdale 429), the poem relates the events of a single day in the life of a farm family, from the cock's "unwelcome call" (14)[12] to the farmer's grateful return to bed. Home in this quotidian narrative is the center from which all activity emanates and to which it returns. There is in fact no activity without the sheltering, engendering space of home. Of course for Baillie the converse is equally true: home is inconceivable without the ebb and flow of human activity that defines and fills its dimensions. Thus even in the relative stillness of morning, the house is already awake with the thoughts of those who occupy and define its spaces:

> The labouring hind, who, on his bed of straw
> Beneath the home-made coverings, coarse but warm,
> Locked in the kindly arms of her who spun them,
> Dreams of the gain that next year's crop should bring;
> Or at some fair, disposing of his wool,
> Or by some lucky and unlooked-for bargain,
> Fills his skin purse with store of tempting gold;
> Now wakes from sleep. . . . (7–14)

Of all household activities described in the poem, labour is clearly the most pervasive. From the security of its past, the home-made bed coverings, are spun the dreams of what its future ("next year's crop") may bring. Yet the dreams of labour's spoils end in the cold reality of the hind's waking and rising, his immediate tending to the "smothered fire" (24), and his elucidation, again through labour, of home's adjoining spaces:

> First [he] sees that all be right among his cattle,
> Then hies him to the barn with heavy tread,
> Printing his footsteps on the new-fallen snow.
> From out the heaped-up mow he draws his sheaves,
> Dislodging the poor red-breast from his shelter
> Where all the live-long night he slept secure;
> But now, affrightened, with uncertain flight,
> Flutters round walls, and roof, to find some hole
> Through which he may escape.
> Then whirling o'er his head, the heavy flail

> Descends with force upon the jumping sheaves,
> While every rugged wall and neighbouring cot
> The noise re-echoes of his sturdy strokes. (26–38)

One movement begets another and each in turn reveals the properties and dimensions of home. The hind's "heavy tread" links house to barn; his selection of sheaves rouses a bird that, like him, is woken into hurried motion, its wings, like the beating flail, testifying to the enclosure of "rugged" walls and roof. All life in effect bears witness to the centrality and solidity of home.

In detailing the affairs within the house, Baillie counterbalances physical solidity and motions of force with light and warmth and playfulness. Whereas the hind's threshing divides wheat and chaff as well as man and bird, the wife's morning chores emphasize togetherness and community, a tender sharing of space:

> The family cares call next upon the wife
> To quit her mean but comfortable bed.
> And first she stirs the fire and fans the flame,
> Then from her heap of sticks for winter stored
> An armful brings; loud crackling as they burn,
> Thick fly the sparks upward to the roof,
> While slowly mounts the smoke in wreathy clouds.
> On goes the seething pot with morning cheer,
> For which some wistful little folk await,
> Who, peeping from the bedclothes, spy well-pleased
> The cheery light that blazes on the wall,
> And bawl for leave to rise.
> Their busy mother knows not where to turn,
> Her morning's work comes now so thick upon her.
> One she must help to tie his little coat,
> Unpin another's cap, or seek his shoe
> Or hosen lost, confusion soon o'ermastered!
> When all is o'er, out to the door they run
> With new-combed sleeky hair and glistening faces,
> Each with some little project in his head. (39–58)

Although the wife, like her husband, moves reluctantly from bed to work and toils at first in solitude, her "family cares" quickly surround her with emotional as well as physical warmth. The crackling fire and seething pot speak "morning cheer." The noise of her work does not, like the beating flail, scatter life but instead draws it near; indeed, her "well-pleased" children "bawl for leave to rise." In this convivial atmosphere even once rugged walls begin to blaze with "cheery light." Baillie's sentimental portrait of the inner home, centered on the "busy mother," is one of abundant energy and life where work and busyness come "thick" but are ultimately "o'ermastered" by the transcendent joy of community.

Notwithstanding the poem's intimations of distinctly gendered household spaces—the outer home of barn and pasture representing an essentially solitary, even alienating sphere of masculine labour and the inner home of the hearth, a female-centered domain of "family care(s)"—Baillie's conception of home hinges ultimately much less on a division of its space than on a broad distinction between home and the outside world. This distinction subordinates above all nature itself, in this case a winter landscape reminiscent of Thomson's, to the consolations of the hearth:

> But let us leave the warm and cheerful house
> To view the bleak and dreary scene without,
> And mark the dawning of a Winter day.
> The morning vapour rests upon the heights,
> Lurid and red, while growing gradual shades
> Of pale and sickly light spread o'er the sky.
> Then slowly from behind the southern hills
> Enlarged and ruddy comes the rising sun,
> Shooting athwart the hoary waste his beams
> That gild the brow of every ridgy bank,
> And deepen every valley with a shade,
> The crusted window of each scattered cot,
> The icicles that fringe the thatched roof
> The new-swept slide upon the frozen pool,
> All keenly glance, new kindled with his rays;
> And even the rugged face of scowling Winter
> Looks somewhat gay. But only for a time
> He shows his glory to the brightening earth,
> Then hides his face behind a sullen cloud. (66–84)

The transition from inner warmth to outer dreariness, from cheery radiance to "pale and sickly light," is abrupt and absolute. In effect, what Baillie offers in this third portrait of waking life—"the dawning of a Winter day"—is a protraction or retardation of the inspiring activity of home. The day's dawning is not merely sluggish; it is a somnambulant creeping of vapour and half-light over a "hoary waste." Even the rising sun, while it does contribute to a softening of winter's ruggedness, brightens the day only "somewhat" before again disappearing. Its "glory," as Baillie notes, is most pronounced only where it touches the human space of home—"each scattered cot," "crusted window" and "thatched roof." Even here, however, the light of nature neither warms nor, like the fire in the hearth, provides nourishment. The birds that hop to and fro in the sun's flitting beams "[c]an find no seeds to stop their craving want" (93) and thus "bend their flight to the low smoking cot, / Chirp on the roof, or at the window peck, / To tell their wants to those who lodge within" (94–96). They, like the "poor lank hare" (97) that steals coleworts from the hind's garden, seek sustenance not from nature but from the bounty of home.

That bounty, as Baillie makes clear, comprises emotional as well as physical nurture. The cottage on the hoary waste is indeed a beacon of help and healing for those broken by the outside world. The description of children playing on the ice, for example, ends in a dramatic return to the embrace of home:

> Then by degrees they scatter to their homes,
> Some with a broken head or bloody nose,
> To claim their mother's pity, who, most skilful!
> Cures all their trouble with a bit of bread. (176–179)

Children scattering from play are not alone in seeking the sanctuary and "pity" of home. The onset of evening brings even those who have no hereditary claim to the spaces of familial care, those who seek not home per se but simply "[a] house to screen them from the piercing cold" (185). Baillie's description of such a visitant to the hind's cottage foregrounds on one hand the dignity of want in terms that anticipate Wordsworth's idealized portraits of mendicants in the *Lyrical Ballads* and *The Prelude*, while also illustrating, on the other, the gentle welcome of home:

> Lo, o'er the frost a reverend form advances!
> His hair white as the snow on which he treads,
> His forehead marked with many a careworn furrow,
> Whose feeble body bending o'er a staff,
> Shows still that once it was the seat of strength,
> Though now it shakes like some old ruined tower.
> Clothed indeed but not disgraced with rags,
> He still maintains that decent dignity

> Which well becomes those who have served their country.
> With tottering steps he gains the cottage door;
> The wife within, who hears his hollow cough,
> And pattering of his stick upon the threshold
> Sends out her little boy to see who's there.
> The child looks up to mark the stranger's face,
> And, seeing it enlightened with a smile,
> Holds out his tiny hand to lead him in. (186–201)

Baillie's location of power in apparent frailty extends as readily to the child as to the beggar. Much as the latter's "feeble body" is still possessed of "decent dignity," so the boy, despite his age and size, opens with a "tiny hand" the universe of home. By conducting the stranger inside, moreover, he initiates a series of additional consolations, each centered on the security and fellowship of home. The stranger is asked to sit and warm himself by the fire in the "chief seat" (226) of the house; he is "Flock[ed] round" (211) by the excited children, welcomed by the father, invited to share a "homely meal" (228) and offered lodging for the night. The domestic tableau of the family and the stranger spending the evening hours in conversation recalls the circular community of "The Cotter's Saturday Night":

> When all are satisfied, about the fire
> They draw their seats and form a cheerful ring.
> The thrifty housewife turns her spinning-wheel;
> The husband, useful even in his hour
> Of ease and rest, a stocking knits, belike,
> Or plaits stored rushes, which with after skill
> Into a basket formed may do good service,
> With eggs or butter filled at fair or market.
> Some idle neighbours now come dropping in,
> Draw round their chairs and widen out the circle;
> And everyone in his own native way
> Does what he can to cheer the social group. (233–244)

It is notable that Baillie's circle, much more so than Burns's, engenders not only conversation but also "useful" labour. As she suggests, it is both a "cheerful ring" and one of "good service." The specific services it facilitates, namely spinning, knitting and basket weaving—all of them literal and symbolic acts of bonding—are here shared across gender lines. Indeed, the evening family circle is so united in purpose that individual differences and gender roles are subordinated to the shared goal of establishing and maintaining community. The familial circle is also, of course, inclusive. Not only is a stranger asked to contribute to the stories spun in its midst, but idle neighbours join and "widen out" its physical and social dimensions, thereby diffusing the "cheer" generated within.

This widening embrace of home does not, however, compromise or diminish the unique fellowship, intimacy and, most importantly, the wondrousness of the family circle. As Baillie points out, with the inevitable dispersal of the neighbours, each to his or her own home, the cottage assumes a markedly different character:

> But where the song and story, joke and gibe,
> So lately circled, what a solemn change
> In little time takes place!
> The sound of psalms, by mingled voices raised
> Of young and old, upon the night air borne,
> Haply to some benighted traveller,
> Or the late parted neighbours on their way,
> A pleasing notice gives, that those whose sires
> In former days on the bare mountain's side,
> In deserts, heaths, and caverns, praise and prayer,
> At peril of their lives, in their own form
> Of covenanted worship offered up,
> In peace and safety in their own quiet home
> Are (as in quaint and modest phrase is termed)
> Engaged now in *evening exercise*. (284–298)

This passage, which Baillie did not include until the poem's second edition, citing it as a "great omission" (Breen 51), foregrounds not only the safety but, more importantly, the sanctity of home. Whereas in "former days" private or nonconformist worship was forbidden, the sheltering space of home enables the freedom of religious expression—what Baillie glosses in everyday parlance as "evening exercise." This exercise, by mingling the voices of young and old, quite literally draws the family together. As Baillie notes, moreover, the effects of such worship redound upon the community as a whole, for where the sounds of devotion spill beyond the boundaries of home, they diffuse the blessing of private exercise publicly and contribute, through the shared recollection of bygone generations, to a revitalization of familial and communal bonds. The devotional family circle is thus inherently stabilizing and fructifying; it secures within and blesses without. On a still broader scope, the "pleasing notice" of "praise and prayer" serves momentarily to subdue the ruggedness of nature itself, mingling with the "northern blast" (305) and carrying an indelible sense of warmth across the "wreaths of snow heaped up on every side" (303). Home in this context becomes a signifier of intimate excess, its light, its song, its physical and spiritual warmth transcending the rugged enclosure of roof and walls while simultaneously preserving the security and sanctity of familial space. The gifts of home, though freely—indeed, ceaselessly—given away, never compromise or deplete the sheltering space within which such gifts, such bounties, are daily (re)generated. Superabundance is thus predicated on the security of limitation, and transcendence, on the intimacy of space. The poem's final lines indeed return to and reinforce the enclosure and closeness of home, in a sense completing its circle: "He shuts his door, / And, thankful for the roof that covers him, / Hies him to bed" (309–311).

The closing of home's door and consequent completion of its boundaries represents of course only a beginning in the exploration of domestic space and quotidian sublimity. To situate the home in its natural and indeed cosmological setting, to cross the domestic threshold and survey the enclosure of walls, roof and door, each in a sense substantiated by the activity of everyday life, is to reify the "mystic circle" but to leave its distribution and distinction of space—its depth, if you will—unelaborated. That depth, as I will suggest, is produced not by boundaries or geometric area but by the objects, the details, the minutiae of everyday life. Coleridge's emphasis on particularity, on the sublimity of kindling coal and pipe smoke, speaks to the aesthetic richness of the ordinary and the close scrutiny required to bring its intimate wonders to light. Home as the center of everyday life is particularly conducive to such aesthetic investigations and experiences because, as Wordsworth, Burns and Baillie reveal, it shelters the subject physically, enfolds her/him in the embrace of community and thus facilitates moments of creative self-expression. For Wordsworth, the simultaneously enclosing and liberating space of Grasmere vale inspires on first sight a wish for home and, in after-years, a poetic musing on the inspirations of home. Burns and Baillie likewise construe home as a sheltering space for individual creativity. They describe, in the intervals between domestic labour, episodes of story-telling and family worship, each engendered by and arising out of the security and fellowship of the family circle. Notwithstanding their exclusive emphasis on inner or "household" creativity, the outer home, by which I mean the immediate surroundings of garden or countryside, is also clearly significant to experiences and expressions of everyday wonder. Drawing on the security of the house—the "home within a home"—Romantic writers indeed frequently enter into the life and richness of its adjoining spaces. Home, as such, is not one but many circles interlocked; it is in Wordsworthian terms a universe of varying objects and spaces, some expansive and others small, even minute, their wonders elucidated by careful scrutiny, by an immersion in intimate immensity.

Chapter Two
Particularity and "Intimate Immensity"

Coleridge's description of the imagination as a power that reconciles or balances the concrete with the general, the individual with the representative, offers, as I have suggested, a means of widening the compass of Romantic aesthetics to include the particular spaces and objects of everyday life. Such physical manifestations are in Coleridge's terms integral to the imagination's esemplastic teleology because they ground notions of representative form and the concomitant formulations of universal truth in the distinct realities of matter. To dissever truth from these realities would be to dissever it from nature itself, which Coleridge characterizes as "the prime genial artist, inexhaustible in diverse powers [and] equally inexhaustible in forms."[1] The poet, accordingly, who seeks to account for the governing truth of nature's formal inexhaustibility must perforce attend to the particularizing and distinguishing details of individual form. The result, as Mark Storey notes, is a refinement of poetic focus, a penetration of generalized nature, *natura naturata*, to reveal natural essence, *natura naturans* (23). Coleridge in fact describes the relationship between the general and the essential as an *inter*penetration, suggesting that individual form is invested with a power—a truth, if you will—typically associated with representative or, more precisely, with ideal form.

In order to understand the effect of an aesthetic of 'individual form' on the literature of the Romantic period, we are helped, I think, by considering first of all its theoretical assumptions and implications, particularly as they develop in contradistinction to the prevailing eighteenth-century emphasis on generalized or representative form. Indeed, the particular vision of everyday life that takes shape in the work of Mary Russell Mitford, Anna Laetitia Barbauld, Dorothy and William Wordsworth, Robert Burns and John Clare is to some extent grounded in and supported by the aesthetic discourses of Coleridge, Blake and Hazlitt which define not only the role and domain of the Romantic artist but, more generally speaking, ways of seeing and being in the world.

Certainly for Coleridge the emphasis on individual form is as much a critical and philosophical, as it is a poetic, inclination. Attentiveness to distinguishing detail in fact becomes a measure of creative genius, a way not only of writing but also of reading and assessing literary works. His analysis of Shakespeare exemplifies this strategy and, as such, serves to illustrate his theoretical variance from the inherited standards of Augustan criticism, particularly those of Samuel Johnson. Reflecting, for example, on the method of characterization in *The Tempest*, Coleridge concludes that,

> Shakespeare's characters are all *genera* intensely individualized; the results of meditation, of which observation supplied the drapery and the colours necessary to combine them with each other. He had virtually surveyed all the great component powers and impulses of human nature,—had seen that their different combinations and subordinations were in fact the individualizers of men, and showed how their harmony was produced by reciprocal disproportions of excess or deficiency. (*Shakespearean Criticism* I, 122–123)

In both rhetorical and aesthetic emphasis, this passage offers itself as a precisely targeted corrective to Johnson's claim in the 1765 Preface to *The Plays of William Shakespeare* that the playwright's power manifests itself most clearly and profoundly in "just representations of *general nature*" (420, emphasis added). In Johnson's view, Shakespeare's characters

> are not modified by the customs of particular places, unpracticed by the rest of the world; by the peculiarities of studies or professions, which can operate but upon small numbers; or by the accidents of transient fashions or temporary opinions: they are the genuine progeny of common humanity, such as the world will always supply, and observation will always find. His persons act and speak by the influence of those general passions and principles by which all minds are agitated, and the whole system of life is continued in motion. *In the writings of other poets a character is too often an individual; in those of Shakespeare it is commonly a species.* (421, emphasis added)

Notwithstanding their common regard for Shakespeare's depth of characterization, Coleridge and Johnson draw clearly disparate conclusions about the nature and effect of that depth. Whereas Coleridge emphasizes Shakespeare's capacity to individualize the "types" he creates, Johnson lauds the common humanity of his ostensibly individuated characters; Coleridge makes generic or typological characterization the canvas upon which genius throws colours of intense, distinguishing subjectivity, while Johnson subordinates the incidental effects of colour to a commonly accessible pattern of humanity. Moreover, while both critics attribute to Shakespeare a capacity for simultaneously keen and extensive observation, they dispute his employment of that capacity as a dramatist. In Coleridge's view, Shakespeare's powers of human observation are exercised dramatically in the delineation of what he terms "individualizers of men," in other words, such passions and impulses as reinforce the pre-eminence and ineradicability of the subject. Johnson, conversely, by holding to the dictum that the "end of writing is to instruct" (424)—a refinement of Horace's *aut prodesse aut delectare*—distills the effects of Shakespeare's observational acumen to a representation of those "general passions and principles by which *all* minds are agitated" and which convey "the *whole* system of life" (emphasis added). The theoretical differences at work here—and they are by no means slight—manifest themselves perhaps most tellingly in the governing metaphors used by each critic to distinguish Shakespeare's dramatic art. Johnson, adopting what M.H. Abrams identifies as an "archetypal analogy" (*Mirror and Lamp* 31), describes Shakespeare as "the poet of nature; the poet that holds up to his readers *a faithful mirror* of manners and of life" (421, emphasis added). Shakespeare's work, in other words, is comprehensively mimetic, offering a broad and undistorted reflection of human nature in which any reader or viewer can trace universal passions and patterns of behaviour. For Coleridge, however, the symbol of the mirror tends to generalize and thus diffuse the effects of what he characterizes as Shakespeare's "psychological genius":

> Shakespeare has this advantage over all other dramatists—that he has availed himself of his psychological genius to develop all the minutiae of the human heart: shewing us the thing that, to common observers, he seems solely intent upon, he makes visible what we should not otherwise have seen: just as, after looking at distant objects through a telescope, when we behold them subsequently with the naked eye, we see them with greater distinctness, and in more detail, than we should otherwise have done. (*Shakespearean Criticism* II, 98)

By likening Shakespeare's work to a telescope that, through multiple lenses or perspectives, magnifies "what we should not otherwise have seen" and thereby heightens our sensitivity to distinguishing details, Coleridge evokes the complexity, indeed the mystery, of nature, and its inherent resistance to the immediacy of perception. Coleridge's aesthetic interest lies not in the readily apparent, that is, in the general shape and contours of everyday existence, but in the particulars, the "minutiae," whether they pertain to the human heart or to physical nature.

These particulars are of course not ignored by the aesthetic philosophies of the Enlightenment but quite deliberately sacrificed to the interests of artistic unity and formal representativeness—what Walter Jackson Bate glosses in *From Classic to Romantic* as "ideal or general nature" (61). Johnson's emphasis on the priority of general nature derives indeed not from any insensitivity to individuating details, but rather from a judgment of their incommensurability with the aims of universal instruction. Despite conceding in *Rambler* No.36 that nature is formally "inexhaustible," Johnson maintains that "its general effects on the eye and ear are uniform, and incapable of much variety of description" (191). Poetry, accordingly,

> cannot dwell upon the minuter distinctions by which one species differs from another without departing from that simplicity of grandeur which fills the imagination; nor dissect the latent qualities of things without losing its general power of gratifying every mind by recalling its conceptions. (191)

Rhetorically, this passage is strikingly reminiscent of Burke's *Enquiry*. The notion that descriptive particularities destroy a poem's "simplicity of grandeur"—a byword for the sublime—and thereby compromise imaginative fulfilment clearly echoes Burke's emphasis on a uniformity of parts as being conducive to sublimity. Without uniformity, Burke insists, "the imagination at every change finds a check; you are presented at every alteration with the termination of one idea, and the beginning of another; by which means it becomes impossible to continue that uninterrupted progression . . . [towards] infinity" (89). For Burke as for Johnson, an overabundance of detail, no matter how reflective of natural excess, serves rather to distract and waylay the imagination than awe it with a sense of prepossessing unity. Yet notwithstanding Johnson's indebtedness to Burke's analytic of the sublime (Elledge 165), his own aesthetic resistance to particularization extends to all forms of poetic expression, not only those that aim at infinity. Hence the comprehensive scope of Imlac's famous proclamation in *Rasselas* that

> 'The business of a poet [. . .] is to examine, not the individual, but the species; to remark general properties and large appearances: he does

not number the streaks of the tulip, or describe the different shades in the verdure of the forest. He is to exhibit in his portraits of nature such prominent and striking features as recall the original to every mind; and must neglect the minuter discriminations, which one may have remarked, and another have neglected, for those characteristics which are alike obvious to vigilance and carelessness.' (352)

While one must always exercise caution when ascribing to an author the sentiments of one of his characters, in this instance (and indeed throughout the narrative) Imlac's views echo Johnson's poetic strictures from the *Rambler* and the Preface to *Shakespeare* with unmistakable clarity. The enumeration of tulip streaks and forest shades is for Johnson an unpoetic descent to empiricism, a loss, that is, of imaginative vision. Reiterating the belief that the aim of descriptive poetry is always to evoke the "original" or representative, Johnson subordinates all incidental details, regardless of their accuracy, to "prominent and striking features." This should not be taken to suggest that Johnson advocates a poetics merely of generalization—he praises James Thomson in the *Lives of the Poets* (1779–81), for example, for having "a mind that at once comprehends the vast, and attends to the minute" (753)—but rather that he emphasizes the selection only of such details as underwrite representative form and contribute to a sense of unity. Where poetic detail complicates or delays the perception of unity, it is deemed extraneous, even corruptive.

Among eighteenth-century critics Johnson is clearly not alone in his resistance to an aesthetic of particularization. Pope sets the tone early in the period when he declares in *An Essay on Criticism* (1711) that

> In wit, as nature, what affects our hearts
> Is not the exactness of peculiar parts;
> 'Tis not a lip, or eye, we beauty call,
> But the joint force and full result of all.
> Thus when we view some well-proportion'd dome,
> (The world's just wonder, and even thine, O Rome!)
> No single parts unequally surprise,
> All comes united to th'admiring eyes;
> No monstrous height, or breadth, or length appear;
> The whole at once is bold, and regular. (243–252)[2]

What this passage posits is a direct correspondence between unity and ideal form. Whether in the architecture of a human face or a cathedral, only when "peculiar" parts are arranged so as to produce a "whole" do they contribute to a sense of exemplary or "regular" form. The movement from the peculiar to the regular involves a subsumption of the individual by the general. As Carol Christ observes in her study of artistic particularization in the Victorian period, a work to which I will return hereafter in greater detail, underlying the neo-classical predilection for representativeness is a "Platonic view of the universe, in which things denoted by a common term have a similarity that implies a universal meaning, an eternal outline, or a necessary formula behind all of its concrete manifestations" (5). In other words, general form is denotative of an eternally and universally inviolable aesthetic—an outline, a formula—upon which all artistic productions are to be patterned.

For Joshua Reynolds, perhaps the most ardent and arguably the most influential defender of an aesthetic of "universal meaning," the only outline worthy of emulation is perfection itself. His fifteen *Discourses*, comprising "perhaps the most representative single embodiment in English of eighteenth-century aesthetic principles" (Bate 79), establish as both an artistic and a moral imperative the pursuit, as Reynolds puts it, of "that ideal excellence which it is the lot of genius always to contemplate" (8). Ideal excellence is in effect a distillation or intensification of general form; it suggests a return to an originating impulse, an eternally unchanging generality. The difficulty, of course, with such a standard is its tendency to undermine art's mimetic function. Reynolds himself concedes in the Third Discourse that

> [a]ll the objects which are exhibited to our view by Nature, upon close examination will be found to have their blemishes and defects. The most beautiful forms have something about them like weakness, minuteness, or imperfection. (40)

The equation of "minuteness" with "weakness" and "imperfection" sets the stage for a creative process in which art is ultimately divorced not only from natural detail but also from sensory experience. Direct observation, as Reynolds suggests, is only useful as a propadeutic, revealing imperfect models that the mature artist later learns to abandon:

> [L]ong laborious comparison should be the first study of the Painter who aims at the greatest style. By this means, he acquires a just idea of beautiful forms; he corrects Nature by herself, her imperfect state by her more perfect. His eye being enabled to distinguish the accidental deficiencies, excrescences, and deformities of things, from their general figures, he makes out an abstract idea of their forms more perfect than

Particularity and "Intimate Immensity"

> any one original; and what may seem a paradox, he learns to design naturally by drawing his figures unlike to any one object. This idea of the perfect state of Nature, which the Artist calls the Ideal beauty, is the great leading principle by which works of genius are conducted. (41)

Theoretically, this passage threatens to shatter the notion of art mirroring nature. Despite beginning with "laborious comparison"—in other words, the emulation of natural forms—the artist in Reynolds's view ultimately "corrects" nature by supplying with abstract ideas its natural deficiencies. Evidently aware of the risks thus posed to an understanding of art as a mimetic medium, Reynolds attempts to obscure the presupposition of nature's always already "imperfect state" by invoking a standard of natural perfection which he terms "Ideal beauty." The artist, he suggests, learns to design naturally, to approximate this ideal, by drawing his figures—and here is the paradox—"*unlike* to any one object" (emphasis added). The artist, in other words, designs naturally by relying on abstractions, not on nature itself. In a theoretical leap by which Reynolds himself seems somewhat baffled, the literally *un*natural is thus naturalized and idealized.

The residue of this paradox Reynolds never entirely dispels. His explanation of the role of particular detail in the Fourth Discourse, for example, foregrounds what one can only describe as an antagonistic relationship between art's mimetic process and its aesthetic goal, the evocation of a sense of grandeur or sublimity. Having conceded that "circumstances of minuteness and particularity frequently tend to give an air of truth to a piece, and to interest the spectator in an extraordinary manner" (55), Reynolds proceeds to inform the reader of the aesthetic limitations of copying nature too closely:

> if there be any thing in the Art which requires peculiar nicety of discernment, it is the disposition of these minute circumstantial parts, which, according to the judgment employed in the choice, become so useful to truth, or so injurious to grandeur. (55)

By charting a fine line between truth and grandeur, Reynolds in effect divides them and subordinates the former, the ideal product of mimesis, to the latter, the ideal product of abstraction. The movement from truth to grandeur that "real excellence" (55) demands, comes, not surprisingly, at the expense of details: "All smaller things, however perfect in their way, are to be sacrificed without mercy to the greater" (55). Whereas Johnson's work merely implies a link between the "greater" and the sublime, Reynolds makes the connection plain:

> However contradictory it may be in geometry, it is true in taste, that many little things will not make a great one. The sublime impresses the mind at once with one great idea; it is a single blow. . . . (63)

The danger inherent in "little things" is not simply that they compromise general form but that they threaten to enervate the most potent of general forms, the sublime. According to Reynolds, therefore, the truth of details and of mimesis must be levelled by the blow of sublimity. This is a triumph, notably, not so much of aesthetic experience as of aesthetic convention. Reynolds himself acknowledges, for example, in Discourse Eleven that "a painter must have the power of contracting as well as dilating his sight" and that "he that does not at all express particulars expresses nothing" (187); such "excellence" is not, however, recommended because "[it] never did confer on the artist the character of genius" (187). For Reynolds genius is a distinction ultimately bestowed from without rather than perceived and nurtured within; in its purest form, it represents an obedience to and a reinscription of prevailing aesthetic categories, namely the sublime and what he characterizes as "Ideal beauty," both being ostensibly natural forms which are, however, supplemented and refined by abstract ideas.

This refinement by abstraction is intended not only to purify natural objects of their attendant deficiencies but also to typify them. Genius for Reynolds expresses itself in the capacity to make an object—whether sublime or beautiful—instantly recognizable to the viewer or reader: it "gives him by reflection his own mode of conceiving" (187). Genius, in other words, does not provoke new ideas or engender alternate ways of engaging or perceiving the world; on the contrary, by eradicating the accidents and distractions of detail, it reinforces only "what is congenial [. . .] to the mind of man" (187). Particularization, conversely, "pre-supposes *nicety* and *research*" (187), methodologies that Reynolds blithely dismisses as

> the business of the curious and attentive . . . [which] does not speak to the general sense of the whole species; in which common, and, as I may call it, mother tongue, every thing grand and comprehensive must be uttered. (187)

In this defence of generalities Reynolds articulates a conception of genius—unapologetically complacent and inattentive—that many writers of the Romantic period worked determinedly to subvert.

Of Reynolds's various detractors, William Blake was arguably the most vociferous. His marginal annotations to the *Discourses* function in a very literal sense as incursions on Reynolds's aesthetic authority, an authority characterized from the outset as both psychologically and theoretically oppressive. In Blakean terms, Reynolds is an unwieldy Urizenic tyrant "Hired to Depress Art" (Blake 438). Underlying Blake's personal indignation at being "hid" (439) behind such bulk is a marked disdain for the aesthetic of generalization:

> To Generalize is to be an Idiot. To Particularize is Alone the Distinction of Merit. General Knowledges are those Knowledges that Idiots Possess. (440)

> What is General Nature? is there Such a Thing? what is General Knowledge? is there such a thing? All Knowledge is Particular. (442)

The particularization of all knowledge derives, according to Blake, from the power of the individual eye/I to shape the world uniquely. "Every Eye," Blake contends, "Sees differently. As the Eye, Such the Object" (441). Generalities therefore contradict not only individual perception but also the varied world of material objects. Perhaps most significant, however, is Blake's characterization of general form as a hindrance to sublimity itself. Guided by the belief that "Without Contraries is no Progression" (*Marriage* 86), Blake proposes an antithesis to Reynolds's thesis and, by extension, to Burke's: "Without Minute Neatness of Execution The Sublime cannot Exist! Grandeur of Ideas is founded on Precision of Ideas" (442). This argument for what Vincent de Luca calls "a plainly accessible infinite" (38) returns sublimity to the realms of nature and physical perception, to the very details of everyday life. For Blake, particularity and perspicuity "are valued not because they make objects more clear, but because they are the 'real' constituents of objects" (De Luca 41). Whereas the veiling shadows of obscurity are merely fictions imposed from without, all physical details are valuable—indeed, Blake would say *equally* valuable—because they serve to distinguish and individualize objects, in effect giving each object its own character or essence.[3] Given that every eye/I shapes or defines objects uniquely, the enumeration of details from a particular perspective also by extension individualizes the moment of perception and thereby accounts for the differences in "seeing." For Blake, it is precisely in these sublime moments of comprehensive particularization when objective details hearken back to or signify the subject in the state of perception that "all the Great / Events of Time start forth & are concievd" (*Milton* 28.1–2).[4] These are the moments of artistic creation "that Satan cannot find[,] . . . [that] renovate[] every Moment of the Day if rightly placed" (*Milton* 35.42–45). While it may be objected that Blake's aesthetic prescriptions are in some ways "too rigorous for even the most sharp-edged mimesis of objects to satisfy" (De Luca 41), they clearly serve to redeem particularized reality from its position of aesthetic extraneousness by reinvesting it with sublime potential. What Blake recommends is in effect precisely that "curious and attentive" engagement with material objects that Reynolds dismisses from his characterization of genius. A world in a grain of sand will only astonish the subject if s/he takes time to sit wide-eyed amid the details of life.

Like Blake, William Hazlitt renounces the aesthetic strictures proposed in the *Discourses*, citing a "radical defect in Sir Joshua's theory" (*Table Talk* 122). There are in fact two principal defects at which Hazlitt levels his criticism, one being Reynolds's conception of sublimity, and the other, his characterization of genius. Where the sublime is concerned, Hazlitt reiterates Blake's view that

> [t]he greatest grandeur may co-exist with the most perfect, nay with a microscopic accuracy of detail, as we see it often does in nature: the greatest looseness and slovenliness of execution may be displayed without any grandeur at all either in the outline or distribution of the masses of colour. . . . Sir Joshua seems to argue that the grandeur, the effect of the whole object, is confined to the general idea in the mind, and that all littleness and individuality is in nature. This is an essentially false view of the subject. This grandeur, this general effect, is indeed always combined with the details, or what our theoretical reasoner would designate as *littleness* in nature: and so it ought to be in art. . . . (*Table Talk* 132–133)

Hazlitt here establishes a direct correspondence between details in nature and nicety of thought by suggesting that even so-called general ideas are comprised of particularities. Grandeur, therefore, what he designates as "the effect of the whole subject," is always necessarily based in and enriched by detail. The unnatural suppression of details results in an unnatural object, "an inexplicable dumb mass without distinction or meaning" (*Table Talk* 134). Having thus made space for particularities in an aesthetic of grandeur, Hazlitt proceeds to question the exclusive relevance of uniformity to that aesthetic:

> I confess, it strikes me as a self-evident truth that variety or contrast is as essential a principle in art and nature as uniformity, and as necessary to make up the harmony of the universe and the contentment of the mind. Who would destroy the shifting effects of light and shade, the

> sharp, lively opposition of colours in the same or in different objects, the streaks in a flower, the stains in a piece of marble, to reduce all to the same neutral, dead colouring, the same middle tint? [. . .] Ideal expression is not neutral expression, but extreme expression. (*Table Talk* 140–141)

The argument for variety and contrast in expressions of grandeur is offered here as an invitation to return from abstractions to nature itself, to its formal inexhaustibility, its susceptibility to "shifting effects," its "lively opposition" of colours and textures. This descent to the level of intense particularity facilitates the enumeration of precisely those details hitherto associated with a corruption of aesthetic ideals: "the streaks in a flower" which for Johnson represent a merely pedantic or mechanical mimesis, and "the stains in a piece of marble" which Reynolds numbers among those natural deficiencies that true genius learns to correct. Far from compromising grandeur or sublimity, such details serve in Hazlitt's view to redeem the transcendent from a lifeless neutrality, a sort of lukewarm, untextured dreariness of size and scope that conducts neither to infinity nor even to nature. Clearly implicated in this characterization of eighteenth-century grandeur is Reynolds's conception of genius as a filmy-eyed purveyor of commonplaces. For Hazlitt, genius implies a sensitivity to nature's "shifting effects" and a willingness to engage it at the level of precise distinction; that is what he means by "extreme expression." While this is not the mimetic extremism that Blake proposes, whereby every detail is equally significant insofar as it reflects the exact perspective and moment of the subject's engagement with the natural object—Hazlitt in fact invokes the necessity of not "los[ing] sight of the more important and striking appearance of the object as it presents itself to us in nature" (*Table Talk* 133)—it clearly represents an alternative to Reynolds's essentially conservative articulation of the character and responsibilities of genius. What Hazlitt advances is a notion of genius that recognizes in nature not generalities or ideals but fluidity and motion, a sense of constant flux in the midst of which individual objects can be transfixed only with precision, and even then only momentarily. To the mind of genius, the universe is numbered and known one star at a time:

> As it appears to me, all the varieties of nature in the infinite number of its qualities, combinations, characters, expressions, incidents, etc. rise from distinct points or centres and must move in distinct directions, as the forms of different species are to be referred to a separate standard. It is the object of art to bring them out in all their force, clearness, and precision,

and not to blend them into a vague, vapid, nondescript *ideal* conception, which pretends to unite but in reality destroys. (*Table Talk* 144)

What the perspectives of Hazlitt, Blake and Coleridge elucidate is a revolutionary aesthetic that locates in the details of everyday life not artistic relevance or significance merely but sublimity itself. By undoing the longstanding (and what many eighteenth-century theorists regarded as an intuitive) correlation between grand physical dimensions and grand experience, many Romantic writers endeavoured to revitalize their relationship with the world of common objects and spaces. Commenting on this relationship, Carol Christ observes that some Romantics do not simply gesture toward the sublime in their immediate surroundings but actively "*seek* the sublime [. . .] in the minute, in the common, in the particular" (9, emphasis added). This seeking consists typically of an intensive scrutiny of objects and their details, what I have described above as poetic *in*sight. Solitary objects or those 'half-hidden from the eye' are often made the focus of such scrutiny. There is, for example, a proliferation of Romantic verse centered on individual flowers, a by no means exhaustive list of which might include Burns's "To a Mountain Daisy," Anna Seward's "Sonnet: To the Poppy," Harriet Falconar's "The Violet" and "The Snowdrop," Helen Maria Williams's "Sonnet to the Strawberry," Henrietta O'Neill's "Ode to the Poppy," Walter Scott's "The Violet," Mary Robinson's "The Snowdrop," William Wordsworth's "To the Small Celandine," its companion, "To the Same Flower," his three poems "To the Daisy," "The Primrose of the Rock," and "To a Snowdrop," and, from Clare's extensive literary floriculture, "The Ragwort," "The Wild Flower Nosgay," "The Water Lilies" and "The Daisy." What immediately strikes one about this list is the distinction of individual flowers by type or species. No less significant is the fact that many of these poems make some claim for naturalistic authenticity; the poets, in other words, appear to be invoking or drawing on prior moments of direct and often extensive observation. Admittedly, the natural details thus gleaned are not always or necessarily conducive to a sense of the sublime. Many of the poems listed above in fact rely on physical particularities only to the extent that they contribute to and clarify the titular flower's symbolic significance. Burns's reference to the daisy's "snawie bosom sun-ward spread" (26),[5] for example, anticipates the flower's metaphorical transfiguration into an "artless maid, / [. . .] By love's simplicity betray'd" (31–33). In like manner, Anna Seward's description of the poppy's "flaccid vest that, as the gale blows high, / Flaps, and alternate folds around thy head" (6–7)[6] is used in the sestet to sharpen the image of "a love-crazed maid, / Smiling aghast; while stream to every wind / Her garish ribbons"

(8–10). A similar metaphorical pattern, shifting the signification of particulars from one object to another, is apparent in Falconar's and Robinson's 'Snowdrop' poems, as well as in Scott's "The Violet."[7] In each of these poems the natural object is observed and described principally because of its relation to the human; the natural, in other words, is subordinated to, or used to validate, the human. Williams's "Sonnet to the Strawberry," O'Neill's "Ode to the Poppy" and Wordsworth's "To the Daisy" (1815) in like manner use the natural to recall and inform the human. For Williams, the "strawberry bloom[ing] upon its lowly bed" (1)[8] evokes memories of childhood, what she characterizes as "[s]hort calendar joys for ever fled" (8); the strawberry, therefore, is only significant as an affective trigger, reviving a distant happiness that, ironically, accentuates by juxtaposition the "successive sorrows" (14) of later life. In O'Neill's "Ode to the Poppy" physical descriptions are almost entirely occluded by the speaker's grief. Seeking "balsam for a broken heart" (44),[9] she turns to the poppy not with a naturalist's eye for detail but seeking instead its "potent charm" (30) wherewith to "[e]xpel imperious Memory from her seat" (32). Wordsworth's reflections on the daisy, finally, are also informed and inflected by personal anguish. Despite likening the "bright daisy Flowers / [. . .] glittering in [their] bowers" (25–27)[10] to a "starry multitude" (28)—another evocation of earth as a lower heaven—he is not entranced by this vision, given its relation to an event of great sorrow in his life, the death of his brother John. For Wordsworth, John was not a brother by birth merely, but a "Brother, too, in loving [the daisy]" (5). This floral bond, as much as the fraternal, prompts Wordsworth in the end to give up the daisy to his brother. As he suggests, "[t]hou, sweet Flower, shalt sleep and wake / Upon his senseless grave" (69–70). The natural is thus quite literally rooted in and nourished by the human. Carol Christ avers that this subordination of the natural to the human is in fact typical of the Romantic engagement with particular sublimity:

> Because the poet is more interested in portraying the movement of mind than the objective order of nature, detail and imagery need not necessarily signify some universal [i.e. transcendent] characteristic of the object portrayed but may only suggest some aspect of mental experience. (11)

In effect, Christ here adopts the model of the egotistical, or what Mellor characterizes as the masculine, sublime. By shifting the focus of poetic seeking from "the objective order of nature" to the "movement of the mind," she undercuts the prepossessing effects of particular details and, in a move reminiscent of Kant, locates sublimity exclusively in the subject. As I have suggested, however, not all Romantic accounts of sublimity involve a sublimation of objective reality, a blurring of the very details deemed capable of fixing and engrossing the poetic imagination.

If we return to the catalogue of floral portraits, we will see evidence of the subject, the beholder, being almost entirely immersed in the process of objective description. Clare's sonnet "The Ragwort," for example, is stubbornly descriptive, foregrounding not the poetic mind that perceives uncommon powers in a common weed, but the weed itself. The poem as such invites what Tracy Brain characterizes as an "environmental reading," one that emphasizes not metaphorical but referential meaning (151). Environmental or ecocritical readings, as David Mazel points out, are based on the assumption that the environment—the local, physical reality of setting and object—truly matters (1).[11] Certainly for Clare, it is *that* reality, not the perceiving I/eye, which occupies his verse:

> Ragwort thou humble flower with tattered leaves
> I love to see thee come and litter gold
> What time the summer binds her russet sheaves
> Decking rude spots in beautys marigold
> That without thee were dreary to behold
> Sun burnt and bare—the meadow bank the baulk
> That leads a waggonway through mellow fields
> Rich with the tints that Harvests plenty yields
> Browns of all hues—and every where I walk
> Thy waste of shining blossoms richly shields
> The sun tanned sward in splendid hues that burn
> So bright and glaring that the very light
> Of the rich sunshine doth to paleness turn
> And seems but very shadows in thy sight.[12]

Unlike Wordsworth, who, in the first of the two Daisy poems published in 1807, speaks of having derived from his hours spent studying the flower "[s]ome memory that had taken flight; / Some chime of fancy wrong or right; / Or stray invention" (46–48)—in other words, stimuli of his own creative subconscious—Clare devotes his naturalistic scrutiny to an elaboration of the ragwort's unrecognized creativity, its capacity, that is, to turn the waste of "tattered leaves" into littered gold and thus transform "rude spots" of earth into brilliant specks of celestial light. By tracing the scatterings of this "humble flower," Clare himself participates in its creativity; his sonnet indeed manages to effect a revitalization of everyday life, to throw "splendid hues" over objects and spaces hitherto left "Sun burnt and bare" by a sort of senseless familiarity. These hues or ornaments, notably, are not the additions of a feverish imagination but the manifestations rather of nature's own richness and variety, of its inherently illimitable excess.

The evocation of such excess—of a heaven quite literally lying about us—is at the heart of the quotidian sublime. Yet what distinguishes this experience from the egotistical sublime is that the natural object is not sublimated or self-appropriated; its formal otherness, to borrow Weiskel's terminology, is not melted or subsumed by the ego. The sublime encounter, consequently, does not lead to self-apotheosis. On the contrary, it serves in a very literal sense to aggrandize the other through processes of perceptual magnification and to establish a relationship with alterity in which the boundaries between subject and object are left intact. Because this relationship is not governed by opposition or predicated on fear, the quotidian sublime is typically conducive to feelings of comfort, connection, solace and joy. Indeed, it centers on what Gaston Bachelard terms "felicitous space," which he defines as "space that may be grasped, that may be defended, the space we love" (xxxv). For Bachelard, home is the most obvious and immediate example of felicitous space; home is a sheltering sphere where "being [is concentrated] within limits that protect" (xxxvi). These limits, notably, are set not only by the walls, windows and doors of the house but also by much smaller enclosures like wardrobes, cupboards, drawers, chests, and even nests. The value of Bachelard's work to the present study lies precisely in its elaboration of these often overlooked household spaces—spaces, as he observes, that "bear within themselves a kind of esthetics of hidden things" (xxxvii). The quotidian sublime is very much about "hidden things," about what is on one hand too familiar (and sometimes too small) and on the other hand too laden with meaning to be fully apprehended or understood. Bachelard uses the term "intimate immensity" to express this paradox of unfathomable familiarity, of everyday spaces or objects that may be enclosed in one's hand but never in fact grasped.

In Romantic literature, the intimate immensity of domestic space is expressed in ways as various as the arrangement of that space. Often, as I have suggested, the writer's focus rests entirely on a solitary object, its context or surroundings being evoked only initially as a way of locating and distinguishing the object. Sometimes, however, particular objects within a larger space, a room for example, are catalogued one by one in order to convey the divisions and depths of that space. Indeed, one of the central paradoxes of domestic space—and one of the markers of intimate immensity—is the fact that the occupation of space by household objects creates new space. Space divided, in other words, is also space multiplied. Take, for example, Mary

Russell Mitford's introductory description of a rented cottage, modeled very closely on her own house in Three Mile Cross, in *Our Village* (1824). Having taken her readers practically by the hand and led them on a walking tour through the village, which she describes as "a little world of our own, close-packed and insulated" (1), she pauses at

> [a] cottage—no—a miniature house, with many additions, little odds and ends of places, pantries and what not; all angles, and of a charming in-and-outness; a little bricked court before one half, and a little flower-yard before the other; the walls, old and weather-stained, covered with hollyhocks, roses, honeysuckles, and a great apricot-tree; the casement full of geraniums (ah, there is our superb white cat peeping out from among them); the closets (our landlord has the assurance to call them rooms) full of contrivances and corner-cupboards; and the little garden behind full of common flowers, tulips, pinks, larkspurs, peonies, stocks, and carnations, with an arbour of privet, not unlike a sentry-box, where one lives in a delicious green light, and looks out on the gayest of all gay flower-beds. That house was built on purpose to show in what an exceeding small compass comfort may be packed. (6–7)

What Mitford offers here is a comprehensive compartmentalization of the entire home through a process of descriptive miniaturization. Indeed, almost every space and object—not to mention every clause—is "little." This reduction or distillation does not, however, result in a loss of substance or detail; on the contrary, Mitford packs her spaces so that everything from casements to closets to the little garden is "full." The miniature cottage, consequently, is one of material abundance, its tiny spaces teeming with particularities. The cottage is also, however, spatially abundant. Although the area it occupies is relatively small, its domestic space is richly diversified and therefore conveys a sense of almost endlessly divisible vastness. To borrow an analogy from the world of toys, the cottage is like a nesting doll in which space is reproduced in a series of diminutions—from house to room to corner-cupboard, and so on. For Mitford, notably, the cottage's intimate immensity is most clearly illustrated not by its particularization and division of space but rather by its capacity to make that space emotionally appealing—"to show," as she explains, "in what an exceedingly small compass comfort may be packed." The evident enthusiasm of Mitford's description seems in fact to suggest that domestic comfort is facilitated by packing, by a reduction of size and a division of space into cozy "little odds and ends of places." Comfort, like space, in other words, seems to be multiplied even as it is packed.

The evocation of comfort is of course not the only aim of Romanticism's particulate representations of domestic objects and spaces. For some writers, the small pockets of everyday life offer a depth of meaning, a capacity to transfix the imagination, that has very little to do with their consolatory value. Barbauld's "An Inventory of the Furniture in Dr. Priestley's Study" (1773), for example, seizes upon the wondrous juxtapositions created by the clutter of common household and specialized scientific objects in a single room. These juxtapositions of familiarity and strangeness are in a sense embodied in the figure of Priestley himself, who, while serving as a tutor at the Warrington Academy for Dissenters run by Barbauld and her husband and as an early supporter of Barbauld's literary endeavours, also conducted numerous scientific experiments on "dephlogisticated" and "flammable" air (oxygen and hydrogen, respectively), became a follower of the Unitarian movement, and, in the 1790s, sided with the English Jacobins and was forced to emigrate to Pennsylvania. In choosing Priestley's study as the focus of her text, Barbauld is therefore in a sense already foregrounding the propinquity and intersections of the ordinary and the extraordinary. Her "Inventory" begins in fact precisely at one of these intersections:

> A map of every country known,
> With not a foot of land his own.
> A list of folks that kicked a dust
> On this poor globe, from Ptol. the First;
> He hopes,—indeed it is but fair,—
> Some day to get a corner there. (1–6)[13]

By distinguishing as the first object in her domestic catalogue a map of the "known" world—a magical transposition of earthly space into perceptible, graspable boundaries—Barbauld evokes not only the capaciousness of the human intellect but also, and I think no less significantly, the intimate immensity of the room itself. Under Barbauld's particularizing gaze, Priestley's study becomes a miniature universe, its spaces numberless, minute and, like Mitford's cottage, packed. Notably, the most coveted spaces, the lines in texts of history and power, are also the smallest; they are occupied by a privileged few and gained quite literally by one's position in the world rather than by knowledge alone. Ironically, Priestley himself is marginalized in the quest for these spaces; "He *hopes*," as Barbauld notes, "[s]ome day to get a corner" in the crowded pages of his own books. Significantly, the more mundane domestic spaces and objects of his study do in fact entitle Priestley to a degree of influence of which he himself seems unaware. Commenting on a chart of the succession of British kings on Priestley's wall, Barbauld wryly implies that he himself has usurped their might and set them swinging "on a packthread" (8). Domestic space, in other words, is here characterized as a locus of subversive power, one might even say *ultimate* power, insofar as it transcends the ebb and flow of political faction and authority.

The sway of Priestley's domestic space, as Barbauld makes clear, extends in fact far beyond the political sphere. In cataloguing "[a] shelf of bottles, jar and phial" (17), she distinguishes the so-called "Leyden jar," a condenser for static electricity, and relates its "lightning" (19) to the spirit in René Le Sage's *Le Diable Boiteaux* (1707) which, upon its release from a phial, exposes the private lives of ordinary people by lifting the roofs off their houses (Mellor and Matlack 167). While using this allusion on one hand to play upon the common misapprehensions about scientific experimentation and thereby to emphasize the long-standing divisions between the realms of science and everyday life, Barbauld also, on the other hand, deliberately brings these realms together by making the elucidation of domestic space the end of scientific inquiry. The mysteries of science are in effect eclipsed by, and directed to resolving, the even greater mysteries of ordinary life. The poem itself in fact approximates an empirical study of domestic space by lifting the roof off Priestley's private study and exposing its spaces and contents to the public. As Barbauld makes clear, however, such exposure is not in itself conducive to a sense of mastery over the vastness and depth of domestic space; on the contrary, the more objects she enumerates, the more unfathomable and uncontainable the room becomes:

> Papers and books, a strange mixed olio,
> From shilling touch to pompous folio,
> Answer, remark, reply, rejoinder,
> Fresh from the mint, all stamped and coined here;
> Like new-made glass, set by to cool,
> Before it bears the workman's tool.
> A blotted proof-sheet, wet from Bowling.
> —"How can a man his anger hold in?"—
> Forgotten rimes, and college themes,
> Worm-eaten plans, and embryo schemes;—
> A mass of heterogeneous matter,
> A chaos dark, nor land nor water;—
> New books, like new-born infants, stand,
> Waiting the printer's clothing hand;—
> Others, a motley ragged brood,

> Their limbs unfashioned all, and rude,
> Like Cadmus' half-formed men appear. . . . (29–45)

From "embryo schemes" to "infant" books to "half-formed men," material excess—specifically, literary material excess—here begins to take on a life of its own, a life that verges on the grotesque. The proliferation of words on Priestley's shelves and, concomitantly, in Barbauld's poem, assumes a shape of indeterminate substance and dimension, "[a] mass of heterogeneous matter," that threatens to extinguish meaning in a "chaos dark." Particulate vision is inundated and for a moment—a moment of sublime blockage—overwhelmed. What in the end recalls both Barbauld and the reader from this profusion of chaotic detail is a solitary object mysteriously rendered as "[a] thing unknown, without a name, / Born of the air and doomed to flame" (57–58). Whether Barbauld is here referring to an unnamed gas or perhaps to her own collection of poems on Priestley's shelf—a collection awaiting the same dismal transformation from "new-born infant" to "[f]orgotten rimes"—is unclear. By her deliberate silence, Barbauld in effect preserves the mysteries of domestic space even while cataloguing its contents. On another level, however, Priestley's study preserves its own mysteries. Notwithstanding the inevitable decay and destruction of the objects in its midst, all of which, in the language of apocalyptic fervor, are "doomed to flame," the room itself, the inner universe, remains intact; its vastness, its capacity to contain a chaotic jumble of irresolvable, irreconcilable particularities, is uncompromised.

A final example of Romanticism's engagement with the intimate immensity of domestic space is Clare's "Farm Breakfast" (c.1827–35), one of the poet's few descriptive sonnets set entirely indoors. Like Barbauld's "Inventory," the poem lifts the roof off an ostensibly private space and thrusts the reader directly into the midst of its clutter and din:

> Maids shout to breakfast in a merry strife,
> And the cat runs to hear the whetted knife,
> And dogs are ever in the way to watch
> The mouldy crust and falling bone to catch.
> The wooden dishes round in haste are set,
> And round the table all the boys are met;
> All know their own save Hodge who would be first
> But every one his master leaves the worst.
> On every wooden dish, a humble claim,
> Two rude-cut letters mark the owner's name;

> From every nook the smile of plenty calls,
> And reasty flitches decorate the walls,
> Moore's Almanack where wonders never cease–
> All smeared with candle-snuff and bacon-grease.[14]

Drawn at perhaps its busiest hour, the farm kitchen, like Priestley's study, is a chaotic space of growth and decline where all energy is devoted to the consumption of (culinary) creation. There is nothing, however, grotesque about the excessive noises, movements and appetites that characterize and crowd this space. As Clare notes, breakfast is a "merry strife." The kitchen is in fact one of the only spaces of "plenty" in an environment so "humble" that wooden dishes are the sole possessions claimed by name. What Clare describes is not, however, merely a mundane plenitude of chairs and dishes, crusts and flitches. Amid the crowded nooks and clatter—indeed, almost entirely occluded by layers of "candle-snuff" and "bacon-grease"—is a solitary object of unceasing "wonders," a smeared immensity, Moore's Almanac. A compendium of meteorological, geographical, medicinal, horticultural, scientific and even prophetic wisdom, the almanac, not unlike Priestley's map of the world, is a distillation of vastness. Literally covered over with the skin—the snuff and grease—of everyday life, the almanac is descried by particulate vision and its wonders immediately apprehended. Yet while Priestley's map is but one object in a miscellany of specialized and wondrous products of human endeavor, each in effect contributing to a sense of uncontainable excess, the almanac is fascinating because it is set against a backdrop of unremarkable, place-appropriate kitchen supplies. Notwithstanding its smeared cover, the almanac indeed appears to be out of place in an enclosure of flitch-covered walls. Clare's matter-of-fact tone does not, however, betray any surprise at its appearance. The kitchen he describes not only contains the 'out-of-place' but seems in fact to call into question the presumption of place-appropriateness. Domestic space for Clare is inherently variegated and complex, inherently immense, because it is transected by the pragmatic and the marvelous. An almanac in a small farm kitchen speaks to the vastness and depth—the microcosmology—of ostensibly limited domestic space.

As I have suggested, this microcosmology typically comprises exterior as well as interior space. Representations of home in Romantic literature are indeed broad enough to sustain the dialectic of indoors and outdoors—what Bachelard terms a "dialectic of division" (211). Notably, the division between these spheres is not always clearly defined or maintained. Some Romantics in fact conflate interiority and exteriority by seizing upon points of intersection between these realms, what one might classify as liminal spaces that are neither entirely inside nor outside. One such space is the nest. Bachelard, who devotes an entire chapter to birds' nests in *The Poetics of Space*, foregrounds their tendency to collapse spatial distinctions. "A nest," he observes, "like any other image of rest and quiet, is immediately associated with the image of a house" (98). This association, notably, flows in both directions:

> among all the shelter virtues, the roof is the dominant evidence. Under the roof's covering the walls are of earth and stone. The openings are low. A thatched cottage is set on the ground like a nest in a field. (98)

The nest is in effect a further distillation and refinement of human household space, a miniaturization that conveys not only domestic values such as security and community but also the aesthetic values of precision and unity. As Bachelard notes,

> in the world of inanimate objects, extraordinary significance is attached to nests. We want them to be perfect, to bear the mark of a very sure instinct. We ourselves marvel at this instinct, and a nest is generally considered to be one of the marvels of animal life. (92)

This conception of the nest as a physical marvel clearly pervades the work of Dorothy Wordsworth and John Clare, the two Romantic writers who deal most extensively and intimately with nature's own mystic circles. Wordsworth's fascination with nests centers in fact largely around one particular specimen, a swallows' nest whose construction, destruction and eventual rebuilding she traces over a period of three weeks in the *Grasmere Journals* (1800–1803). While previous criticism has tended to subsume this episode within a wider focus on human community, homemaking and marriage,[15] I will suggest, to the contrary, that it exemplifies Wordsworth's aesthetic prioritisation of smallness and intimacy, her desire to account for the world and the life around her on the level of particular details. Indeed, her work in the *Journals* is characterised by what Jill Ehnenn designates as "an alternate mode of perceiving and recording experience" (88). Small details and spaces have value for Wordsworth not because they form part of a larger world but rather because they are in themselves worlds and universes entire. Her fascination with the swallows serves to bring universes great and small—that of Dove Cottage and that of the nest—into propinquity without subordinating one to the other. The parallels between Dove Cottage and the nest, between these spheres of intimate domesticity, are indeed unmistakable. Like the Wordsworths, the swallows are busily engaged in homemaking, in fellowship, in loving communication. Their first appearance in the journal, foregrounded by a description of a young bird, which, having left its nest, "seemed bemazed and not strong enough to strive with [the wind],"[16] is characterised by an irrepressible sense of hope:

> The swallows come to the sitting-room window as if wishing to build but I am afraid they will not have courage for it, but I believe they will build at my room window. They twitter and make a bustle and a little chearful song hanging against the pane of glass, with their soft white bellies close to the glass, and their forked fish-like tails. They swim round and round and again they come. (*Journals* 137)

Whereas all the surrounding events and details of Wednesday, June 16, 1802, are presented in past tense, Wordsworth distinguishes her account of the swallows with present tense narration, thereby imbuing this episode with a sense of enduring immediacy. Indeed, the birds' rhythmic and repetitive movement, their swimming "round and round," is suggestive of an almost primal energy, what William describes in "Lines Written A Few Miles Above Tintern Abbey" as "[a] motion and a spirit that impels / All thinking things, all objects of all thought, / And rolls through all things" (101–103).[17] The apperception of a common "motion" in the everyday phenomena of nature enables Dorothy to find not merely solace or momentary distraction in the lives of swallows but a source of engrossing presence. Having alluded but briefly to their chirping busyness in the entry for June 19, she expatiates on their activities and her own corresponding fascination on June 25:

> As soon as the nest was broad enough, a sort of ledge for them they sate both mornings and evenings, but they did not pass the night there. I watched them one morning, when William was at Eusemere, for more than an hour. Every now and then there was a feeling motion in their wings, a sort of tremulousness and they sang a low song to one another. (*Journals* 142)

The intensity of Wordsworth's focus not only captures detail, like the "feeling motion" in the swallows' wings, but is itself suggestive of captivation or entrancement. For one deeply-focused hour, she is transfixed by the "low song" of everyday life.

Not unlike Wordsworth's evocation of enduring immediacy in the first description of the swallows, the foregoing episode also subverts real time by appearing after the discovery of the fallen nest. In some sense, therefore, it may be read as a nostalgic reminiscence, a commemoration of harmonious homemaking. Clearly, the fall of the nest is the central event of June 25, and Wordsworth's response to it reveals a keenly sympathetic understanding of the value of the space that is home:

> . . . I went just before tea into the garden. I looked up at my Swallow's nest and it was gone. It had fallen down. Poor little creatures they could not themselves be more distressed than I was. I went upstairs to look at the Ruins. They lay in a large heap upon the window ledge; these Swallows had been ten days employed in building this nest, and it seemed to be almost finished. (*Journals* 142)

Wordsworth's sense of connectedness with the daily life of swallows, though it derives on one hand from what is merely a fortuitous sharing of space, an accidental proximity of homes, is also characterised by an internalised spirit of community or neighbourliness. Her references to "*my* Swallow's nest" (emphasis added) and to an equitable sharing of distress elucidate an investment not only of time or attention but also of affection. The swallows' misfortune, notably, elicits both commiseration and commemoration. The remnants of the nest, though ostensibly nothing more than "a large heap upon the window ledge," are distinguished by the title of "Ruins." Their history, though spanning merely ten days, is recounted by Wordsworth with a sense of blighted hope: "it seemed to be almost finished." The inclusion of such a minute event—which Pamela Woof attributes to a voracity of memory that insists on "having everything in" (39)—serves on one hand to call into question the pre-eminence of human spaces and human histories by bringing them on a level with the worlds and narratives of birds, while also, on the other hand, signalling the fragility of sheltering spaces in general and thus enhancing the value of all homes, be they nests or cottages. Clearly, the idea of home is central to Wordsworth's journals. As the hub of felicitous space, the home is root, shelter and solace all in one; it is the space of labour, of love, of community. The home is also, however, as Bachelard points out, a sanctuary for self-expression and imagination. Using "home" and "house" interchangeably, the latter being the physical manifestation of the former, he suggests that "the chief benefit of the house [is that it . . .] shelters daydreaming, the house protects the dreamer, *the house allows one to dream in peace*" (6, emphasis added). Wordsworth seems to convey a similar notion when she writes that "Grasmere . . . calls home the heart to quietness" (*Journals* 17). Dove Cottage, in this conception, becomes the very embrace of that quietness.

Given the centrality of the cottage home to Wordsworth's lived and written life, her affecting response to the fallen nest may be linked to her own fears of homelessness. Certainly the proliferation of beggars and vagrants in the pages of her journals would suggest that such fears are both real and reasonable. Indeed, though her emphasis is on "felicitous space" and the domestic microcosm, the worlds of Grasmere and Dove Cottage are continually traversed and impinged upon by the poor, the dispossessed, the uprooted. Beyond the peace and stillness of home Wordsworth distinguishes "the Beggars' cant and the whining voice of sorrow" (*Journals* 26). Her detailed descriptions of these ambling, tattered supplicants are often juxtaposed by images of her own relative security and comfort. The account of the old sailor, for example, ends with Dorothy, William, Mary and Coleridge sitting "snugly round the fire" (*Journals* 73). A more telling episode is recorded in the entry for February 12, 1802. Wordsworth here recounts the appearance of a begging mother and son at her door, their house having been "unroofed" (*Journals* 89) in a storm. Though she does not relate what, if anything, they were given, Wordsworth concludes the episode with a renewed appreciation of her own comparative well-being:

> Poor creatures! When the woman was gone, I could not help thinking that we are not half thankful enough that we are placed in that condition of life in which we are. We do not so often bless god for this as we wish for this 50£ that 100£ etc. etc. We have not, however to reproach ourselves with ever breathing a murmur. This woman's was but a *common* case. (*Journals* 89)

The parallels between these "Poor creatures" and the "Poor little creatures" on her window ledge are obvious, and, indeed, in Wordsworth's domestic cosmology there is between them little difference. Of significance here is her recognition that the condition of being sheltered or housed is an increasingly *un*common privilege, one that a mere gust of wind may instantly revoke. As she relates, in closing the account, the "wild and melancholy sight" (*Journals* 89) of this dispossessed family passing by her window in the stillness of a snowy evening, one senses rather the anxiety of homelessness than the gratitude of shelter. Indeed, as Anita McCormick notes, the vagrants she describes throughout her journals are "projections of Dorothy's worst anxieties: of losing her home, her role and her sense of self" (482).

If homelessness is an underlying fear in the *Grasmere Journals*, homemaking, or, in the case of the swallows, the rebuilding of home, is a source of unparalleled joy and comfort. Despite three missing entries after that of the fallen nest, Wordsworth continues to attend to the activities of the undaunted birds on Tuesday, June 29:

> It is now 8 o'clock I will go and see if my swallows are on their nest. Yes! there they are side by side both looking down into the garden. I have been out on purpose to see their faces. I knew by looking at the window that they were there. (*Journals* 142)

What begins for Wordsworth as "an uncertain day" (*Journals* 142) on account of unsettled weather is quickly composed and brightened by a scene of domestic fellowship in the nest. Previously content to describe the swallows by their white bellies and forked tails, Wordsworth here seeks the faces of her neighbours as though expecting to see in them the joy of imminent shelter. When their home is at last finished, the event is related by coupling the domestic spheres of nest and cottage: "The swallows have completed their beautiful nest. I baked bread and pies" (*Journals* 145). Clearly, the image here conveyed is of contiguous and compatible universes, of harmony within and between. The parallels between life in the cottage and life in the nest extend not only to scenes of domestic bustling but also to moments of rest and recuperative fellowship. The image of the birds sitting together side by side and singing low to one another, for example, is mirrored by an earlier (June 2, 1802), and perhaps the journals' most affecting, passage on sibling love:

> After we came in we sate in deep silence at the window—I on a chair and William with his hand on my shoulder. We were deep in Silence and Love, a blessed hour. (*Journals* 130)

It is, as Bachelard points out, in these blessed hours, these spots of time within the sheltering space of home, that one "experiences all the qualities of intimacy with increased intensity" (41).

For Wordsworth, the travails and apparent joys of nest-life do not merely echo those of life in the cottage but come to be associated with the very ideal and essence of home. On the eve of her departure for London, a trip which will culminate in William's marriage to Mary Hutchinson and thus in the irrevocable alteration of the domestic cosmology of Dove Cottage, Dorothy reflects with an admixture of regret and nostalgia on the life and spaces she must leave behind:

> The Swallows I must leave them the well the garden the Roses, all. Dear creatures!! They sang last night after I was in bed—seemed to be singing

to one another, just before they settled to rest for the night. Well, I must go. Farewell. (*Journals* 146)

For Dorothy, the swallows have come to epitomise domestic fellowship and devotion, their low song continuing uninterrupted as before, seemingly unfazed by the perturbations of life around them. Unlike the changing world of Dove Cottage, the nest maintains its integrity, its habitual spheres of motion and emotion. By attending to these spheres and to the enclosing circle of the nest that is both shelter and home, Wordsworth elucidates the intimate immensity of everyday space. "Intimate" in this context is of course suggestive not only of small, domestic spaces, but also of a method of aesthetic engagement, a perceptual thoroughness, that allows the subject—the ranging I/eye—to be arrested by and to re-envision the apparently common or seemingly mundane, the immense world in a ring of mud and spittle. Wordsworth's visual and textual attentiveness to the nest and its inhabitants, her ability to evoke wonder from apparent plainness, to recognise a home in a little space and to make of it a universe—all of this enables her to transfix the reader much as she herself is transfixed. Indeed, part of her 'journalistic genius,' to paraphrase Alan Liu (115), lies in her capacity to transmit the very fascination which seizes upon the details of intimate space and swells them into worlds.

For Clare, as for Wordsworth, the nest is an emblem of the numinous everyday. His literary engagement with birds and their nests is, however, rather more diverse and extensive than Wordsworth's, comprising over fifty poems in addition to numerous journal entries and nature notes. Most of the poems, as Anne Tibble observes in her introduction to *Birds Nest*, one of the first collections of Clare's ornithological verse, were not published until the 1970s, a reflection surely of the poet's historically contested place in the Romantic canon. In an apt commentary on his still dubious propinquity to the "Pantheon" of nineteenth-century literature, Eric Robinson and Geoffrey Summerfield write that "Clare, probably more happy there, is pottering about in the garden outside" (14). To this I would add that Clare is not merely pottering about but actively looking for nests, for to trace him to the garden is invariably to trace him to nests. The poet's fascination with these intimate domestic spheres manifests itself not only in the number and variety of nests he describes but also in the fastidious precision with which they are rendered. The following passage on nest construction is a showpiece of particularization, a veritable bird's-eye view of home:

> Long tailed titmouse and Chaffinch and red cap make a most beautiful outside to their nests of grey lichen linnets and hedgsparrows make

> a loose ruff outside of coarse green moss wool and roots the first are like the freestone fabrics of finished ellegance the latter like the rough plain walls of a husbandman's cottage yet equally warm and comfortable within Pinks use cowhair and some feathers for their inside hangings redcaps get thistle down hedge sparrows use wool and cowhair intermixed linnets use wool and cowhair and the furze linnet uses rabbit down these four sorts of birds never (I think) are known to use horse hair while yellow hammers ground larks yellow wagtails and skylarks never use wool or cowhair but on the contrary small roots and horse hair and this universaly bulfinches make a slight nest of sticks and small roots very shallow whitethroats use dead hariff stalks linked with cobwebs and lined with fine roots and horsehair [sic][18]

What immediately strikes one about this excerpt is the juxtaposition of precise, observed detail—as though Clare were pulling the various nests apart, twig by twig, hair by hair—and a rhetorical and stylistic nonchalance, a loose cobbling together of facts based not only on direct observation but also on recollection, deduction and conjecture, all without the benefit of full stops or capitals. In essence, what Clare assembles here is a nest of his own, a sort of verbal bricolage tending to the elucidation not of one detail or one moment of natural observation but of many simultaneously. The effect on the reader, even with the inclusion of gaps between sentences, is overwhelming; one is inundated by particularities, rushed headlong from one object (or bit thereof) to the next, never able to formulate the image of an entire nest. It is important to note, however, that Clare is not solely interested in objects or material details. His focus also comprises the actions, the movements—the verbs—that serve to hold raw materials together. The nest is after all *made* to be a home. Materials are collected ("redcaps get thistle down"), mixed ("whitethroats use dead hariff stalks linked with cobwebs and lined with fine roots and horsehair"), shaped ("bulfinches make a slight nest of sticks and small roots very shallow") and even used ornamentally for "beautiful outsides" and "inside hangings." Clare's descriptions indeed foreground an aesthetic of nest-making based on human models of domesticity. He likens the exteriors of titmouse, chaffinch and red cap nests to "the freestone fabrics of finished ellegance" and distinguishes them from the humbler constructions of linnets and hedge sparrows whose "rough plain walls" evoke images of a "husbandman's cottage." As Clare points out, moreover, the primary aim of nest-making, as of house-holding, is to make a space that is "warm and comfortable," to enclose and enfold those within, to facilitate a sense of physical and emotional security.

The emphasis on domestic security naturally presupposes the perception of a threat to that security, and, indeed, much of Clare's fascination with nests hinges on their extreme fragility and susceptibility to the accidental and often wilful incursions of human hands. Much as Wordsworth's representation of domestic space is informed by a realization of its growing scarcity and impermanence, so Clare's depictions of birds' nests are set against a backdrop of human insensitivity and even hostility. Of the twenty poems in *Birds Nest*, more than half make direct reference to human hunters, variously styled as "clowns," "birdboys," "schoolboys" and "nesting boys." Sometimes, as in "Impromptu on finding a birds nest," the threat is disarmed as suddenly as it is evoked:

> Fear not little younglings no robber is nigh ye
> No unfeeling clown wipes they screening boughs bye
> The poor harmless bees in the flower blooming by thee
> Are not more unlikley to wrong ye then I (1–4)[19]

On other occasions, however, Clare details the deleterious effects of unwelcome curiosity. In the sonnet "The sailing puddock sweeps about for prey," the titular bird's nest is ravaged with unmitigated cruelty:

> The schoolboy often hears the old ones cry
> & climbs the tree & gets them ere they fly
> & takes them home & often cuts their wing
> & ties them in the garden with a string (11–14)[20]

Despite his assurances of benignity, Clare himself at times assumes the menaces of a plunderer. In "There is a small woodpecker red & grey," for example, he details his own efforts to secure the woodpecker's rarely seen eggs:

> Ive stood nor seen them till they flew away
> I've swarmed the grain & clumb with hook & pole
> But scarce could get three fingers in the hole
> They build on grains scarce thicker then ones legs
> Ive found the nests but never got the eggs
> But boys who wish to see what eggs they lay
> Will climb the tree & saw the grain away (8–14)[21]

The only thing that here distinguishes Clare from wanton boys is an unwillingness to fell trees, the last extremity of grim determination. In all other respects, he is equally invasive. His "three fingers in the hole" represent a profound assault on the peace and security of domestic space. One could in fact argue that Clare's particularizing aesthetic depends to some extent on disassembling the nest in order to study and describe its constituent parts. Unlike Dorothy's strictly watchful communion with the humble lives and worlds that intersect her own, Clare pursues an often tactile, even pugnacious, method of engaging everyday reality. His notes and poems are written, as it were, with dirty fingers—fingers like those that Dorothy's brother used to pen his recollections of plundered ravens' nests and ravaged hazel bowers. It is only in their responses to such violations that Clare and William differ, for Clare pries into nature like a naturalist not a moralist. His conduct in fact anticipates Ruskin's aesthetic strictures in *Modern Painters* (1856), a text in which it is proposed that "to break a rock with a hammer in search of crystal may sometimes be an act not disgraceful to human nature, and that to dissect a flower may sometimes be as proper as to dream over it" (412). For Ruskin as for Clare, full and accurate perception depends on empirical rigour, on a willingness to dismantle, if need be, nature's wondrous constructions in order to better understand and appreciate them. Particulate vision, as Ruskin's first example implies, may also serve to reveal rather than destroy wonder.

Where the revelation of natural wonder is not helped by hammers or fingers, Clare adopts other investigative methods that convey a profound sensitivity to the nest's precarious place in the world and a sympathy for its inhabitants. Birds, as he designates them in various poems, are his "neighbours," and their nests represent an integral part of the poet's landscape of home in and around Helpstone. Often therefore, as in "The Nightingales Nest," he approaches the nest not with benign intent merely but in postures of reverence and awe:

> Creeping on hands and knees through matted thorn
> To find her nest, and see her feed her young.
> And vainly did I many hours employ:
> All seemed as hidden as a thought unborn.
> And where those crimping fern-leaves ramp among
> The hazel's under boughs, I've nestled down,
> And watched her while she sung; and her renown
> Hath made me marvel that so famed a bird
> Should have no better dress than russet brown. (13–21)[22]

There is something indeed almost penitential about the poet's cowed advance through dirt and thorn, his prostration before a nest in the woods.

Undertaking the journey with no certainty of success, he resigns himself to a wait of "many hours"—a sort of prayerful watch—before at last spying the "famed" bird. Keenly aware of the preciousness of the moment, Clare extends on this occasion no prying fingers but instead effects a momentary kinship with the bird by "nestl[ing]" down in an enclosure of ferns and hazel boughs—literally a nest of his own—and watching. Through self-restraint he attests to a relationship with the nightingale, the natural other, in which the boundaries of domestic space are preserved and protected. It is in fact only through such restraint, such a yielding of the self to the other, the subject to the object, that the "marvel" of the nightingale's song is experienced. As Clare observes, "if I touched a bush or scarcely stirred / All in a moment stopt" (28–29). A watchful, peaceable coexistence, notably, yields another marvel no less profound than song: a more expansive view of the world. Suggesting that the nightingale's "joys are evergreen, her world is wide" (41), Clare seems to imply that listening in and of itself, listening as a sort of rudimentary empathy, ushers one into that joy, that vastness. The nightingale's song indeed alters the landscape around the nest. As Clare observes,

> . . . melody seems hid in every flower,
> That blossoms near thy home. These harebells all
> Seems bowing with the beautiful in song;
> And gaping cuckoo-flower, with spotted leaves,
> Seems blushing of the singing it has heard. (71–75)

Like the harebells and the cuckoo-flower, the poet himself, nestled down and transfixed by song, is for a moment "[l]ost in a wilderness of listening leaves" (32).

His wonderment notably is not, like that of countless poets before him, aroused by the nightingale's music alone. Evincing a marked disdain for the generic praises bestowed on the famed bird—which he dismisses as "[p]oor idle tales of idle minds / Who never seek for truth" (25–26)[23]—Clare turns at poem's end to the elaboration of a marvel only gleaned by direct observation, the marvel namely of the nest itself:

> How curious is the nest; no other bird
> Uses such loose materials, or weaves
> Their dwellings in such spots: dead oaken leaves
> Are placed without, and velvet moss within,
> And little scraps of grass, and, scant and spare,
> What scarcely seem materials, down and hair;

> For from men's haunts she nothing seems to win.
> Yet Nature is the builder, and contrives
> Homes for her children's comfort, even here;
> Where Solitude's disciples spend their lives
> Unseen, save when a wanderer passes near
> That loves such pleasant places. Deep adown,
> The nest is made a hermit's mossy cell.
> Snug lie her curious eggs in number five,
> Of deadened green, or rather olive brown;
> And the old prickly thorn-bush guards them well.
> And here we'll leave them, still unknown to wrong,
> As the old woodland's legacy of song. (76–93)

For Clare, the nightingale's uniqueness and wondrousness have as much to do with its "curious" nest as its "sobbing songs" (25). Woven sparsely of "loose" materials and set not high in trees but on the ground itself, the nightingale's nest is in some ways the most humble and precarious of domestic spaces. Likened rather to a "hermit's mossy cell" than to a thatched cottage, the nest occupies a marginal place on the forest floor—isolated, unseen and unwelcoming to passers-by. Clare's scrutiny, however, reveals "comfort, even here." Peering "[d]eep adown," he discerns five eggs lying snugly in the bosom of the nest. Despite the meanness of their surroundings, the eggs partake of an idyllic existence, an enviable state, in that they are, as Clare points out, "still unknown to wrong." The nest thus shelters not only life but innocence; wondrously constituted and situated, it is a self-sufficient sphere of songs and dreaming.

While some nests are so well hidden that they demand of the viewer a willingness to crawl on hands and knees, to wait and even suffer, in order to partake of their wonders, others, as Clare points out, lie scattered around us in such improbable proximity that their mere existence is a marvel. Clare claims, for example, to have "found larks nests in an old cart rut grassed over and pettichaps close on the edge of a horsetrack in a narrow lane where two carts could not pass and two oxen would even have difficulty in doing so but yet I never found a nest destroyed" (*Poems and Prose* 147). The closer that nests are built to the 'tracks' of human beings, the more precarious and also marvellous is their existence. Nowhere is this idea made clearer than in "The Blackbird":

> The Blackbird has a thousand whims
> In choosing places for her nest
> In spots that so unlikely seems

> As want of skill and hardly taste
> Upon the bindings of the hedge
> On water grains of high oak tree
>
> In roots oer looked by kecks and sedge
> On thorns where every eye may see
> And on gateposts very top
> Oerhung with boughs will wonder stare
> To find them—shepherds laughing stop
> And think that boys have placed it there
>
> On woodstacks in a cottage yard
> Nay shelved upon an hovel stone
> Ive marked them with a strange regard
> As nests some foreign birds might own
> My wonder I could scarce conceal
> And what surprised me more than all
>
> Between the spokes of an old wheel
> That leaned against an hovel wall
> Some moss was seen I thought it laid
> By boys to make each other stare
> But bye and bye a nest was there
> And eggs like fairy gifts were there[24]

With what seems to Clare a careless whimsy, the blackbird builds its nests "where every eye may see," as if inviting into its domestic sphere the very destruction that other species such as nightingales work so assiduously to prevent. It is, however, precisely this negligence or brazenness which in the end saves the nest. As Clare notes, "shepherds laughing stop" but do not inspect the nest, thinking it already discovered and plundered by birdboys. Thus the nest survives in wondrous propinquity to the human space of home—on gateposts, woodstacks, even on a hovel stone—"shelved" as if it were a common household object. Only an uncommonly scrupulous eye, a "strange regard" such as Clare's, recognizes the nest for what it is. Yet just as he protects the secret location of the nightingale's nest, keeping it "unknown to wrong," so he endeavours to "conceal" his great astonishment at finding the blackbird's home "[b]etween the spokes of an old wheel / That leaned against an hovel wall"—literally bound up in the domestic spaces and diurnal rounds of human existence. What so astonishes Clare, however, is more than the bird's unexpected adaptation of human space. The transformation of "[s]ome moss" into a wondrous nest containing "eggs like fairy gifts" is for the poet a miraculous metamorphosis of substance, as though the moss itself had been turned to eggs by unseen hands. Indeed, both the spaces and the materials of everyday life offer "gifts" to those who take the time to study the shifting face of apparently familiar surroundings and allow themselves to be transfixed by what they have seen, or think they have seen, before. Such gifts are not, however, simply to be claimed from "fairy" hands and self-appropriated. The miracle of the eggs' appearance is brief and attests to a mutually sustaining contiguity between domestic spheres, a relationship of security that depends on a willingness to share space. To claim the eggs would be to violate the bond of shared space, the very ethic of home. In an apt commentary on the necessity of preserving this ethic, Jonathan Bate observes in *Romantic Ecology* that "if 'the nonhuman' is to do something for us, we must do something for it—not least give it space, allow it to continue to exist" (56).

While most nests, as Clare points out, are subject to violations and depend for their survival on the concealment of their gifts, some are wondrous because of their *in*violability, their capacity quite literally to transcend the schemes and machinations of human hunters. "The Ravens Nest," for example, details the improbable, indeed almost legendary, survival of "a curious nest / Of twigs made up a faggot near in size" (2–3).[25] Although the nest's considerable size makes it an easy target for the eye, its position "[u]pon the collar of an hugh [sic] old oak" (1) ensures a rather more difficult assault for the hands and feet of intrepid birdboys. "[D]own they sluther," Clare notes, "soon as ere they try" (9). These failed attempts "[y]ear after year" (2) become in a sense as familiar and renowned as the nest itself:

> . . . old men
> When passing bye will laugh and tell the ways
> They had when boys to climb that very tree
> And as it so would seem that very nest
> That ne'er was missing from that self same spot
> A single year in all their memorys (10–15)

The nest not only contributes to the narratives of local history but in fact becomes a focal point of both personal and communal recollection: it unites the village in the effort of attempt, the inevitability of failure, and the pleasures of reminiscence. It is a landmark no less distinctive, no less bound up with the history of a community than human dwelling places. The nest also of course has a history of its own, a history namely as a home. As Clare points out, the villagers' fondness for rehearsing that history is suggestive of its integrality to their own notions of home and community:

> And they will say that the two birds are now
> The very birds that owned the dwelling then
> Some think it strange yet certaintys at loss
> And cannot contradict it so they pass
> As old birds living the woods patriarchs
> Old as the oldest men so famed and known (16–21)

As living symbols of immutability, the ravens are invested with a mystical or "strange" authority that defies both time and reason. Likened to the village's "oldest men" who seem by age alone to have risen to positions of unassailable renown, the birds are acclaimed as "the woods patriarchs," governors not only of their nest but of the entire scene below them. The nest is nonetheless the locus or epicenter of their power in that it is the visible manifestation of the ravens' seemingly timeless existence. As Bachelard suggests, "the nest found in natural surroundings [. . .] becomes for a moment the center—the term is no exaggeration—of an entire universe, the evidence of a cosmic situation" (94). Upon ending his account, Clare returns to this center and reinvokes its structural and temporal transcendence:

> every spring
> Finds the two ancient birds at their old task
> Repairing the hugh nest—where still they live
> Through changes winds and storms and are secure
> And like a landmark in the chronicles
> Of village memorys treasured up yet lives
> The huge old oak that wears the ravens nest (43–48)

The nest's intimate immensity is here expressed in its dual function as a private shelter and a repository of "village memorys." Much as its architecture protects "two ancient birds" from the natural and climatological changes brought on by winds and storms, so its unaltered presence atop the oak serves to remind the village elders of the "adventureous days" (40) of their youth. No more than a little repair, a little effort of recollection, serves to maintain the nest's central place in the village and, with it, a sense of a still living past.

While the nest is at once an emblem of the numinous everyday and a physical manifestation of the mystic circle of home, it is by no means the culmination or, if you will, the terminus of the Romantic aesthetic of particularity.

From crowded cottages to cluttered rooms to nests, the Romantic preoccupation with details traces everyday life to a still more refined and particulate realm of existence—that of the insect. Adopting Timothy Brownlow's discussion of 'insect views,' which he borrows from a passage in Henry David Thoreau's journals in which the author comments on nature's capacity to "bear the closest inspection" and her invitation to us "to lay our eye level with her smallest leaf and take an insect view of its plain" (*Journals* I.81), I would like to consider the entomological writings of the English Romantics and their relation to the intimate immensity of the very soil under our feet. After all, the insect view proposed by Thoreau demands not merely an intensification of visual attention but an entire alteration in one's physical relation to the earth, a prostration akin to Clare's. This willingness to lay the self quite literally beside the other and adopt a posture of radical empathy with it serves to distinguish such works as Burns's "To a Louse" and Clare's varied reflections on insects in his *Nature Notes* and *Natural History Letters* from more typical or what I would define as more "self-centered" engagements with insect life such as William Wordsworth's "To a Butterfly" and Barbauld's "The Caterpillar." These latter works, as I will suggest, establish a relationship with natural alterity that always returns to and re-establishes the priority of the human.

Wordsworth's "To a Butterfly," a title affixed to two companion poems composed in Grasmere in the spring of 1802, adopts an insect view rather for the purpose of commemorating the speaker's (and poet's) relationship with his sister than of celebrating the butterfly itself. What draws him to the "gay creature" (7)[26] in the first of these poems is its unlikely reflection of himself. The butterfly, as he suggests, is a "Historian of my infancy" (4) capable of reviving "Dead times" (6). From the outset, therefore, the speaker uses the titular insect to slip out of the present, to withdraw from the very moment of encounter into a long lost and wished for past. He begs it to "[s]tay near me" (1) only to absorb it in a memory of childish play, a time when

> My sister Emmeline and I
> Together chased the butterfly!
> A very hunter did I rush
> Upon the prey;—with leaps and springs
> I followed on from brake to bush;
> But she, God love her! feared to brush
> The dust from off its wings. (12–18)

The substitution of one butterfly for another that accompanies the shift from present to past in effect diminishes the experience and significance of particulate reality: one butterfly is merely a copy of another, an unindividuated double. Notably, it is Emmeline who offers an alternate, a quite literally more *in*sightful (not to mention ecological) response to natural otherness. Her fear of brushing "[t]he dust from off its wings" is indicative not simply of a moral but also of a visual sensitivity to the details of everyday life. The link between the speaker's Emmeline and the poet's Dorothy is unmistakable. Commended in *The Prelude* for having "preserved me still / A Poet, made me seek beneath that name / My office upon earth, and nowhere else" (X.919–921), Dorothy, like Emmeline, is associated with a self-effacing approach to natural otherness, with a perceptual sensitivity that both discerns and preserves in the other the slightest of distinguishing details.

The second of the two poems may be read as an attempt by Wordsworth, at least in the opening lines, to adopt his sister's sensitivity. He begins, fittingly, in a state of apparent entrancement:

> I've watched you now a full half-hour,
> Self-poised upon that yellow flower;
> And, little Butterfly! indeed
> I know not if you sleep or feed.
> How motionless!—not frozen seas
> More motionless! and then
> What joy awaits you, when the breeze
> Hath found you out among the trees,
> And calls you forth again! (1–9)[27]

Intent solely on describing what is before him and fascinated by nothing more than perfect stillness, Wordsworth writes in the thrall of the present moment, himself as motionless as the "[s]elf-poised" butterfly. The spell, however, the "full half-hour," is broken with the butterfly's departure on the breeze, at which point the poet likewise begins to stir again, moving from present captivation to an enumeration of all that is around him—"This plot of orchard-ground [. . .] / My trees [. . .] my Sister's flowers" (10–11)—and finally to the "dead times" of the previous poem, the "summer days, when we were young" (16). His invitation to the butterfly to "[c]ome often near us" (14) echoes the pleading voice of the first poem and may be read as a yearning not for the insect per se as for the innocent past with which it is inextricably associated. In other words, the butterfly's literal significance, its capacity to fill a half hour with wonder, is ultimately subordinated to its symbolic significance, its capacity to transport the poet back to those "[s]weet childish days" (18) spent in company with his sister. For Wordsworth the butterfly is valuable rather as a reminder of an age of wonder than as a wonder in itself; it serves to direct him to the fount of his consolations and creative powers without necessarily supplying their want in the present moment. As Christine Kenyon Jones notes, "the meeting of Wordsworth's 'egotistical sublime' with the radically different egotisms of beasts and birds [and insects] sets up tensions and complexities" (87)—tensions and complexities, one might add, that are often resolved, if not in a subsumption, then in a blurring of individual details and essence.

Barbauld's insect view in "The Caterpillar" (1825), while it does not conduct to the sort of personal recollections that characterize Wordsworth's engagement with everyday particularity, is likewise adopted primarily for the purpose of elucidating human experience. The poem in fact functions as an extended simile on the subject of "grow[ing] human" (39)[28] in the most unlikely of circumstances. The event that triggers these reflections is the poet's encounter with a solitary caterpillar, an otherness seen as it were for the first time:

> No, helpless thing, I cannot harm thee now;
> Depart in peace, thy little life is safe,
> For I have scanned thy form with curious eye,
> Noted the silver line that streaks thy back,
> The azure and the orange that divide
> Thy velvet sides; thee, houseless, wanderer,
> My garment has enfolded, and my arm
> Felt the light pressure of thy hairy feet;
> Thou hast curled round my finger; from its tip,
> Precipitous descent! with stretched out neck,
> Bending thy head in airy vacancy,
> This way and that, enquiring, thou hast seemed
> To ask protection; now, I cannot kill thee. (1–13)

The poet's initially destructive intention is as readily altered as it is intimated, the crucial change between "now" and then being effected by nothing more than an engagement with otherness at the level of particular detail. As Barbauld explains, "I have scanned thy form with curious eye." Her scrutiny, notably, not only ensures the enumeration of distinct colour patterns and textures (eg. "velvet sides") but also facilitates direct contact: the caterpillar is literally "enfolded" by her. Such contact is critical to Barbauld's development of sympathy for "little life" while also precipitating a process of mutual scrutiny. Indeed, even as Barbauld traces the insect's movements on her skin, she herself is traced from arm to fingertip. It is this mutual discovery that in the end wins the caterpillar "protection" from "the slaughter . . . / Of tribes and embryo nations" (15–16), a slaughter undertaken by the poet herself:

> I have sought
> With sharpened eye and persecuting zeal,
> Where, folded in their silken webs they lay
> Thriving and happy; swept them from the tree
> And crushed whole families beneath my foot;
> Or, sudden, poured on their devoted heads
> The vials of destruction. (16–22)

The "sharpened eye" bent on destruction is clearly not the same eye that subsequently detects streaks of silver, azure and orange on the insect's back; distorted by a "persecuting zeal," it details not the other so much as a systematic process of annihilation enacted by the self. The details of alterity and individuality are literally crushed beneath Barbauld's foot. Not until she is unavoidably confronted by those details does she in fact cease her assault:

> when thou,—
> A single wretch, escaped the general doom,
> Making me feel and clearly recognize
> Thine individual existence, life,
> And fellowship of sense with all that breathes,—
> Present'st thyself before me, I relent,
> And cannot hurt thy weakness. (23–29)

The power of "individual existence," as Barbauld explains, consists in conveying not only distinctiveness but also a "fellowship of sense with all that breathes." The caterpillar, in other words, is recognized as much for its likeness as for its otherness. United with Barbauld and indeed with all of nature in a "fellowship of sense"—a shared reliance on a similar set of perceptual tools and protocols, a similar way, that is, of negotiating one's way through the world—the insect is spared the "general doom" of its species.

As the poem's ending makes clear, however, Barbauld's ultimate object is not to direct our gaze to the "little life" beneath our feet but rather to turn it inward, upon ourselves. Notwithstanding her emphasis on the value of insect views and of the creatures they bring to light, Barbauld returns finally to the greater value of the human condition. Having described her thought- and pity-provoking encounter with the caterpillar, she concludes with an analogy of more familiar, more human, dimensions:

> So the storm
> Of horrid war, o'erwhelming cities, fields,
> And peaceful villages, rolls dreadful on:
> The victor shouts triumphant; he enjoys
> The roar of cannon and the clang of arms,
> And urges, by no soft relentings stopped,
> The work of death and carnage. Yet should one,
> A single sufferer from the field escaped,
> Panting and pale, and bleeding at his feet,
> Lift his imploring eyes,—the hero weeps;
> He is grown human, and capricious Pity,
> Which would not stir for thousands, melts for one
> With sympathy spontaneous:—'Tis not Virtue,
> Yet 'tis the weakness of a virtuous mind. (29–42)

The visions and tales of "embryo nations" are here quite literally swept away by "the storm of horrid war"—that is, by human history itself. What ensues is not a triumph of particulate vision but rather an obfuscation of detail. The "single sufferer" is not endowed with any but the most generalized attributes; he is merely one of indistinguishable "thousands," unnamed, unknown, and finally saved not through a process of mutual scrutiny, a relation of self to other, but rather by "capricious Pity." Having previously emphasized the value of "clearly recognizing the other's individual existence," Barbauld seems here to base that value on nothing more than affective fluctuations. Her insect view thus leads ultimately to a scrutiny of human motivations and ethical impulses, specifically those that constitute "the weakness of a virtuous mind." Indeed, the lesson that appears to preoccupy Barbauld has much less to do with the qualities of otherness that provoke "sympathy" than with the qualities of human-ness that extend or withhold it.

A markedly different use is made of the insect view in Burns's "To a Louse" (1786), a poem that offers a whimsical reversal of the power dynamic between humanity and earth's "embryo nations." In choosing for the subject of his verse a louse, in human terms one of the lowliest and most reviled members of the insect world, its name a very byword for moral turpitude, Burns engages in "an extraordinary poetic act of empathy" (Bold 227). His account is of course not only thematically but also perceptually extraordinary in that it details the movements of so miniscule a creature. Notably, the poem's full title, "To A Louse, On Seeing one on a Lady's Bonnet at Church" (from the Kilmarnock Edition), asserts that what Burns is describing is an actual event, not a delightful fiction or an embellished recollection. As Bold

(227) contends, the poem's most likely setting is Mauchline Kirk, where Burns (in an ironically louse-like predicament) had done penance in 1785 for fathering his first illegitimate child with Elizabeth Paton. Burns does not, however, use the poem as an apologia, instead directing his attention entirely to the "crowlin ferlie" (1)[29]—the 'crawling wonder'—before him. What elicits Burns's astonishment is not only the juxtaposition of seeing a louse in "sic a place" (6)—meaning the church as well as the bonnet—but the apparent "impudence" (2) with which the insect imposes itself on the physical and spiritual spaces of human existence. Burns is not, however, outraged by such an incursion; on the contrary, he recognizes the louse even in its brazenness as a "blastit wonner" (7). Although "ugly, [and] creepin" (7), "[d]etested, [and] shunn'd" (8), the louse is an irresistible spectacle of mite conquering might. Its precipitous ascent of Jenny's bonnet—specifically a "Lunardi" bonnet, extremely fashionable and expensive—is marked by Burns with the acute eye of a naturalist:

> Now haud ye there! ye're out o' sight,
> Below the fatt'rils, snug an' tight;
> Na, faith ye yet! ye'll no be right,
>   Till ye've got on it—
> The vera tapmost, tow'ring height
>   O' Miss's bonnet. (19–24)

Keenly aware of the scandal the louse is causing and thoroughly riveted by its audacious progress, Burns seems only to wish it "out o' sight" in order to protect it from "[t]hae winks an' finger-ends [that] . . . / Are notice takin" (41–42). Indeed, whereas the outrage of his fellow parishioners is directed at the louse and their sympathy at the unfortunate Jenny who "little ken[s] what cursèd speed / The blastie's makin" (39–40), Burns offers a rather different perspective on the affair, one that is informed and refined by the insect view:

> O wad some Power the giftie gie us
> To see oursels as ithers see us!
> It wad frae monie a blunder free us,
>   An' foolish notion:
> What airs in dress an' gait wad lea'e us,
>   An' ev'n devotion! (43–48)

For Burns, the louse's encroachment on our intimate and sacred spaces represents an opportunity "[t]o see oursels as ithers see us"—the end of which is not only to know ourselves more truly but also to establish a relationship with the "ither" that hinges on an act of vicarious seeing, a sort of sensory empathy. In this instance, the most obvious 'ithers' are the parishioners who are enabled through the louse's movements to penetrate the surfaces of "gauze and lace" (4) to a corporeal truth that Jenny herself does not recognize—a truth, as Burns points out, that is ultimately far less injurious than the "blunders" of affectation. The "ither" is also, of course, the louse itself which does not discriminate between rich and poor, sacred and profane, in its daily peregrinations. Unfazed by airs of dress or piety, the louse approaches all humans equally—namely, as potential hosts. For Burns, such an impartial perspective is a "giftie" worth wishing for, a sort of miraculous mirror onto the self and the other. Despite insignificance of size and contemptibility of reputation, the louse is to him a "wonner" because it exposes precisely those superficial distinctions and "foolish notions" that regularly bedim our vision and delimit the range of our sympathy.

Like Burns, Clare manages to render the world of insect life and its unexpected gifts with astonishing precision. His *Nature Notes* and *Natural History Letters* offer glimpses of an otherness so captivating that the self, the viewing subject, is almost entirely effaced in the process of description. Indeed, the only way that Clare may be said to adopt an insect view in order to elucidate the human condition is by foregrounding our ignorance and misconceptions concerning the life beneath our feet. His descriptions of ant colonies in the *Nature Notes* (1825–37), for example, begin with a repudiation of traditional authority on the subject:

> It has been a commonly believd notion among such naturalists that trusts to books & repeats the old error that ants hurd up & feed on the curnels of grain such as wheat &barley but every common observer knows this to be a falsehood I have noticed them minutely & often & never saw one with such food in its mouth they feed on flyes & caterpillars which I have often seen them tugging home with & for which they climb trees & the stems of flowers. . . . (199)[30]

Much as he disparaged the poets of the nightingale who "never seek for truth," Clare here sets himself and indeed all "common observers"[31] against those who trust rather in books or opinions than in their own active senses. It must, of course, be noted that Clare's standards of common observation exceed a merely rudimentary perceptual intercourse with the objects and scenes of everyday life. Offering himself as an example, he elaborates on the sort of naturalism that yields truth: "I have noticd them *minutely & often*" (emphasis added). Common observation, in other words, entails habitual concentration on particularities; it reveals movements as fine as those of an ant on the stem of a flower. Clare's fascination with ants in fact leads to a focus of such microscopic intensity that even their intimate communications are accounted for:

> I have often minded that two [ants] while passing each other woud pause like old friends longparted see & as if they suddenly recollected each other they went & put their heads together as if they shook hands or saluted each other. . . . (199–200)

Rather than using ants to elaborate on the human condition, Clare uses human models to better understand insect behaviour. What he elucidates in this case are patterns of social intercourse whose minuteness of scale and apparent meaninglessness to the casual observer belie a complexity, a depth of feeling and experience, that humans typically associate only with themselves. As Clare suggests elsewhere in his *Natural History Letters*, "Insects have a language to convey their Ideas to each other & it always appears that they possess the faculty in a greater degree than the large animals" (194).[32] In "The Ants," one of Clare's early sonnets from *The Village Minstrel* (1821), he in fact seizes on the ants' capacity for language as a sign of their mystical heritage, a 'remnant,' more broadly speaking, of an age of wonder:

> Surely they speak a language whisperingly,
> Too fine for us to hear; and sure their ways
> Prove they have kings and laws, and that they be
> Deformed remnants of the Fairy-days. (11–14)[33]

Marvellously descended, socially complex and linguistically refined, ants, according to Clare's ento-mythology, are nearer than humans to nature's originative magic. Their wonders, moreover, consist not merely in 'whisperings' but also in more tangible displays of constructive ingenuity. Their nests, for example, combine security with astonishing architectural grandeur:

> [T]hese little creatures will raise a large tower of earth as thick as a mans arm in the form of a sugar loaf to a foot or a foot & a half high in the grain & long grass for in such places they cannot meet the sun on the ground so they raise these towers on the top of which they lay their eggs & as the grass or grain keeps growing they keep raising their towers till I have met with them as tall as ones knee[.] (201)

Clare's focus on the ants' persistence in building towers that keep pace with the growth of grass and grain serves to invest the very soil of everyday life with an indomitable energy that obtrudes on, and alters, the spaces of human existence. This passage may in fact be taken as a gentle warning to "[c]arless observers" (200) to attend to the details of everyday life lest they fall headlong over its wonders.

Few passages bring these wonders more vividly to light than Clare's description of the Glow-worm in his *Nature Notes*. Combining observational precision with a poetic sensitivity to the numinous, the following excerpt teases out the worm's natural magic:

> The Gloworm is a sort of catterpillar insect and thousands of them may be seen on Casterton Cowpasture on a summer night they appear as if a drop of dew hung at their tails which had been set on fire by the fairys for the purpose of a lanthorn—and I have often gathered them up and put them into leaves to see if they shone by daylight but when day came they were nothing but a little dark looking insect apparently half dead and as it were shrivelled up another insect is as commonly and infact more commonly known as the gloworm among the common people because it frequents their houses shining very brilliantly anights like liquid silver and leaving if touchd part of its shining qualities littered about where it crawled this when seen by day light is a red long insect with a great quantity of legs and therebye called the forty legged worm[.][34]

Unconcerned with the niceties of scientific classification—which Clare associates elsewhere with a merely bookish naturalism[35]—he describes the glow-worm as it appears to "common people" in the natural daylit world, namely as "a sort of catterpillar insect." The setting of the sun, however, transforms these common caterpillars into mystical wonders: "they appear as if a drop of dew hung at their tails which had been set on fire by the fairys for the purpose of a lanthorn." Again, Clare begins by describing what he sees, but in this instance, as in his accounts of the blackbird's eggs and the ants' social refinement, he appends a conditional clause that introduces the possibility of supernatural agency. Evidently overwhelmed and unable to conjure a natural or rational explanation for what is a recurring natural phenomenon, Clare can only revert to the possibilities of imagination, to a world even tinier than that of the insect, a world of "fairys" and magic. He mingles these imaginative forays, however, with the evidence of his own senses, the evidence, that is, of the glow-worm's dual existence. By daylight, as he notes, it is "nothing but a little dark looking insect apparently half dead." The glow-worm's natural magic thus appears to derive in part from the improbability and unexpectedness of such an unremarkable creature giving off light. The juxtaposition of its plainness in daylight and its brilliance at night is indeed indicative of the workings of quotidian sublimity. Everyday objects, even shrivelled up insects, are for Clare never simply what they appear to be; they may possess "shining qualities," traces of a wondrousness, an energy, so improbable and dynamic that it exceeds the grasp of ready comprehension. The shining qualities of everyday life are, moreover, "littered about," waiting to be "touchd" and discovered. Sometimes they are as plainly visible as glow-worms at night but more often they require of the subject a sensitivity to, and a willingness to engage, everyday reality at its lowliest and most minute levels. For the full wonder of the glow-worm, as Clare's description implies, derives not only from its light but also from its darkness. The passage's conclusion indeed serves to remind the reader that "liquid silver" runs on forty legs.

For many Romantics, the recognition that everyday spaces and objects—everything from closets and cupboard corners to maps and books, from nests to eggs and insects—can simultaneously elicit a sense of the familiar and the unknown, the pragmatic and the marvellous, contributed to a renaissance of the home, an aesthetic reinvestment in scenes deemed by many Enlightenment critics to be unworthy of serious literary endeavour. Given that these scenes typically exist on a much smaller plane than the objects of natural sublimity evoked by Burke and Kant—often, indeed, they are entirely hidden from view—their revelation demands of the subject not merely a perceptual and artistic subtlety or meticulousness, but a readiness to wait on hands and knees, to yield the self to the presence of the other, in order to be astonished. Commenting on this need to arrest the self in the contemplation of what surrounds it, Bachelard writes that "[a]s soon as we become motionless, we are elsewhere; we are dreaming in a world that is immense" (184). The self-preoccupation, in other words, that attends both our physical and cognitive motions tends to diminish our sensitivity to the subtle details, variations and changes in a seemingly static and familiar environment. Often such changes, like the accrual of moss between the spokes of an old wheel, signal the depth and immensity of everyday spaces, the extent, that is, to which they are literally inhabited by an otherness of wonder. Whereas the sublime of mountain-tops and torrents, rolling seas and boundless skies, is in a sense unavoidably and immediately accessible, the quotidian sublime, despite the proximity of its objects, may be daily, indeed habitually, overlooked. Thus the domestic verse and insect views of local Romantic writers serve as reminders to those who have forgotten, and invitations to those who have perhaps never known, the astonishment of first seeing what has since grown so familiar as to become

Particularity and "Intimate Immensity"

entirely unnoticed. Insect views also of course represent a way of seeing and engaging the everyday that is innovative and without precedent; such views indeed call into question our assumptions of familiarity and facilitate a shift, in Hegelian terms, from '*Bekenntnis*' to '*Erkenntnis*.' Although this shift is momentary and never in fact complete because sublimity by its very nature exceeds '*Erkenntnis*,' the sublime event nevertheless awakens in the subject, the poet, a consciousness of life's shining qualities. These qualities, as I will suggest, inhere as readily in the actions and the movements through which everyday space is shaped as in the objects that fill and multiply that space.

Chapter Three
Sublime Transport and the Making of Space

The foregoing emphasis on what may loosely be defined as objective space, meaning space that is shaped, multiplied and defined by material reality, by the walls of cottages, for example, or the twigs of birds' nests, ought not to suggest that the Romantic subject merely occupies space without affecting its dimensions and constitution. Not only do physical bodies transect the spaces of everyday life through the innumerable motions, most of them habitual and subconscious, that comprise the regimens and routines of living, but Romantic subjects also in a sense create space through their physical and mental negotiations of it. As Michel de Certeau observes in *The Practice of Everyday Life*, our daily movements, everything from dwelling, walking, reading, cooking and shopping, "weave places together. . . . They are not localized; it is rather they that spatialize" (97). Quotidian perambulations, in other words, from one room to the next, from house to garden and garden to house serve to make and localize a home no less than the wood and brick and glass of which that home is built. According to de Certeau, we "furnish" homes with acts and recreate them in later years with memories (xxi). The specific arrangement or configuration of our homes and, indeed, of our neighbourhoods thus depends as much on a subjective as on an objective ordering and definition of space. The subject's capacity to "weave places together," literally to make homes and neighbourhoods, or alternately, to "condemn[] certain places to inertia or disappearance" (de Certeau 99) by choosing to pass them by, invests even the most mundane, habitual and seemingly meaningless actions with generative and transformative potential. For de Certeau, that potential is primarily of a political nature and expresses itself in subversive "reappropriat[ions] [of] the space organized by techniques of sociocultural production" (xiv). Invoking the Foucauldian idea of a grid of bureaucratic, legal and institutional discipline devoted to the maintenance of socio-economic order, de Certeau contends that

> it is all the more urgent to discover how an entire society resists being reduced to it [i.e. the grid], what popular procedures (also 'miniscule' and quotidian) manipulate the mechanisms of discipline and conform to them only in order to evade them, and finally, what 'ways of operating' form the counterpart, on the consumer's (or 'dominee's'?) side, of the mute processes that organize the establishment of socio-economic order. (xiv)

The countervailing "ways of operating" upon which he centers his discussion are those everyday behaviours or "tactics" by which the subject resists conformity to, and assimilation by, the grid of power. Pedestrianism, already a radical activity by the late eighteenth century (Jarvis 27), is perhaps the most obvious example and the one to which de Certeau recurs most frequently. Characterizing alternate modes of transport such as trains as "travelling incarceration[s]" (111), de Certeau sees in the walker the essence of navigational freedom and, consequently, political enfranchisement. The vagrant, the jaywalker, the roadside fruit vendor—each of these becomes a figure of resistance in de Certeau's countercultural topography. The effect and scope of their resistance is of course debatable. Indeed, one of the obvious limitations of the political agenda of de Certeau's cultural analytic is its diffuseness, its tendency to operate exclusively on the margins of society. As Kristin Ross points out, de Certeau's "tactics"

> add up to no larger strategy. . . . [They are] a lot of pinprick operations separated from each other in time and space. . . . *The resistance of an escapee from the panopticon can only be individual, or at best part of a culture of consolation—which is to say, ultimately, aesthetic.* (71, emphasis added)

What Ross articulates here as a critique of de Certeau's paradigm serves also, and I think somewhat ironically, to accentuate its theoretical contributions to the study of everyday life both in the Romantic period and in our own. Indeed, the strength of de Certeau's work, particularly as it relates to the literature of everyday life, lies in its recognition of the consolatory, the creative, even the wondrous potential of those experiences and activities traditionally excluded from aesthetic discourse. For de Certeau, the simple act of walking inscribes meaning onto spaces that otherwise would not be "marked, opened up by a memory or a story, signed by something or someone else" (106). The mystic circle of home is itself a product of such habitual motions, of steps that demarcate, enclose and connect those within. These motions, moreover, are related not only to the creation of space but also to the creation of story and text. As de Certeau suggests, "*a theory of narration is indissociable from a theory of practices*" (78). Everyday movements thus not only make a home but tell its story. Movement in fact tells many stories, some familiar like the stories of home, some already forgotten, and others newly invented:

> Physical moving about has the itinerant function of yesterday's or today's 'superstitions.' Travel (like walking) is a substitute for the legends that used to open up space to something different. What does travel ultimately produce if it is not, by a sort of reversal, 'an exploration of the deserted places of my memory[?].' . . . [I]t is a fiction, which moreover has the double characteristic, like dreams or pedestrian rhetoric, of being the effect of displacements and condensations. As a corollary, one can measure the importance of these signifying practices (to tell oneself legends) as practices that invent spaces. (106–107)

For de Certeau, walking or "travel" is not simply a metaphor for story-telling but an instantiation of it. Our everyday movements literally "open up" and "invent" space. This creativity or inventiveness extends likewise to the recollections of travel and, moreover, to the textual inscriptions of such recollections, to journals, descriptive prose or verse, autobiography, travel narratives, et cetera. Indeed, the writing of everyday life is inherently *re*-creative, assembling, ordering and configuring the motions and spaces of our yesterdays. For the reader, unless s/he is intimately familiar with the locations described, the text serves to invent space. Reading allows one to reverse the process of experience-recollection-transcription, to walk, as it were, retrospectively into new worlds.

Yet before turning to the spatial interactions between the reader and the Romantic text, I want to consider the preliminary relationship between author and space. For what de Certeau characterizes as "everyday creativity" (xiv) begins with the physical movements by which the author defines and develops space. Although writing is clearly one of these movements and the text is one of these spaces, writing necessarily draws on prior motions, prior experiences. What I am interested in exploring are everyday activities through which writers of the Romantic period experience and convey a sense of the sublime. In other words, how do their daily movements, recounted in writing, open up spaces of wonder? Under the rubric of 'everyday activities' are included examples of work and leisure, with especial attention devoted to walking or pedestrianism, an activity, as Robin Jarvis notes, that was undertaken in the 1780s and 90s not only for athletic or political purposes (the latter variety he designates as "radical walking" [34]), but also increasingly for the sake of aesthetic pleasure. As he suggests, "the Romantic period witnessed a dissociation of the idea of [pedestrian] travel from the meanings integral to its parent linguistic form, 'travail'" (28). Instead, walking enabled local and descriptive writers to deepen their aesthetic connection with their natural surroundings by providing "enhanced opportunities for careful observation and methodical record-keeping" (Jarvis 47), a process integral to the aesthetic of particularity. As I will suggest, however, walking was not the only means of sublime transport in the Romantic period. In addition to the rather more rare instances of numinous play, such as Wordsworth's description of skating in Book I of *The Prelude*, common activities like travelling by coach—what de Certeau would characterize as another form of "incarceration"—also opened up spaces of wonder and awe.

While such modes of leisure and travel necessarily connote a move away from the mystic circle of home, the movements and spaces of work in the nineteenth century are typically contained within that circle. The maintenance or perpetuation of home as localized space is in fact dependent on the motions of work. Indeed, the very conception of home is founded on imagined labour. A poem, for example, such as John Thelwall's "Lines, written at Bridgwater, in Somersetshire, on the 27th of July, 1797; during a long excursion, in quest of a peaceful retreat" foregrounds the role of labour in developing and accentuating home's wondrous spaces. Written in the afterglow of a ten-day visit with Coleridge and the Wordsworths at Alfoxden, from a soul, as Thelwall notes, "sick of public turmoil" (72),[1] the poem articulates both a yearning for "peaceful retreat" and a speculative spatialization of its boundaries. That spatialization begins, notably, with imagined labour: "Ah! let me, far in some sequester'd dell, / Build my low cot . . ." (85–86). Notwithstanding the emphasis on a "sequester'd" location, Thelwall's wish is not for solitary, isolated labour; his vision of the construction of home is one of shared creativity, of a communal space shaped in fellowship with Coleridge, his "best-belov'd of friends" (88):

> Ah! 'twould be sweet, beneath the neighb'ring thatch,
> In philosophic amity to dwell,
> Inditing moral verse, or tale, or theme,
> Gay or instructive; and it would be sweet,
> With kindly interchange of mutual aid,
> To delve our little garden plots, the while
> Sweet converse flow'd, suspending oft the arm
> And half-driven spade, while, eager, one propounds,

> And listens one, weighing each pregnant word,
> And pondering fit reply, that may untwist
> The knotty point—perchance, of import high—
> Of Moral Truth, of Causes Infinite,
> Creating Power! or Uncreated Worlds
> Eternal and uncaus'd! or whatsoe'er,
> Of Metaphysic, or of Ethic lore,
> The mind, with curious subtilty, pursues—
> Agreeing, or dissenting—sweet alike,
> When wisdom, and not victory, the end. (91–108)

What Thelwall describes here is a coupling of physical and discursive labour, each as it were enlivened by the other. Delving garden plots and discussing "Causes Infinite" are complementary activities that involve a search for roots and open up as yet "Uncreated Worlds"—*terrae incognita*. Much as the mind seeks ways of untwisting "knotty" points of debate in order to facilitate mutual understanding and an arrival at "wisdom," so the spade must sever and unearth the knotted roots of trees if the ground is to be made ready for sowing. The harmonious exchange between Thelwall and Coleridge is echoed by the harmonies between labour and leisure, spade and tongue—the latter being the very instruments of everyday creativity. The "Creating Power" at work in Thelwall's poetic reverie is in fact so comprehensive that home, metaphysical insight and community are forged simultaneously.[2] These products and the individual activities that bring them into being are for Thelwall interdependent. He cannot, for example, imagine sitting around "the blazing hearth, social and gay" (120) until the dues "to toil . . . to study . . . / And literary effort, ha[ve] been paid" (115–116). The "Golden Age" (147) he envisions is one that "mingl[es] Arcadian sports / With healthful industry" (145–146). Indeed, the poem seems to suggest that "industry" is integral to the creation not only of the space of home but also of its spirit.[3] The act of digging, of literally making room in the soil of everyday life, serves to open up spaces of dialogue, debate and reflection, and it is in these latter realms that "Uncreated Worlds" begin to take shape.

The labours that Thelwall only imagines are for other Romantic writers the stuff of daily life and, as such, of verse. Drawing upon personal experience and the immediate contexts of home, poets like Barbauld elucidate movements and spaces of work that have the potential rather to exhaust than enliven the body and depress the spirit instead of elevating or ennobling it. Barbauld's "Washing Day," for example, first published in 1797 in the *Monthly Magazine*, takes to task with an admixture of irony, wit and unfeigned outrage the "prattling" (4)[4] household verse of her day that sings solely and wistfully "[o]f farm or orchard, pleasant curds and cream" (5) and reduces domestic hardships to "drowning flies, or shoe lost in the mire / By little whimpering boy, with rueful face" (6–7). In order to redress the perceived imbalance, Barbauld turns her attention to the one chore—a diurnal round all its own—to which "nor peace belongs / Nor comfort" (12–13): the washing day. Although she addresses herself to male and female readers alike, her sympathies (and expectations of support) lie clearly with those who "full well [. . .] ken the day" (10) through their own bitter experience— the housewives, namely, "who beneath the yoke of wedlock bend, / With bowed soul" (9–10). Where washing is concerned, the effects of unrelenting pressure and obligation redound upon the body as well as the soul, bowing it low to search and scrub out "dirt and gravel stains" (25). The author of such pressure, as Barbauld suggests, is not only the idle master who asks, amid the din, to have his stockings mended (37), but also the very elements themselves. Indeed, the "last evil" (22) is the "lowering sky" (21), which, if it should break on washing day, would unleash "all the petty miseries of life" (28). In a playful analogy that dramatizes both the pettiness and miseries of the housewife's lot, Barbauld likens her suffering to that of smiling saints "stretched upon the rack" (29)—the difference being that "never yet did housewife notable / Greet with a smile a rainy washing-day" (31–32). Having, as it were, righted the scales of domestic and poetic justice by emphasizing the yoke and lash of housewifery instead of its "pleasant curds and cream," Barbauld here reminds her readers of the folly of tipping the balance too far by exaggerating perceived hardships.

What she turns to in the end to help her assess these hardships is her own experience of them—not as an adult but as a child. Significantly, it is the child's perspective which teases out almost from the beginning the unacknowledged wonders of washing:

> I well remember, when a child, the awe
> This day struck into me; for then the maids,
> I scarce knew why, looked cross, and drove me from them:
> Nor soft caress could I obtain, nor hope
> Usual indulgencies; jelly or creams,
> Relic of costly suppers, and set by
> For me their petted one; or buttered toast,
> When butter was forbid; or thrilling tale
> Of ghost or witch, or murder—so I went
> And sheltered me beside the parlour fire. . . . (58–67)

Sublime Transport and the Making of Space 117

For the young Barbauld, washing day is an event of incomprehensible, indeed, *awe*-inspiring significance; it triggers an abrupt and unexplained alteration in the world that is home, turning soft caresses to cross looks, forbidden pleasures to mere forbidding, thrilling tales to frightful reality. Perhaps most important, however, is the fact that washing brings detachment and, with it, a space for reflection. Recalling the "Uncreated Worlds" of Thelwall's garden debates with Coleridge, one might say that washing in this instance opens up a realm for self-reflection, for a re-evaluation of the home and the child's place within it; the bustle of washing, in other words, allows the child to reposition itself in the domestic cosmology. Amid the ringing of her mother's voice and the din of "hands employed to wash, to rinse, to wring, / To fold, and starch, and clap, and iron, and plait" (76–77)—a machine-like rhythm that anticipates Thomas Hood's "The Song of the Shirt"—the child makes space for thought. As she writes, "[t]hen would I sit me down, and ponder much / Why washings were" (78–79). For the child at least, these ruminations are no less compelling or profound than Thelwall's words "of import high"; the fact that washing has quite suddenly and inexplicably managed to reconstitute the established order of the entire domestic sphere would seem to suggest that it is indeed an activity of considerable "import" in the home. Though unable to resolve "[w]hy washings were," the child does in the end participate playfully in this mysterious activity, and it is the experience of play, recalled in adulthood, which serves to open up further spaces of wonder:

> Sometimes through hollow bowl
> Of pipe amused we blew, and sent aloft
> The floating bubbles; little dreaming then
> To see, Mongolfier, thy silken ball
> Ride buoyant through the clouds—so near approach
> The sports of children and the toils of men.
> Earth, air, and sky, and ocean, hath its bubbles,
> And verse is one of them—this most of all. (79–86)

By collapsing the products of toil, play, science and art into soap-bubble dimensions, Barbauld seems on one hand to foreground their insignificance and want of substance while also, on the other, intimating their wondrous capacity to transcend our "dreaming." The "bubbles" set adrift by the wringing of soapy rags, by a child's breath, by the daring of scientific innovation or, alternately, by the idle poet's pen, although prone to misdirection and inevitable destruction, nevertheless manage for a time to charm and captivate our thoughts, to waft their way in airy splendour across the noise and sweat and blankness of the day. No less than their figurative counterparts, the literal bubbles of washing and child's play represent wondrous transpositions and reconstitutions of everyday space; the former are created incidentally by the exertions of human hands as a sort of sublime excess, an unbidden magic that attends and also transcends the most wearisome of labours; the latter, meanwhile, are inspired by the very breath that sustains life, are created as it were within, and issued heavenward as if from ocean depths as visible signs of presence. The very insubstantiality of such bubbles ensures their transcendence. The same may be said of the verse that bodies forth this image of wondrous space. Notwithstanding Barbauld's guarded estimation of the value or weight of her words, their metaphoric evocation of the bubble as the quintessence of human endeavour serves to ensure that even the tangible text rises beyond the reader's ready grasp, that though its wonders may be spatialized, they can never be definitively held.

What the examples of Thelwall and Barbauld make clear is that the sublimity of labouring movements often inheres rather in the incidental spaces they create—the "Worlds" or "bubbles" of conversation, reflection and play—than in the products to which their energy is ostensibly directed. There is, in other words, a creative surplus that attends our physical activities that is unrecognised, unanticipated, accidental. Even activities that we would typically classify as unproductive or haphazard are to some extent inherently creative in that they reveal hitherto unseen spaces and alter the spaces we already know. Pedestrianism is perhaps the most obvious example. Commenting on the creative power of the walk, de Certeau suggests that the intertwined paths of our footsteps "give their shape to spaces" (97). Yet such paths alone do not tell the tale of pedestrian travels, for though paths may be traced on maps so as to ascribe trajectories and distances, "[s]urveys of routes miss what was: the act itself of passing by" (de Certeau 97). Surveys are in a sense the sparsest of histories, revealing neither the walker, the experience of walking, nor the details of the walk, by which I mean both the physical surroundings (the spaces opened and bypassed) and the creative surplus of which the walker is her/himself often only dimly aware (i.e. the incidental rearrangements of physical and/or cognitive space produced by acts of passing). Owing to their preoccupation with mere points of geographical space and the measured lines that connect those points, surveys may in fact be conceived as narrative detours or distractions—de Certeau calls them "procedures for forgetting" (97)—by obscuring both the walker and the act of walking.

Pedestrian travel literature, on the other hand, offers rather more comprehensive peripatetic maps. As I have suggested, in the Romantic period such maps charted not only the act but also the aesthetics of walking. Speculating on the genesis of the increasing shift in emphasis from "radical" to reflective or pleasurable walking, Jarvis suggests that

> the peculiar intimacy of pedestrian travellers with the environments they pass through, and the way in which walking fosters a sense of proportion between human beings and the rest of nature unflattering to the anthropocentric fantasies of the former, renders them more susceptible to aesthetic stimuli from landscape. . . . (53)

The walk, therefore, this "quintessentially Romantic image" (Robinson 5), involves not only political but also aesthetic levelling by facilitating a sense of "proportion" between the subject and the landscape. What this means in the discourse of sublimity is that the walk is particularly suited to experiences of relationship or community with nature, not the self-apotheosizing conquests intimated by the Burkean and Kantian paradigms of transcendence. In a compelling passage on the psychology of perambulation, Jeffrey Robinson goes so far as to suggest that the walk is rather about "self-forgetting" than self-aggrandizement:

> On a walk one is continually encountering the new and, by the 'despotism of the eye,' the tyranny of bodily pleasure, willingly forgetting the old. Every forgetting is an assertion of freedom from which the mind goes on another journey. Every forgetting is, in addition, a self-forgetting, an assertion of renewed innocence and pleasure. As we forget, and forget ourselves, we become aware of the gradual fact of hoarding of encounters, impressions, and discoveries. We begin to experience our world as a growing plenitude. . . . (67)

The self-forgetting by which we grow more aware of what is around us—a redemptive strategy analogous to Blake's notion of 'Self Annihilation'—reveals the world as "a growing plenitude," a vibrant and ever-changing display of inexhaustible forms and particular details. By walking, the subject in effect opens her/himself up to the possibility of sublime inundation. The desire for such numinous experiences, for freedom not only from socio-political but also from prevailing aesthetic strictures, may indeed be theorized as playing a significant role in the Romantic preoccupation with pedestrian travel. As Robinson contends, the power of the walk as both Romantic image and experience lies in its capacity to engender "the mental polarity of critical thinking all the way to wonderment" (4). Walking, simply put, is a canvas broad enough for sublime expression.

One of the first extended examples of what one might label a peripatetic aesthetic is found in Wordsworth's *An Evening Walk*, a work written in the poet's youth (1787–89) and generally associated not with the sublime but the picturesque. Robert A. Aubin's *Topographical Poetry in Eighteenth-Century England*, for example, highlights in cursory strokes the poem's "conventional" use of picturesque subjects, sentiments and perspectives (219), a conclusion confirmed more recently by Alan Liu in his rather more detailed examination of the poem's "tapestry view[s]" (*Wordsworth* 132). It would indeed be fruitless to deny the influence upon the young Wordsworth of such diverse Lakeland travel writers as John Brown, Thomas Gray, William Hutchinson, Thomas West, William Gilpin and James Clarke,[5] all of whom contributed to what he would later characterize in *The Prelude* as "a strong infection of the age" (XI.156), a tendency, namely, to distill nature's inexhaustible forms and movements to a series of spatially balanced aesthetic templates or snapshots, each tending to the promotion of what Liu calls "gentle quietude" (75). *An Evening Walk* does not, however, offer a case-study merely of one aesthetic response but, as I will suggest, a range of responses that includes the sublime. Indeed, this "history of a poet's evening" (36)[6] is as much about the frustration as the culmination of gentle quietude. As Jarvis contends, *An Evening Walk* is a poem "where there is no consummation" (93); instead, the poetic eye roves errantly from scene to scene, stilled only to be stimulated, and stimulated without end. Wandering in effect reveals the limitations of a strictly picturesque approach to nature, the difficulty, that is, of finding rest. Indeed, every intimation of repose, as the following passage attests, serves as an invitation to wander on:

> As by enchantment, an obscure retreat
> Opened at once, and stayed my devious feet.
> While thick above the rill the branches close,
> In rocky basin its wild waves repose,
> Inverted shrubs, and moss of gloomy green,
> Cling from the rocks, with pale wood-weeds between;
> And its own twilight softens the whole scene,
> Save where aloft the subtle sunbeams shine
> On withered briars that o'er the crags recline;
> Save where, with sparkling foam, a small cascade
> Illumines, from within, the leafy shade;
> Beyond, along the vista of the brook,
> Where antique roots its bustling course o'erlook,
> The eye reposes on a secret bridge,

> Half grey, half shagged with ivy to its ridge;
> There, bending o'er the stream, the listless swain
> Lingers behind his disappearing wain. (55–70)

One may in fact trace here a series of unconsummated gestures to repose, beginning with what the poet describes as a staying of his "devious feet." Jarvis points out that the poet's cessation of movement is at best partial, for where his feet are fixed, "the eye is made to wander instead" (93). Indeed, Wordsworth's optical perambulations—the poem's predominant mode of travel—allow him to sketch a vibrant, living scene whose energy appears to transcend the picturesque frame of closing branches and embowered obscurity. The paradoxical image of "wild waves [in] repose" serves to foreground the tensions between desire for, and the apparent impossibility of, rest. The "withered briars that o'er the crags recline" likewise reinforce the difficulties of rest, the degree to which even inactivity is charged with tension or potential energy, a sort of precursor to movement itself. The scene's focal point, "a small cascade" (64) modelled on the Lower Falls at Rydal, also fails to compose the poet or arrest his attention. He tracks its descent into a brook whose "bustling course" (67) he traces to a bridge, whereon his eye again "reposes" (68) but for a moment, before taking note of a "listless swain" (70) bending over the water. And even here, at what appears the last concrete image of rest before a more generalized apostrophe to the "wild stream" (73), Wordsworth's eye continues to stray to something behind the swain, something that gestures beyond the picturesque canvas itself—the already "*disappearing* wain" (71, emphasis added). Wordsworth's gaze in effect bores through the canvas to that which is not wholly contained by it, an object, a simple cart, whose half-seen presence intimates a space beyond, an as yet unexplored horizon.

It is of course not only the profusion or variety of nature's visual stimuli that frustrates the attainment of gentle quietude but also their wondrousness, their mystery, their *im*penetrability. Shifting from description to narrative, from a mode of visual wandering to one that is historical, Wordsworth recounts a local legend whose dubious claim on truth contributes to a sense of growing unease:

> In these secluded vales, if village fame,
> Confirmed by hoary hairs, belief may claim;
> When up the hills, as now, retired the light,
> Strange apparitions mocked the shepherd's sight.
> The form appears of one that spurs his steed
> Midway along the hill with desperate speed;

> Unhurt pursues his lengthened flight, while all
> Attend, at every stretch, his headlong fall.
> Anon appears a brave, a gorgeous show
> Of horsemen-shadows moving to and fro;
> At intervals imperial banners stream,
> And now the van reflects the solar beam;
> The rear through iron brown betrays a sullen gleam.
> While silent stands the admiring crowd below,
> Silent the visionary warriors go,
> Winding in ordered pomp their upward way,
> Till the last banner of their long array
> Has disappeared, and every trace is fled
> Of splendour—save the beacon's spiry head
> Tipt with eve's latest gleam of burning red. (192–211)

Based on a description in Clarke's *Survey of the Lakes*, this passage signals a definitive move beyond the borders of the picturesque. Whereas the picturesque is wholly reliant on a visual representation and composition of space—occasionally enhanced by recourse to a Claude glass[7]—the "Strange apparitions" here described are such as *mock* sight and thus thwart the quest for a framed and gentle quietude. There is indeed little in Wordsworth's delineation of the "visionary warriors" that soothes or stills. Poet and reader are made one with those that "[a]ttend, at every stretch" the drama of "horsemen-shadows moving to and fro" in an uncertain display of "pomp" and power. The oxymoronic title of "horsemen-shadows" already in a sense foregrounds the inapplicability, indeed, the outright collapse, of ontological and epistemological frameworks. The scene's capacity to frustrate and transcend conventional modes of signification is further enhanced by its governing silence—a silence that enfolds both the warriors and the "admiring crowd" and is transmitted to the poet himself. Unable to resolve the meaning of this flitting woodland tableau, of a "Splendour" that slips as suddenly away as it appears, Wordsworth leaves in the reader's eye only a "gleam" of its fullness.

A similarly transcendent encounter with nature's spectral powers occurs at poem's end as Wordsworth contemplates the dance of day's "farewell light" (287) on the surface of an unnamed lake. Immediately preceded by the pathetic image of the Female Beggar weeping over the lifeless infants that lie "coffined in [her] arms" (278), a moment whose unexpectedly stark reality, as Liu notes, is "excessive of picturesque arrest" (119), the poet's description of twilight serves no less definitively or profoundly to transcend the expectations, the very framework, of picturesque experience. Where before the poet's wandering eye and feet opened up the scenes around him, on this occasion it is nature's own perambulatory creativity that helps to bring the wondrous to light:

> The half-seen form of Twilight roams astray;
> Shedding, through paly loop-holes mild and small,
> Gleams that upon the lake's still bosom fall;
> Soft o'er the surface creep those lustres pale
> Tracking the motions of the fitful gale.
> With restless interchange at once the bright
> Wins on the shade, the shade upon the light.
> No favoured eye was e'er allowed to gaze
> On lovelier spectacle in faery days;
> When gentle Spirits urged a sportive chase,
> Brushing with lucid wands the water's face:
> While music, stealing round the glimmering deeps,
> Charmed the tall circle of the enchanted steeps. (292–304)

Beginning with Twilight's "half-seen form" and roaming presence, this passage conveys precisely that sense of unease, that undercurrent of unframeable and uncontainable energy, which, as noted earlier, frustrates by its conceptual excess the experience of picturesque calm. The mingling of Twilight's elusive and uncertain presence with that of the "fitful gale"—a sort of conspiracy of natural agitation—casts even over the lake's "still bosom," the scene's central image of repose, a "restless interchange" of light and shade. In a move reminiscent of Clare, Wordsworth reverts to a world of mystical agency in an attempt to characterize this restlessness. His evocation of "faery days" serves in effect as an acknowledgment of the scene's signifying excess, of the numinous contiguities between the natural and the mystical. The poet's apperception of these contiguities or interpenetrations reveals itself in his reinterpretation of twilight's "lustres pale" as "gentle Spirits" and the restless wind as "lucid wands" fanning the surface of the lake. Significantly, nature's wilful restlessness is here juxtaposed by the poet's relative stillness. Like the "tall circle" of surrounding hills, Wordsworth is "enchanted" by the spectacle before him; having wandered spellbound into the regions of myth and imagination, he is for a moment "[c]harmed"—that is, transfixed.

What follows serves most clearly and definitively to distinguish the poet from the picturesque tourist and his experience from a mere quest for tapestry views. Although the vision of water Spirits and the poet's resulting enthralment are momentary, he shows little interest in recommencing either his physical or visual perambulations. Instead of seeking fresh stimulation, he dwells on that which is no more: "The lights are vanished from the watery plains: / No wreck of all the pageantry remains" (305–306). Like the spectacle of "horsemen-shadows," the source of his transfixion is inherently fleeting, leaving him on this occasion without even a gleam of its prepossessing magic. Yet instead of consoling himself, as the picturesque traveller might do, with the quest for new vistas, the poet acknowledges that his "wearied vision" (308) fails to find inspiration in a world "Lost in the thickened darkness" (312). Although he strives, with typically Wordsworthian resilience, to conjure within himself a "sympathetic twilight" (316) to replace that which he has lost, the attempt only exacerbates the pang of loss and deepens his enfolding gloom:

> Stay! pensive, sadly-pleasing visions, stay!
> Ah no! as fades the vale, they fade away:
> Yet still the tender, vacant gloom remains;
> Still the cold cheek its shuddering tear retains. (319–322)

The visions of sublimity gone, the poet has only the palpable evidence of his own disappointment to remind him of what was. Cherishing the "vacant gloom" and "shuddering tear," he casts his eyes dimly around as one awakened from a dream. What eventually re-inspires movement (first optical, then physical) is the gradual appearance of nature's own "sympathetic twilight," namely the moon. Indeed, not until Wordsworth discerns its "half-veiled, . . . lovely face" (334) and traces its "fondest ray" (347) to an imaginary cottage home to be shared with his sister, does he in fact continue his evening walk. The home, at once a source of the sublime, is also the supreme consolation for its loss. In the absence of arresting twilight, the hoped-for home becomes the "Sole bourn, sole wish, sole object" (348) of the wandering poet's way.

It is perhaps not surprising that Wordsworth's interest in poetic pedestrianism was also shared by his sister, for whom, according to Jarvis, walking was not simply "a given of existence" (162) but also a means of "reaffirming and deepening a sense of belonging to the local environment in which a sheltered space has been discovered" (164). Walking, in other words, has for Dorothy the function of confirming the boundaries of home and embedding or securing the self within those boundaries. The confirmation of home's boundaries, it must be noted, is the result of a certain kind of walking, what Jarvis distinguishes as "the regular perambulation of an intimately known and partly domesticated terrain" (162). Regular perambulation, as this definition suggests, is as much about habitual routes as habitual movement. It is the kind of walk often described in Dorothy's *Journals*, a walk like that, for example, undertaken on February 7, 1798, while she and William were living at Alfoxden:

> Turned towards Potsham, but finding the way dirty, changed our course. Cottage gardens the object of our walk. Went up the smaller Coombe to Woodlands, to the blacksmith's, the baker's, and through the village of Holford. Still misty over the sea. The air very delightful. We saw nothing very new, or interesting. (*Journals* 5–6)

Comprising an "object" or destination, a series of stops or route markers, in addition to one detour, Dorothy's quotidian travelogue is notable for its factual and historical, but not its aesthetic, detail. The phrase "nothing very new," while it may intimate the potential of even well-trodden ways to surprise the walker, registers on this occasion only the vague disappointment of finding that potential unfulfilled. Indeed, one of the consequences of regular perambulation is that the "very new" is often difficult to find, even for an eye as exquisitely precise as Dorothy's.

There is, however, evidence in Dorothy's work of other varieties or modes of walking that do not so readily succumb to the rubric (and aesthetic disappointment) of regular perambulation. Take, for example, the arrestingly vague entry for March 30, 1798: "Walked I know not where" (*Journals* 11). Aside from being literally aimless, such a walk exceeds the "intimately known" parameters of home. And even where walking transpires within those parameters, it may yet stray into regions of indeterminacy, as in "Walked a considerable time in the wood" (*Journals* 14). Notwithstanding the reference to a general topographical space—"the wood"—there is here little sense of a precise destination or purpose, or, for that matter, of a familiar path being retraced. Although the act of walking in the wood may be habitually undertaken, the individual journeys must be assumed to differ from one another in duration and direction, time of day and season, to say nothing of the varied psychological states that impel the walker out of doors. The phrase 'walking in the wood' also encodes a kind of vagrancy, directionlessness and freedom that differs sharply from what is associated with other forms of wood-walking such as 'walking by the wood,' 'walking to the wood,' 'walking around the wood' or 'walking through the wood.' To walk in the wood is to walk *around in* it, to meander, to ramble, perhaps even to become lost; it is movement without arrival or departure. One of the striking differences between the Alfoxden and Grasmere Journals is the degree of linguistic specificity and variety that

Dorothy begins to assign to acts of perambulation, specifically to those that imply the leisureliness of 'walking in the wood.' Whereas the Alfoxden Journal is almost entirely threaded together by the verb 'to walk,' typically employed in the past tense, the Grasmere Journal, in but its first week of entries, details two acts of sauntering (May 17 and 19) and one of strolling (May 19). Perhaps most significant, however, is the mention of a ramble on June 3:

> Sent off my letter by the Butcher—a boisterous drying day. I worked in the garden before dinner. Read R[ichar]d Second—was not well after dinner and lay down. Mrs Simpson's grandson brought me some gooseberries. I got up and walked with him part of the way home, afterwards went rambling by the lake side—got Lockety Goldings, strawberries etc., and planted. After tea the wind fell. I walked towards Mr Simpson's. Gave the newspapers to the Girl, reached home at 10. No letter, no William—a letter from R[ichar]d to John. (*Journals* 23)

The fact that Dorothy distinguishes the act of "rambling by the lake side" from two other instances of walking clearly suggests that rambling is for her a variant mode of perambulation. Indeed, while the walks follow a predetermined route (i.e. to the Reverend Joseph Simpson's house at High Broadrain on the Keswick Road) and are undertaken for specific purposes of hospitality, namely to accompany the Simpson's grandson 'Tommy' and, later, to drop off newspapers for the Simpson's daughter, the ramble is at best loosely confined to the "lake side" and pursued for no clearer purpose than that of recreation or aesthetic pleasure. The gathering of globe-flowers and strawberries, whether it occurs at the lake side or further along Dorothy's homeward journey, is but an act of caprice, a natural detour, if you will, in the ramble's inherently indeterminate itinerary. Indeterminacy or route-lessness is precisely what distinguishes rambling from the more teleological acts of walking (and working) that fill Dorothy's day. Rambling may in fact be conceived as a wished-for release from mere walking, that is, from the duties of neighbourliness and the confinements of footpaths.[8] There is indeed sufficient cause for reading relief into Dorothy's sudden turn from walking with Tommy to rambling alone by the lakeshore when one considers the Journal's previous entry, where she bemoans the company of Mrs Nicholson on her return from Ambleside to Grasmere. "This was very kind," she declares, "but God be thanked I want not society by a moonlight lake. . . ." (*Journals* 23).

Rambling and the wish for solitude are inextricably linked not only in Dorothy's Journals but also in her verse. In "A Winter's Ramble in Grasmere

Vale" (c.1805), for example, a poem whose date of composition and thematic interest in sketching the boundaries of home make it a provocative companion-piece to William's *Home at Grasmere*, she recounts one of her first solitary excursions upon arriving in Grasmere:

> A stranger, Grasmere, in thy vale,
> All faces then to me unknown,
> I left my sole companion-friend
> To wander out alone.
>
> Lured by a little winding path,
> Quickly I left the public road,
> A smooth and tempting path it was,
> By sheep and shepherds trod.
>
> Eastward, towards the lofty hills,
> This pathway led me on
> Until I reached a stately rock,
> With velvet moss o'ergrown.
>
> With russet oak and tufts of fern
> Its top was richly garlanded,
> Its sides adorned with eglantine
> Bedropped with hips of glossy red.
>
> There, too, in many a sheltered chink
> The foxglove's broad leaves flourished fair,
> And silver birch whose purple twigs
> Bend to the softest breathing air.
>
> Beneath that rock my course I stayed,
> And, looking to its summit high,
> 'Thou wear'st,' said I, 'a splendid garb—
> Here winter keeps his revelry.
>
> Full long a dweller on the plains,
> I griev'd when summer days were gone;
> No more I'll grieve, for winter here
> Hath pleasure-gardens of his own. (1–28)[9]

Dorothy's very precise emphasis on her decision "[t]o wander out alone," particularly in a context of already profound social isolation, is one of the more striking examples of self-assertion and independence in her entire literary corpus. Wandering or rambling, as she makes clear, entails not only the desertion of "the public road" but also a prior separation from William, her "sole companion-friend." At its core, wandering is an act of distinction, a way, that is, of defining both nature and the self by regarding them in isolation, one set nakedly against the other. Nature, or in this case, the localization of the broader space of home (namely Grasmere Vale), is clearly Dorothy's primary reason for setting out. And here again one must note the importance of travelling alone, of determining the boundaries and dimensions of home subjectively. While it may be read in company, home for Dorothy (as for William) is a text written in solitude; it bears the indelible marks of individualized movement and unique perception. In Dorothy's case, that movement and perception lead her to eschew not only the public road, but also the "lofty hills" towards which the "little winding path" appears to tend. Indeed, she is drawn not to nature's conventionally sublime heights, which are also part of her landscape of home, but instead to the seemingly unremarkable appearance of "a stately rock / With velvet moss o'ergrown." While early critics of the poem have tended to lament this turn from obvious sublimity to apparent ordinariness, characterizing it as "poetic stultification" (Homans 53), Dorothy's experience of the rock is, as I would like to suggest, clearly anything but stultifying. In exploring the rock's features and its significance to the topography of home, she relies less on a roving than a gleaning eye, one that sifts the readily apparent for distinguishing details and penetrates commonness to discover its underlying wonders. What appears, for example, to be a mere covering of moss is revealed under Dorothy's searching gaze as "a splendid garb" of oak, fern, eglantine, foxglove and silver birch. Piercing even the "sheltered chink[s]" of this garment, Dorothy marks variations in colour and texture that make it, as she suggests, "gayer than an April mead" (30). And it is this unexpected gaiety or "revelry" that subdues her grief for summer's passing. One might suggest that it also serves to soothe the displacement of one who has been, as she notes, "long a dweller on the plains." Indeed, her encounter with the "stately rock" is very much about re-placing or re-embedding the self in a congenial environment, in a relationship with nature, in a wondrous space of home. Transformed at poem's end into "an inmate of this vale" (39), Dorothy is fixed in place, her "youthful wishes all fulfilled" (37). The routelessness of wandering yields at last a joyful re-rooting of the self at home.

The wandering that shapes the space of home, inscribing and confirming its boundaries and the self's place therein, is also juxtaposed in the Romantic canon by modes of perambulation whose aesthetic pleasure or value seems to inhere in their capacity to defamiliarize both home and self. These latter walks are precisely what de Certeau has in mind when he likens pedestrian travel to a form of story-telling that "open[s] up space to something *different*" (emphasis added). Pedestrian travel, in other words, is not only recreational but also rec-reative; it allows the subject to reconsider the apparent familiarity or certainty of home, neighbourhood and self. Walking, one might say, allows the subject to escape both home and self, to plunge into an otherness of space and being. That, clearly, is the theme of what Jarvis characterizes as "one of the greatest short pieces of walking literature" (192) in the period, Hazlitt's "On Going a Journey," from *Table Talk* (1821). Guided by the conviction that "We go a journey chiefly to be free of all impediments and of all inconveniences; to leave ourselves behind" (181), Hazlitt presents the walk as an opportunity for radical self-refashioning. The act of "leaving ourselves behind" depends, notably, on a series of prior disentanglements, the most important being the society of others. Insofar as companionship brings with it not only the impediment of conversation—glossed by Hazlitt as "attempts at wit or dull common-places" (182)—but also the inconvenience of shared experience, of precisely that knowledge, however mundane, which the traveller wishes to leave behind, it undermines that "perfect liberty, to think, feel, do, just as one pleases" (181). It is only in silence, in nature, and with adequate elbow-room that the subject, in Hazlitt's opinion, can begin to consider (or reconsider) what exactly s/he is, has been or might become:

> Give me the clear blue sky over my head, and the green turf beneath my feet, a winding road before me, and a three hours' march to dinner—and then to thinking! It is hard if I cannot start some game on these lone heaths. I laugh, I run, I leap, I sing for joy. From the point of yonder rolling cloud, I plunge into my past being, and revel there, as the sunburnt Indian plunges headlong into the wave that wafts him to his native shore. Then long-forgotten things, like 'sunken wrack and sumless treasuries,' burst upon my eager sight, and I begin to feel, think, and be myself again.(182)

Hazlitt's image of thoughtful perambulation, a veritable running over oneself, depends clearly on a juxtaposition or productive tension between desired liberty and the spatial and temporal boundaries, the "blue sky" and "green turf" and the window of a "a three hours' march to dinner," within which that liberty is exercised. An analogous tension is evident in the author himself, a tension, namely, between expressions of childlike giddiness such as play and revelry, and a more mature, almost fretful determination to make the most of silence and solitude, to begin "thinking" as speedily and purposefully as possible. A reconciliation of these disparate impulses occurs only when Hazlitt "plunge[s] into [his] past being," when he returns in thought, as he has already in deed, to a playful childlike self. Walking in effect begets this other journey or plunge of self-discovery that ends at his "native shore." Given the inherent circularity of this journey, its turn to the native rather than the new, it is perhaps best characterized as a *recovery* of self, enabling the walker, as he suggests, to "be myself *again*" (emphasis added). For Hazlitt, as for Wordsworth, the childhood self is the truest self and its recovery is only possible by escaping, even if only briefly, the trappings of age, custom, duty and society. The recovery of self, simply put, is only possible by walking, by "going a journey."

There is, of course, another rather more inventive mode of self-fashioning that Hazlitt associates with travel, particularly when travel takes one well beyond the reaches of familiarity. This he characterizes as the "*incognito* of an inn":

> Oh! it is great to shake off the trammels of the world and of public opinion—to lose our importunate, tormenting, everlasting personal identity in the elements of nature, and become the creature of the moment, clear of all ties—to hold to the universe only by a dish of sweet-breads, and to owe nothing but the score of the evening—and no longer seeking for applause and meeting with contempt, to be known by no other title than the 'Gentleman in the parlour'! One may take one's choice of all characters in this romantic state of uncertainty as to one's real pretensions, and become indefinitely respectable and negatively right-worshipful. *We baffle prejudice and disappoint conjecture; and from being so to others, begin to be objects of curiosity and wonder even to ourselves.* (Noyes 664, emphasis added)

The anonymity of travel, its capacity, that is, to open up spaces of uncertainty—a sort of topography of negative capability—here becomes a playful incitement to refashion the self into a "creature of the moment," a flitting ego that takes its cue from the ever-varying "elements of nature." Indeed, insofar as walking heightens the sense of nature's changeableness by constantly shifting both scene and perspective, it is particularly suited to the perambulatory role-play that Hazlitt envisions. The value of such role-play, as he makes clear, redounds as readily upon the self as upon others, for not only do we thereby enhance our public interest but we become "objects of curiosity and wonder even to ourselves." The association of walking and wonder lies at the heart of Hazlitt's perambulatory aesthetic. Indeed, it is by walking, perhaps the most quotidian of all human activities, that the subject learns to rise above "hackneyed commonplaces" (Noyes 664), to free him/herself to re-imagine the world, to push back the boundaries of both geographical and social space. Imagination itself, in fact, is susceptible to the expansive effects of perambulation. As Hazlitt suggests, "[t]here is hardly anything that shows the short-sightedness or capriciousness of the imagination more than travelling does. With change of place we change our ideas; nay, our opinions and feelings" (Noyes 665). Travel or walking, in other words, expands our mental image of the world by revealing, with each new scene or prospect, the limits of that which preceded it. Thus if, as Hazlitt claims, "[t]he world in our conceit of it is not much bigger than a nutshell" (Noyes 665) the aesthetically impoverished obverse of seeing a world in a grain of sand—walking enables one to think, as it were, outside the shell, to transcend the stagnancy and littleness of our conceptions, our social role, indeed, our very identity.

Like Hazlitt, Leigh Hunt emphasizes the recreative potential of perambulation; as he makes clear in his 1828 essay "Walks Home By Night" (from *The Companion*), however, that potential may be realized without leaving behind all traces of familiar society. This represents a particularly striking departure from Hazlitt's, to say nothing of the Wordsworths', perambulatory aesthetic, when one considers that Hunt's social environment and milieu are distinctively and unapologetically metropolitan. Indeed, the journey he describes in "Walks Home By Night" takes him from London's West End to his suburban home in Highgate, making him, at least in de Certeau's terms, a much more representative or "modern" pedestrian than his Romantic counterparts. His suggestion, for instance, that a walk by night "does not always do us good"[10] seems to encode a clear understanding of the attendant perils of urban walking that, as contemporary readers well know, have nothing to do with the difficulty of the terrain, the length of the journey or (as Hunt wryly implies) the relative "stoutness" of one's constitution. Hunt's walker is, moreover, a much more social creature than Hazlitt's solitary rambler; far from relishing his escape from the embrace of civil society, he deems that separation "[t]he worst part of . . . setting out" (321). As if to assuage the pang of departure he emphasizes the power of farewell words to "last us all the way home, and [. . .] make a dream of [the journey]" (321). The traveller's wish for distracted perambulation, for a walk that closes out the world, is, however, immediately juxtaposed by an experience of heightened, almost numinous, sensitivity to his surroundings.

Startled out of his walking dream by the wonders of enveloping stillness, he describes a scene of prepossessing *un*familiarity:

> Inanimate objects are no calmer than passions and cares now seem to be, all laid asleep. The human being is motionless as the house or the tree; sorrow is suspended; and you endeavour to think that love only is awake. (322)

Recalling Coleridge's vexed meditations on "extreme silentness"[11] in "Frost at Midnight," this passage registers the difficulty of reading or interpreting silence. Bereft of all clues of motion, all sense of familiarity, all certainty, the walker can only "endeavour" to impose on the world around him a wishful fiction of suspended sorrow and slumberless love. From one dream he effectively wanders into another. This second dream, notably, is as brief as the first, for even though the night inspires thoughts of wondrous rest from care, it also bears quiet evidence of rest's undoing. A mere shift in direction reveals to the traveller the red lamp shining over the apothecary's door, a sign, as he suggests, of "help" (322) for those who cannot sleep.

Thus roused anew, the traveller turns his attention from the world without to that within, the actual physiological experience of walking. In order to elucidate this most routine and automatic of activities, he seizes upon the walk that is struggle, the "walk [that] cannot well be worse"—the walk "alone, and in bad weather, and with a long way to go" (323):

> There is a pleasure in overcoming obstacles; mere action is something; imagination is more; and the spinning of the blood, and the vivacity of the mental endeavour, act well upon one another, and gradually put you in a state of robust consciousness and triumph. Every time you set down your leg you have a respect for it. The umbrella is held in the hand like a roaring trophy. (323)

The transformation of perambulation from mere transport to "triumph" is, as Hunt suggests, a product of coordinated physical and mental endeavour, of spinning blood and imagination. In essence, what Hunt describes here is an amalgam of athletic and aesthetic pedestrianism, the effect of which is to invest the 'tools' of everyday life, such as the leg and the umbrella, with a renewed sense of power and purpose. Walking begins, one might say, by making us cognisant of these tools and continues, with every step, to raise our consciousness of their productive potential until we are fully aware of the act of walking and persevering. Hunt's notion of "robust consciousness" is nothing less than

Hegelian 'Erkenntnis'—a shifting of the obscure, untheorized, unconscious everyday into the stark and sudden light of realization. Indeed, walking is as much a triumphant assertion of the everyday as of the walker who persists in finding his way despite inclemencies of weather and terrain.

Robust consciousness pertains to the walker's relationship not only with his body, his most immediate physical environment, but also with the cityscape and those that occupy its darkened spaces. Indeed, Hunt's concluding account of the various watchmen he passes on his night-time rambles reveals a keen sensitivity to distinguishing detail. Despite insisting in his introductory deprecation of the type that differences in watchmen are few, Hunt concedes upon further reflection that "[t]hey are not all mere coat, and lump, and indifference" (323). The varieties he enumerates—the "Dandy," the "Metallic," the unnamed third "who cried the hour in Bedford Square" (323)—are distinguished principally by their vocalizations, their impression, that is, on the walker's ear. Noting discrete variations in pronunciation, intonation and pitch, Hunt draws a series of characters who literally startle the walker into a recognition of his physical surroundings. Not only does he mark their voices but each voice serves by its association with a specific location—Oxford Street, Hanover Square, Bedford Square—to mark (and of course time) the walker's homeward journey. In noise as in silence, therefore, the nightwalker experiences a conflation or elision of the human and the inanimate—in this case, a voice and a street corner—which serves to defamiliarize his environment and also, paradoxically, conduct his way home. As though to reiterate this experience of the world 'made strange'[12] in the context of an after-hours walk, Hunt concludes his essay with a description of "the oddest of all [watchmen]" (324): the so-called Sliding Watchman. Appearing to the walker as "a sort of bale of a man in white [. . .] sliding [forward] with a lantern in one hand, and an umbrella over his head" (324), the Sliding Watchman represents the very collapse of the boundaries between familiarity and the surreal, between walking and dreaming. Hunt is indeed powerless to resolve this "oddest mixture of luxury and hardship, of juvenility and old age" (324), to distill from it any but the most tenuous truths. Characterizing him as "a watchman for Rabelais" (324), Hunt intimates the slippage between perambulatory role-play and pure fiction, between walking *as* text and walking *into* text. If the Watchman's role in this narrative of perambulation is uncertain, that is, either too real or too absurd, so too is the walker's. Indeed, their fates or 'truths' are inextricably intertwined; for if the Watchman's claim, unspoken but attributed to him by Hunt, is true, namely that "'Everything's in imagination'" (324), the walker is himself merely a fiction, as insubstantial and uncertain as the sliding spectre before him. What in the end distinguishes the two is nothing more or less than the nature of their movement. For whereas the Watchman's sliding motion accentuates his tenuous grip on reality, on the physical world—Hunt comments, for example, that "[t]he slide seemed to bear him half through the night at once"— the walker's regular perambulation, "A few strides on a level," brings him finally home and deposits him, as he suggests, "in his own nest" (324). Thus literally embedded in material reality, in the everyday, the walker finds rest; he becomes as still, as substantial, as "the house or the tree."

The foregoing episode underlines what one might call the paradox of walking, its tendency, namely, to accommodate the wondrous, the sublime, while also maintaining contact with the soil of everyday life. Walking, like digging and washing, opens up spaces of wonder *in the real world*; it is at once creative and toilsome, leisurely and practical, aimless and always tending somewhere. The walk may lead to the sublime, but it also returns from it. Indeed, even 'walking in the wood' must be understood as the midpoint of a journey that begins by walking *to* the wood and, ultimately, walking *from* the wood. This conceptual capaciousness, what I have earlier characterized as walking's 'broad canvas,' seems quite clearly to underlie our critical eagerness to distinguish the walk as "quintessentially Romantic." As image, as symbol, as activity, the walk accomplishes much and leaves much more to be accomplished. For the purpose of the present study, however, it must be noted that walking, notwithstanding its symbolic fecundity, is but one of many activities or canvases that make up the much larger scene of everyday life. Indeed, where the spaces, experiences and wonders of our diurnal round are concerned, walking alone cannot elucidate them all. Even de Certeau's study, despite its emphasis on pedestrianism, reminds the reader that the fabric of quotidian life is also threaded together by acts of cooking, dwelling and reading, to name but a few. Moreover, as I would like to suggest, there are modes of everyday transport other than walking that serve to reveal the contiguities between the mundane and the mystical.

One such mode, intimated by the figure of the Sliding Watchman and already more fully developed in the 1805 *Prelude*, is the act of ice-skating. Although far less common than acts of perambulation, skating, like the blowing of wash bubbles, is one of life's innumerable variations of play, a category of experience as intrinsic to the everyday as labour itself. Play, indeed, is perhaps best conceived not as the opposite but rather the obverse of labour; it is a complementary activity to acts of digging or washing (or sewing or cooking, etc.) likewise characterized by the creative division of time and multiplication of space. While the spaces of play may be imaginary, that is, created entirely within, they also of course, like spaces of work, exist in the real world. Physical play such as skating, therefore, serves to spatialize the subject's environment in much the same way that domestic labour spatializes a home or walking defines its boundaries. Wordsworth's account of skating on Esthwaite Water while a student at Hawkshead, for example, is set in proximity to the blazing cottage windows of home, "visible," as he writes, "for many a mile" (I.453). In Wordsworth's case, notably, the act of skating is as much a repudiation as a reification of the boundaries of home. Indeed, he likens himself in the exultation of play to "an untired horse / That cares not for its home" (I.459–460). Both the space and the experience of play are in effect defined in contradistinction to home. Skating transpires in the "frosty" (I.452) outdoors, away from cottage warmth, and is characterized by a series of unfettered movements—"wheeled about" (458), "hissed along" (461), "spinning still" (481)—that defy the regular "summons" (I.455) of home, the tolling, namely, of the village clock. For the young poet, skating is a mode of self-expression and adventurous inquiry that signals growth beyond the child's world of home. He likens it in fact to the adult pleasures of hunting (I.462), the only difference being that skating is inherently generative or creative; it animates the spaces and objects of its own discovery. As Wordsworth writes,

> So through the darkness and the cold we flew,
> And not a voice was idle; with the din,
> Meanwhile, the precipices rang aloud;
> The leafless trees and every icy crag
> Tinkled like iron; while the distant hills
> Into the tumult sent an alien sound
> Of melancholy not unnoticed, while the stars
> Eastward were sparkling clear, and in the west
> The orange sky of evening died away. (I.465–473)

The motions and incidental sounds of play serve in effect to shape the enveloping darkness, to bring its unseen precipices, trees, crags and distant hills by echo into being. Significantly, this composition by movement and sound is one that returns to the poet's ear not merely the tinkling of his own skate blades but also a sense of nature's inherent otherness, what he characterizes as its "alien sound." Here, as in the raven's nest episode, childish pursuits usher the boy-poet quite unexpectedly into a world that exceeds his imaginings and preconceptions, a world that does not merely mimic the subject but communicates itself, intones its own profound "melancholy."

The poet's experience of natural alterity through play leads ultimately to an awareness of the self as being in relationship with nature. This relationship, significantly, is predicated not on motions of unfettered discovery that shape the other incidentally, but on a stillness, an enthrallment, through which the poet perceives the other in motion. Wordsworth's consciousness of his surroundings is heightened the moment he leaves "the tumultuous throng, / To cut across the image of a star / That gleamed upon the ice" (I.476–478). Drawn, as in *Home at Grasmere*, to the prospect of a nether heaven, to starlight scattered at his feet, Wordsworth turns from "games / Confederate" (I.461–462) to a solitary encounter with everyday wonder. So prepossessing is the image of the reflected star that the poet feels impelled to "cut across" it in order to reassure himself of its actual location and, by extension, of his own. Movement in this case is indeed as much about localizing or centering the self as about facilitating an encounter with natural otherness—particularly when one considers that the natural consequence of skating across the star is not to sharpen but rather to obscure and bedim its image. The perception of nature's true agency or animating force is only possible, as the poet discovers, through a momentary cessation of movement:

> and oftentimes,
> When we had given our bodies to the wind,
> And all the shadowy banks on either side
> Came sweeping through the darkness, spinning still
> The rapid line of motion, then at once
> Have I, reclining back upon my heels,
> Stopped short; yet still the solitary cliffs
> Wheeled by me—even as if the earth had rolled
> With visible motion her diurnal round!
> Behind me did they stretch in solemn train,
> Feebler and feebler, and I stood and watched
> Till all was tranquil as a dreamless sleep. (I.478–489)

Beginning with the skaters playfully yielding their "bodies to the wind," this passage traces a reversal or shift of agency from the human to the natural, the subject to the other. The poet's sudden stop, his severance of the "rapid line of motion," completes this shift and induces an awareness of a motion far more thoroughgoing or "deeply interfused"[13] than his own: the earth's "diurnal round." Although Wordsworth realizes that his perception of a spinning world is triggered by the act of "[s]topp[ing] short," his response of wonderment registers an appreciation of the underlying and awesome truth of that perception. A mere moment of play has evoked what he describes so famously in "Lines Written a Few Miles Above Tintern Abbey" as "a sense sublime"[14] in which motion and animating spirit ("Ye Presences of Nature" [I.490]) are perceived as one. The poet's response to this most fundamentally quotidian of sublime experiences is, notably, to maintain his motionlessness: "I stood and watched." So engrossing is the spectacle of "visible motion" that even the din of play is swallowed in transcendent tranquillity. No longer conscious of the ice, his playmates, the stars or distant cottages, the poet discovers himself in communion with nature's primal forces, the "[s]ouls of lonely places" (I.492). Having always already, as he claims, "[h]aunt[ed] me thus among my boyish sports" (I.495), these powers are for Wordsworth inherently quotidian, permeating and animating every facet of existence and discernible only by those who take the time to stop short amid the bustle of life.

Stopping short, as I would like to suggest, may be conceived not only as a literal cessation of movement but also as an aesthetic readiness, even in the midst of motion, to turn from self-revolving thoughts to nature's diurnal rounds, to the wonders, that is, of otherness in motion. Stopping short, in other words, does not preclude walking in the wood. A perhaps better (that is to say, less paradoxical) example of how one may travel while at rest is that of riding in a coach, also an increasingly common activity in the nineteenth century but one rarely associated with aesthetic experience. The reasons for this neglect have perhaps less to do with what de Certeau characterizes as the incarcerating quality of vehicular travel than with its attendant cost. As Jarvis points out, even with the introduction of Obadiah Elliot's elliptical spring in 1805, a device which made for speedier and more comfortable carriages and consequently increased passenger traffic, regular coach travel in the Romantic period was still "the preserve of a small social élite" (21)—whom Wordsworth in *The Excursion* designates merely as "the luxurious" (II.97).[15] By 1820 this trend had changed. Leigh Hunt's "Coaches and their Horses," for example, published in *The Indicator* in August of that year, makes the claim that while travel by carriage is "too convenient, too exacting, too exclusive," other forms of coaching such as stage-coach and mail-coach travel are cheap substitutes in which even "the poor are well met" (*Leigh Hunt* 222, 226). Hunt, interestingly, makes no direct claim for the potential of coach travel to broaden one's aesthetic horizons. The nearest he comes to such a notion is to recommend the use of gigs and curricles to those who seek danger in their travels, danger being, as he suggests, "a good thing for giving a fillip to a man's ideas" (*Leigh Hunt* 223). His description of the post-chaise, glossed as "home in motion" (*Leigh Hunt* 224), highlights a series of benign pleasures among which aesthetic stimulation, briefly and cursorily evoked, is but one:

> The smooth running along the road, the fresh air, the variety of scene, the leafy roads, the bursting prospects, the clatter through a town, the gazing gape of a village, the hearty appetite, the leisure (your chaise waiting only upon your own movements), even the little contradictions to home-comforts, and the expedients upon which they set us, all put the animal spirits at work, and throw a novelty over the road of life. If anything could grind us young again, it would be the wheels of a post-chaise. (*Leigh Hunt* 224)

As this passage makes clear, "the variety of scene" and "bursting prospects" which the view from a coach window affords serve not exclusively or primarily as aesthetic, but more generally as physical, stimulants. For Hunt, the pleasure of coach travel is reducible to its effects on the "animal spirits." Whatever "novelty" is incidentally thrown over the road of life appears to derive rather from the traveller's enlivened physical perception than from a quickened imagination. In effect, Hunt echoes Burke's commentary in the *Philosophical Enquiry* on the contributions of gentle motion to the experience of beauty. According to Burke, coach travel facilitates "that agreeable relaxation which is the characteristic effect of beauty":

> Most people must have observed the sort of sense they have had on being swiftly drawn in an easy coach on a smooth turf, with gradual ascents and declivities. This will probably give a better idea of the beautiful, and point out its probable course better than almost anything else. On the contrary, when one is hurried over a rough, rocky, broken road, the pain felt by these sudden inequalities shows why similar sights, feelings, and sounds are so contrary to beauty. . . . (153–4)

Burke's traveller, like Hunt's, experiences the aesthetic effects of coach travel physically—as swiftness, smoothness and general ease. Where these effects are thwarted by one's passage over uneven terrain and in fact transformed into direct physical discomfort, the aesthetic experience ceases entirely. For Burke at least, coach travel has no relation to the sublime; it is either beautiful or painful.

An alternate perspective on the aesthetics of coach travel does not emerge until somewhat later in the nineteenth century with the publication of Thomas De Quincey's *The English Mail-Coach* in 1849. Described by Vincent de Luca as the chief document in De Quincey's literary corpus that establishes the author "among the major English writers in the visionary tradition" (*De Quincey* 83), *The English Mail-Coach* is a rhapsodic meditation on coach travel as an instantiation and experience of power in motion. The nature of said power is at once concentrated and diffuse; it rests ostensibly in the state and expresses itself in the project of nation-building but its manifestations also comprehend the purely physical or mechanic, the aesthetic, the spiritual, even the apocalyptic. Moreover, as de Luca points out, De Quincey's approach to the representation of power is inherently ambivalent and polarized; power is treated alternately "as attraction and as threat" (*De Quincey* 99). To translate this polarity into the language of aesthetics, one might say that De Quincey's notion of coach travel accommodates both the beautiful and the sublime. His account of a particularly memorable journey through Hertfordshire in 1809, for example, culminating in a description of the coach's arrival at an unnamed village, is richly ornamented with the tropes of Burkean beauty:

> We saw many lights moving about as we drew near; and perhaps the most striking scene on the whole route was our reception at this place. The flashing of torches and the beautiful radiance of blue lights (technically, Bengal lights) upon the heads of our horses; the fine effect of such a flowery and ghostly illumination falling upon our flowers and glittering laurels; whilst all around ourselves, that formed a centre of light, the darkness gathered on the rear and flanks in massy blackness: these optical splendours together with the prodigious enthusiasm of the people composed a picture at once scenical and affecting, theatrical and holy. (22)

Juxtaposed against such soothing snapshots of power at rest, however, are scenes of awe-inspiring wonder, scenes capable, as De Quincey notes, of "tyrannis[ing] over [one's] dreams" (2). Where that tyranny is allied with the mail-coach's "awful political mission" (2) of communicating the news of England's military campaigns abroad, it is generally experienced as sublime terror. "The mail-coach it was," De Quincey writes, "that distributed over the face of the land, like the opening of apocalyptic vials, the heart-shaking news of Trafalgar, of Salamanca, of Vittoria, of Waterloo" (2). The coach's association with its own dreadful tidings transforms it into a living symbol of hope and despair, a materialization, as de Luca suggests, of "the thundering irresistible chariot [. . .] variously rendered in the Scriptures, in Dante, Milton, Blake, and Shelley" (98). De Quincey's 'chariot,' notably, is a conflation of the mechanic and the organic; more than a mere "glorified object" (2) of indomitable force and velocity, the coach is a nexus of physical, animal and spiritual sensibilities:

> [W]e heard our speed, we saw it, we felt it as a thrilling; and this speed was not the product of blind insensate agencies, that had no sympathy to give, but was incarnated in the fiery eyeballs of the noblest among brutes, in his dilated nostril, spasmodic muscles, and thunder-beating hoofs. The sensibility of the horse, uttering itself in the maniac light of his eye, might be the last vibration of such a movement; the glory of Salamanca might be the first. But the intervening links that connected them, that spread the earthquake of battle into the eyeball of the horse, were the heart of man and its electric thrillings—kindling in the rapture of the fiery strife, and then propagating its own tumults by contagious shouts and gestures to the heart of his servant the horse. (12)

Whatever moves in De Quincey's universe is wedded to life, animated, run through by a flash of rapturous energy; the coach's flight is an inevitable, irresistible aftershock from an originating impulse, an epicentre of war. These "inter-agencies" (12), as De Quincey calls them, are, more importantly, a locus of numinous experience. Commenting on the subtle communication between horse and master, he suggests that out of this symbiotic relationship are derived "many aspects of sublimity under accidents of mists that hid, or sudden blazes that revealed, of mobs that agitated, or midnight solitudes that awed" (12). The heart, in other words, depends for its "electric thrillings" on a sense of connectedness to the greater organ or spirit of motion. Travel by steam-engine conversely—and here De Quincey anticipates de Certeau—is dismissed because it "disconnect[s] man's heart from the ministers of his locomotion" (12); train travel thus becomes an unnatural and soulless mode of transport, capable neither of thrilling the imagination nor of galvanizing public interest.

The aesthetic impact of the traveller's experience of connectedness to the "ministers of locomotion" is perhaps most clearly elucidated in 'The Vision of Sudden Death,' a narrative sequence in which the mail-coach is presented not as a public organ for the communication of destruction abroad but as a direct threat of private destruction at home. The coach's evocation of terror is therefore diminished in scope but intensified in degree; it is collapsed into a single moment, a single vision of collision that comes upon both traveller and reader with the inexorability of rumbling wheels. The incident occurs on a routine trip from London to Glasgow, near the town of Preston, when the driver inadvertently falls asleep and, to the horror of an apparently helpless De Quincey, sets the coach on a collision course with an approaching gig. The sublimity of this experience, notably, is not reducible to the visionary moment of imminent death but rather begins in the surreal calm that precedes this moment. Indeed, what heightens the terror of approaching destruction is the sense of harmony and connectedness to life that the author experiences in the early hours of the journey. "[T]he night," as De Quincey recalls, "was one of peculiar solemnity and peace. . . . I had so far yielded to the influence of the mighty calm as to sink into a profound reverie" (32). The author's reverie is characterized once again by an awareness of nature's inter-agencies, on this occasion described as the "orchestral part" which all natural manifestations play in the production of an "exquisite state of unity" (33). As De Quincey makes clear, such unity comprehends both earth and heaven:

> In the clouds, and on the earth, prevailed the same majestic peace; and in spite of all that villain of a schoolmaster has done for the ruin of our sublimer thoughts, which are the thoughts of our infancy, we still believe in no such nonsense as a limited atmosphere. Whatever we may swear with our false feigning lips, in our faithful hearts we still believe, and must for ever believe, in fields of air traversing the total gulf between earth and the central heavens. Still, in the confidence of children that tread without fear *every* chamber in their father's house, and to whom no door is closed, we, in that Sabbatic vision which sometimes is revealed for an hour upon nights like this, ascend with easy steps from the sorrow-stricken fields of earth, upwards to the sandals of God. (33)

This startling vision of sublimity, so reminiscent of the author's description in *Suspiria De Profundis* (1845) of swooning by his dead sister's bedside and rising "as if on billows"[16] to the throne of God, derives its power from its confirmation of the limitless possibility of childish thought. For De Quincey, the child's ideas are "sublimer" because they acknowledge the inter-agency between earth and heaven, the human and the divine, and thus allow for moments of passage beyond the "limited atmosphere" of empirical science. This particular moment of passage is of course also facilitated by the freedom that comes from being a passenger on the coach, by the leisure, that is, to indulge in reverie—a version of adult play—while the reins of mastery are in the driver's hands. De Quincey's position on the box, prized, as he suggests, by young passengers in particular, allows him to experience his surroundings more fully while also maintaining the vital connection between himself and the horses. For a dreamer, his is the most enviable position on the coach.

When the driver succumbs, however, to an almost trancelike slumber, De Quincey's position quickly becomes the most dreadful, his dreams of sublime transcendence turning to a nightmare of sublime terror. Listening, as he writes, "in awe" (33) to the approach of distant hoofbeats, De Quincey recognizes the night's soothing calm as the prelude to a storm:

> this accursed gift I have, as regards *thought*, that in the first step towards the possibility of a misfortune I see its total evolution; in the radix of the series I see too certainly and too instantly its entire expansion; in the first syllable of the dreadful sentence I read already the last. (34)

The "Sabbatic vision" is here transformed into one of imminent apocalypse. Held in the thrall of terror as much by his confidence in his "accursed gift" as by the immovable figure of the driver, from whose "viced" (35) hand De Quincey cannot free the reins, he gives himself, the couple in the approaching carriage, and the reader over to the inevitability of collision. And it is precisely this resignation to destruction which makes the outcome—a loud but harmless bump of carriage wheels in the night—all the more resonant. Having comprehended what is in the end only the limited inter-agency between a slumbering driver and runaway horses, De Quincey is startled, indeed awed, by the culmination of a larger, miraculously benign inter-agency between the two carriages. The failure of what he prophesies as the "total evolution" of the event is a failure ultimately to anticipate otherness in motion—the reactions, namely, of the occupants of the approaching gig. Only after the mail-coach passes the gig, thereby distinguishing the destinies of travellers fated to collide, does De Quincey in fact acknowledge and commiserate with the other in the lingering terror of averted misfortune. His reaction to the spectacle of the young couple in the first moments after certain death registers not only the astonishment of escape and foiled prophecy, but the awe of participating in a miracle greater than death, that of deliverance. It is indeed the confluence of the vision of sudden life with that of sudden death which so impresses itself on De Quincey and is carried, as he suggests, "into my dreams forever" (39). As before, the mail-coach's destructive potential is offset by its generative capacity to open up for the traveller scenes and experiences of visionary power. One impulse, one moment, one cog in a larger machinery of motion, the runaway mail-coach serves by its course to reveal the limitations of a subjective construct of "total evolution" in which the other's fate is inextricably bound up and comprehended by the self; by bringing the traveller rather to an acknowledgment than an annihilation of the other, the speeding coach—or rather, coach*es*—adumbrate an inter-agency of miraculous design and possibility. The vision of sudden death in effect culminates in a realization of the self's and the other's "orchestral parts" in a greater symphony of motion.

Sublime Transport and the Making of Space 143

The notion of sublime transport in the Romantic period is itself such a symphony, comprised of distinct and variegated movements—those of labour, pedestrianism, play and travel, among others—each serving to shape geographical and, as I suggested in the introduction to this chapter, textual space. This latter space is at once a product and an instantiation of the inherent creativity of everyday movement or travel; for if travelling creates space, weaves it together, then the transcription of recollected travel results in a further re-creation of space. The nature of such textual re-creation is twofold, involving what de Certeau characterizes on one hand as "displacements and condensations" (107), and what I would designate on the other as subjective expansions. The process of displacing and condensing space, of shifting woods or mountains onto a page, is authorial and depends on the intentional and at times accidental selectivity of memory. Recollected space, although built upon the actual experience of moving in and around a particular environment, is therefore inherently fictive; it is the product, in De Quinceyean terms, of tracing and interpreting the vestigial marks and smudges on a palimpsest. The second form of recreated space, subjective expansion, is likewise fictive, insofar as it is not recollected by the author but rather created or visualized entirely by the reader. Whereas the author displaces and condenses a physical environment into textual space, the reader works in reverse, constructing an imagined place or setting from the clues of text. Such construction, although necessarily idiosyncratic, operates in general terms by a species of expansion or enlargement. The process is described perhaps most famously in Keats's "On First Looking Into Chapman's Homer" (1817), where reading is re-envisioned as a mode of travel culminating in moments of discovery:

> Then felt I like some watcher of the skies
>   When a new planet swims into his ken;
> Or like stout Cortez when with eagle eyes
>   He stared at the Pacific. . . . (9–12)[17]

The act of reading is for Keats geographically expansive; it pushes back the conceptual boundaries of heaven and earth and, recalling de Certeau, "opens up space to something different." The text, then, is a site for the exploration and expression of that difference, whether it is achieved through displacement, condensation or expansion.

For the author, as I have suggested, the exploration of different space is predominantly retrospective, involving, in de Certeau's terms, a reconstruction and creative negotiation of "the deserted places of [. . .] memory" (106). These places of memory not uncommonly have their origin in childhood. As de Certeau suggests, "[t]o practice space is [. . .] to repeat the joyful and silent experience of childhood" (110). For Romantic writers of the everyday, the recovery of place is likewise coincident with a recovery of self, typically a purer childhood self such as Wordsworth's 'best philosopher.' To borrow Hazlitt's metaphor, one cannot arrive at one's native shore without plunging along the way into one's past being. The inspiration for localized or spatialized recollection in the Romantic period—for strolls down memory lane—is not, however, reducible solely to a nostalgic longing for self. The return to what are expressly "*deserted* places of memory" (emphasis added) must also be understood more broadly as a desire to people those places—that is, to replace the self and the other in relationship, in community.

Few works elucidate the subtle interrelationships between recollected place, self and community, as well as the spatial creativity of memory, more vividly than Coleridge's "This Lime-Tree Bower My Prison" (1797), a poem which, according to Raimonda Modiano (*Concept of Nature* 57), marks the poet's first and perhaps only successful reconciliation of subjective idealism and naturalism, which may be characterized in general terms as the assimilative powers of self or imagination and those of external nature, including the human other. Coleridge's establishment of a balance, that is, an ideal communion, between the demands of self and nature in the poem depends on the mediation of memory, on the recollection of a series of connecting steps, literally the common ground, between the embowered self and the wandering other. Notwithstanding the extra-textual claims of the Advertisement that the author "composed the following lines in the garden bower" or the textual use of deictic markers to suggest an immediate *in situ* moment of poetic creation—"Well, they are gone, and *here* must I remain, / *This* lime-tree bower my prison!" (1–2, emphasis added)[18]—the role of memory is clearly central to an understanding of the poem's evocation of place and community. "This Lime-Tree Bower" is, after all, as much about a visionary landscape pieced together by acts of memory and imagination as it is about an actual site of composition.

Prevented from attending his visiting friends, Charles Lamb and the Wordsworths, on a ramble over the Quantocks by the misfortune of having a pitcher of boiled milk spilled on his foot on the morning of their arrival, Coleridge uses the medium of verse to accompany his friends imaginatively in a way he cannot manage physically. Indeed, from the outset the poem articulates an inherently descriptive longing for space elsewhere, outside of bower and page, for moments other than those of secluded composition:

> I have lost
> Such beauties and such feelings, as had been

> Most sweet to have remembered, even when age
> Had dimmed mine eyes to blindness! They, meanwhile,
> My friends, whom I may never meet again,
> On springy heath, along the hilltop edge,
> Wander in gladness, and wind down, perchance,
> To that still roaring dell of which I told;
> The roaring dell, o'erwooded, narrow, deep,
> And only speckled by the midday sun;
> Where its slim trunk the ash from rock to rock
> Flings arching like a bridge; that branchless ash,
> Unsunned and damp, whose few poor yellow leaves
> Ne'er tremble in the gale, yet tremble still,
> Fanned by the waterfall! (2–16)

The move from isolation to vicarious experience is so sudden and, indeed, so convincing by its enumeration of detail that the distance between the displaced poet and his friends is narrowed with one visionary stride. Anticipating not only the course of their journey—a course already in fact laid out for them—but also the very experience of walking ("[o]n springy heath," "in gladness"), Coleridge relies on an "empathetic imagination" (Jarvis 148) as well as his own particularized memories of the landscape to walk in words with his companions and thus experience those "beauties" and "feelings" whose loss he initially laments. He trusts additionally of course in the self-perpetuating rhythms of nature to maintain for the walkers the landscape of his own experience. His references to the "*still* roaring dell" and to leaves that "tremble *still* / Fanned by the waterfall" (emphasis added) encode an understanding of nature's imperviousness to the corruptions of time, its enduring consistency, one might say, as a setting for human exploration. Coleridge's reliance on natural stability and, moreover, on the fastidious precision of memory to reproduce a specific physical landscape, allows him to reconstruct his friends' journey step by step, sight by sight:

>   And there my friends
> Behold the dark green file of long lank weeds,
> That all at once (a most fantastic sight!)
> Still nod and drip beneath the dripping edge
> Of the dim clay-stone.
>   Now my friends emerge
> Beneath the wide wide heaven—and view again
> The many-steepled tract magnificent

> Of hilly fields and meadows, and the sea,
> With some fair bark, perhaps, which lightly touches
> The slip of smooth clear blue betwixt two isles
> Of purple shadow! (16–26)

Significantly, the work of memory is here supplemented by that of imagination, a union that superimposes an aesthetically pleasing but presumably fictive image of a bark "betwixt two isles" onto the mental map of the sea. Explained by Anne Mellor as a brief picturesque stop on a comprehensive progression through the aesthetic categories of the day ("English Landscape" 259), this momentary idealization of landscape may also be read, particularly in light of the overarching emphasis on imagined community, as the poet's wish (materialized into reality) that his friends experience the full and varied pleasures of the walk, that their journey, in other words, comprise every element of joy that Coleridge himself has experienced on his various rambles over the same ground. The imagined journey in this paradigm of wish fulfilment thus becomes a composite of many actual journeys, a map built of many memories, and the walkers' "gladness," a distillation of the poet's own varied joys in traversing a landscape so rich in aesthetic pleasures. The addition of the bark in this economy of pleasure serves as an aesthetic gift from Coleridge to ensure and secure his friends' delight. The emphatic claim that immediately follows—"Yes, they wander on / In gladness all" (26–27)—may be read as an expression both of the earnestness of his wish and his self-imposed belief in its realization.

The transmission or gift of joy from the imprisoned poet to the liberated walkers (and indeed, back again) is clearly central to the poem's facilitation of community. Insofar as joy is here linked to aesthetic pleasure, namely to an experience of natural beauty and variety, it is a gift dependent on and comprised of the poet's own recollections of landscape. The gift of joy, in other words, is a gift of memory, *a gift of space*, ornamented, as I have suggested, by the works of imagination. It is a gift, moreover, particularly precious to Charles Lamb, who, as Coleridge insists, "pined / And hungered after nature many a year / In the great city pent" (28–30). Recalling Coleridge's own stultifying childhood experience of being "pent mid cloisters dim,"[19] Lamb's relation to (urban) space is characterized by deprivation and an attendant longing for elsewhere. The gift of space he is given, a gift re-created in text, amply supplies these wants. Moreover, by ensuring that the poetic landscape is stocked with irresistible sources of wonderment such as the sun's "glorious" (33) setting, Coleridge achieves a communion of sentiment with his friend, a shared joy that obliterates the distance between them:

Sublime Transport and the Making of Space

> So my friend,
> Struck with deep joy, may stand, as I have stood,
> Silent with swimming sense; yea, gazing round
> On the wide landscape, gaze till all doth seem
> Less gross than bodily, a living thing
> Which *acts* upon the mind—and with such hues
> As clothe the Almighty Spirit, when he makes
> Spirits perceive His presence. (37–44)

Founding a community of joy on his own memories of witnessing a sunset and on Lamb's 'present' experience thereof, Coleridge envisions his friend standing for a moment "as I have stood," the initially tentative "may" becoming an insistent "yea" as the re-created scene begins to act upon his mind. The recollected here in effect becomes the re-lived as Coleridge's memory and Lamb's experience meld into a single expression of wonder. Occupying the same physical space, indeed, almost the same body, the two friends are held in thrall by the perception of divine "Presence"; their "gazing" is unindividuated, their senses, a common pool. The communion of common experience brings them in the end to a yet deeper communion, a oneness not merely with each other but with a "Spirit" that underlies and animates every living thing. Fittingly, the joy of the experience redounds as much upon Coleridge as upon the "sad yet patient soul" (31) of Lamb. The poet's own gift of visionary landscape, of re-created space, enables him to transcend his present embowerment and to be "glad / As I myself were there" (44–46). Thus the displacement of physical space onto a page, initially feared as a loss of beauty and feeling, results through the poet's own displacement from bower to hilltop in a profound recovery of beauty and feeling, and, what is more, of community.

It must of course be noted that Coleridge's escape from present isolation to the landscapes of memory is temporary. Indeed, what Modiano characterizes as his poetic success in mediating between self and nature is marked by his return to the bower, his willingness to explore and derive solace from his immediate physical environment much as he has from the spaces of the past. Coleridge seems in fact to intimate an awareness of the bower and its aesthetic consolations even in the midst of his visionary transcendence of it:

> Nor in this bower,
> This little lime-tree bower, have I not marked
> Much that has soothed me. Pale beneath the blaze
> Hung the transparent foliage; and I watched
> Some broad and sunny leaf, and loved to see

> The shadow of the leaf and stem above
> Dappling its sunshine! (46–52)

As if recalling himself to the present, Coleridge retraces all that he has "marked" while ostensibly engaged in an act of imaginative sympathy with his wandering friends. As before, the setting he recounts so acts upon his mind as to become animated through the very process of description. Indeed, the movements of nature, heretofore described in past tense, obtrude with sudden irresistible presence on the poet's consciousness:

> And that walnut tree
> Was richly tinged, and a deep radiance lay
> Full on the ancient ivy which *usurps*
> Those fronting elms, and now with blackest mass
> Makes their dark branches gleam a brighter hue
> Through the late twilight; and though now the bat
> Wheels silent by, and not a swallow twitters,
> Yet still the solitary humble-bee
> Sings in the bean-flower! (52–60)

Much as the ivy "usurps" the elms, miraculously turning "dark branches" with its "blackest mass" to a "brighter hue," so it creeps with wonder-working agency across the poet's distracted mind, rousing him to an aesthetic awareness of what is "now" before him—the transformative powers of nature's everyday manifestations. These powers in fact usurp the conventional sublimity of the sunset itself, effecting in the poet a change no less profound than is evinced by his "swimming sense." Cognisant, as before, of nature's timelessness, its undiminished rounds of motion, its tireless song, Coleridge finds solace in the epiphany that solace lies everywhere:

> Henceforth I shall know
> That nature ne'er deserts the wise and pure—
> No scene so narrow but may well employ
> Each faculty of sense, and keep the heart
> Awake to love and beauty! (60–64)

Having been forced into a "narrow" scene by one of the innumerable accidents of daily living, the poet learns in the midst of his confinement to "employ / Each faculty of sense" in the aesthetic appreciation of the narrow and the ordinary. It is in effect by suffering the everyday that he is redeemed by it.

Sublime Transport and the Making of Space

In a final remarkable mediation between self, nature and the human other, Coleridge turns at poem's end from the embrace of personal solace to its extension or diffusion beyond the self. While the act of writing in itself accomplishes this diffusion, the poet also chooses a more direct messenger to communicate what nature in the midst of want has given him: the "lively joy" (67) that comes from contemplating the source of joy itself. His lively joy, drawn from spaces past and present, spaces extraordinary and mundane, is ultimately expressed in the making of community, in a gift not primarily of memory, as before, but of imagination:

> My gentle-hearted Charles! when the last rook
> Beat its straight path along the dusky air
> Homewards, I blessed it, deeming its black wing
> (Now a dim speck, now vanishing in the light)
> Had crossed the mighty orb's dilated glory
> While thou stoodst gazing; or, when all was still,
> Flew creaking o'er thy head, and had a charm
> For thee, my gentle-hearted Charles! to whom
> No sound is dissonant which tells of Life. (68–76)

Turning from the creativity of recollection to the mediating forces of nature, Coleridge establishes a link, literally through a flight of imagination, between himself and Lamb, between the past and the present. His blessing of the passing rook, an act perhaps even more resonant with redemptive potential than the Mariner's blessing of the sea snakes because it is performed consciously, joins the self to the other by joining it first to nature. Passing directly out of Coleridge's immediate surroundings and into Lamb's, the rook is a reminder of the narrowness of human separation, a solace that by its loud "creaking" is no less tangible than the sun's "dilated glory." The poet's selection of a rook as his messenger is also of course significant because the rook, as Donna Landry points out, is an inherently sociable bird that lives typically in large flocks (228). Coleridge's choice, therefore, of a solitary rook flying "[h]omewards" is suggestive of a return to community. The "charm" it carries to Lamb may accordingly be read not only as a reminder of community and fellowship but also as an invitation to return home, to deliver the poet physically, as he has already managed imaginatively, from his embowered seclusion.

A success that critics rarely mention in their discussions of the poem's facilitation of community and its promotion of spatial and experiential intercourse between the poet and the other is its anticipation of, and responsiveness to, the perambulations of another traveller, an always already implied explorer of the text's topography: the reader. Indeed, the "beauties" and "feelings" that Coleridge endeavours to recreate for his friends are also in turn created for the reader who enters the textual landscape, much like Lamb, as an uninitiated walker. The poet's gift of recollected space, his invitation to explore, is therefore widely diffused. Significantly, the more profound gifts of fellowship and community are already in a sense embedded in the act of reading. By virtue simply of our breadth of perspective, our capacity, that is, to command the viewpoints of the embowered poet as well as the liberated walkers, we bring them into communion by passing from one to the other, much like the rook. As readers, we also of course participate more directly in the communion between Coleridge and Lamb by sharing simultaneously in their experiences of the landscape; at once dependent on the topographical details that the poet supplies, we are also at liberty, like the walker, to range over the landscape beyond the immediate boundaries of the lime-tree. Although the reader's experience of textual space is always necessarily imaginative and therefore 'unreal,' it is also, by virtue of that imaginative freedom, amenable to the gifts of aesthetic idealization. Because we cannot refer to the truth of lived experience in refuting Coleridge's placement of a bark betwixt two isles, we become opportune wanderers through the poem's textual spaces, ideal recipients, that is, of the poet's gifts. Included among these gifts is also that which redounds upon the poet himself, the solace, namely, of nature's "narrow" scenes. Much as Coleridge in the midst of creative recollection is recalled to his immediate surroundings by a sudden perception of their wondrous aesthetic potential, so the reader is invited by the poet's epiphany to return from imagined spaces and the illusion of perambulation to the narrow space of text and the present reality of reading. For although "This Lime-Tree Bower My Prison" is ostensibly a walking poem, it also clearly foregrounds the value of reading through its insistent return to the present site and space of textual production. The sudden obtrusion of the here and now on the poet's recollections and his consequent return to the bower and (thus) to the act of composition speak to the inescapability, one might say the "charm," of text. For the reader, that charm is experienced as a series of paradoxical gifts: the gift of space through narrowness of dimension; the gift of unfettered movement despite stillness; the gift of community in midst of solitude. The text in some sense epitomizes the unexpected plenitude and consoling wondrousness of everyday life. Indeed, one may suggest that of all narrow scenes it is the text that most consistently "keep[s] the heart / Awake to love and beauty," and of all quotidian journeys it is reading that covers the most ground, shortening with each word, each step, the distance between self and other.

Chapter Four
Simple Flowers and Familiar Soil: The Consolations of Everyday Life

The effects of turning from expansive vistas to the narrow, particular scenes of daily life transcend the obvious physical, perceptual and aesthetic refinements that such a shift in perspective necessitates. As Coleridge illustrates in "This Lime-Tree Bower My Prison," an awareness of and re-immersion in our immediate and present surroundings have the potential, by reinvigorating our sense of connectedness to life, to assuage feelings of displacement, isolation, even imprisonment. Such moments and experiences are, to be sure, exceptional, epiphanic, uncommon; to borrow Coleridge's term, they depend on a sudden *usurpation* of the familiar by the wondrous. Indeed, it is the wondrous that awakens the subject to the signifying excess, the sublimity, of everyday life. Wonder, one might say, redeems the everyday from the obscurity into which it falls through habituation and familiarity. For Coleridge, notably, the wonder of everyday life is also associated with the redemption of the subject—a redemption effected by a revitalized sense of "love and beauty." Wonder, albeit a momentary state, is thus in itself a consolation; by casting a sudden light upon all that is hidden in full view, all that is familiar but unrealized, it invites a reinterpretation of, and a fundamental shift in the self's relation to, everyday life.

An understanding of the link between wonder and consolation lies in fact at the heart of that admittedly heterogeneous and amorphous body of philosophical and spiritual writing generally glossed as the *consolatio*. Consisting primarily of Greek and Roman models such as Plato's *Phaedo*, Crantor's *On Grief*, Cicero's *Tusculan Disputations*, Plutarch's *Consolatio ad Apollonium* and Boethius's *The Consolation of Philosophy* (all of which incorporate the study of consolation into a broader philosophy of ethics) and later adopted by Cappadocian Christian writers of the fourth and fifth centuries, the *consolatio* represents a reasoned attempt to come to terms with the inevitability of suffering and the grief of death. Although its popularity as a literary genre was short-lived, the *consolatio* survived at least in spirit through a pluralization of form, the result being that its preoccupying themes and questions, as old indeed as human experience, were debated and diffused in such diverse genres as the elegy, the memorial, the hymn and the funeral sermon, to say nothing of such modern incarnations as self-help books and bereavement cards. Today it is perhaps more proper to speak of distinct literatures of consolation rooted in the disciplines of psychology, theology, philosophy and the arts. As Robert C. Gregg observes in *Consolation Philosophy*, one of the paradoxes confronting the modern writer who wishes to compose a letter of consolation for a friend is that s/he has no specific model on which to draw but feels, nevertheless, quietly overwhelmed by a tide of well-known, often hackneyed, sentiments (iii). There is, then, on one hand something quite common about consolatory writing, something indeed dated and trite, something that, by virtue of its familiarity, often fails to console. It is no doubt the despair of arming oneself against anticipated suffering with only clichés that has prompted many modern writers, as Seamus Perry notes, to regard even the possibility of solace as "wholly *passé*" (479). Where consolation is at all effective (or even conceivable), it is generally associated with an unfamiliar or striking idea. As Horace Gregory suggests in his introduction to *The Triumph of Life*, an anthology of consolatory poetry dating largely from the nineteenth and twentieth centuries, "[t]o be consoled is often to discover new aspects of the world in which we live" (ix). The consolations of discovery are, for example, precisely what Elihu recommends to Job in response to the latter's unremitting grief: "Remember that thou magnify his [i.e. God's] work, which men behold" (36:24). Notably, the "work" to which Elihu alludes in his own magnifying fashion is the everyday wonder of a rain shower:

> For he maketh small the drops of water: they pour down rain according to the vapour thereof: which the clouds do drop *and* distil upon man abundantly. . . . [C]an *any* understand the spreading of the clouds . . . ? (36:27–29)[1]

While the Judeo-Christian *consolatio* quite clearly foregrounds everyday wonder as an expression of the sublime wonder of God, its emphasis on the natural and earthly, the immanent and immediate environment of day-to-day life, is incorporated into what M.H. Abrams characterizes as Romanticism's "displaced and reconstituted theology" (65) of nature and imagination. The result is a re-awakening, both aesthetically and spiritually, to the wonders of narrow scenes, to the solace that, quite apart from any explicit evocation of divine presence, is always already there.

This lesson, dramatized so explicitly in Coleridge's "Lime-Tree Bower," also expresses itself more subtly, at times even matter-of-factly, in the works of other Romantic writers. Indeed, as I would like to suggest, an understanding of everyday life as inherently wondrous, solacing and fructifying permeates the literature of the period. The everyday, as Keats observes in his famous letter to Benjamin Bailey on the indivisibility of imagination and truth, lies at the heart not of our fleeting happiness but of our more secure and reassuring contentedness:

> I scarcely remember counting upon any Happiness—I look not for it if it be not in the present hour—nothing startles me beyond the Moment. The setting sun will always set me to rights—or if a Sparrow come before my Window I take part in its existence [sic] and pick about the Gravel. (Keats, *Letters* 69)

Written twenty years after Coleridge's epiphany in the lime-tree bower and in terms decidedly more subdued, this passage evokes that moment of wondrous return to the consolations of the present and the ordinary. For Keats it is not the boundlessness of space or the transcendent might of nature but the merest expression of nature's diurnal round that sets him to rights; he is solaced not by the sublimations of a god-like ego but by the experience simply of a shared existence with nature's humblest other. As Keats reveals in a letter to James Rice a year before his death, the consolations of such an ever-present source of joy are experienced with especial poignancy in moments of suffering:

> How astonishingly does the chance of leaving the world impress a sense of its natural beauties on us. . . . I muse with greatest affection on every flower I have known from my infancy—their shapes and coulours [sic] are as new to me as if I had just created them with a superhuman fancy. It is because they are connected with the most thoughtless and happiest moments of our Lives. I have seen foreign flowers in hothouses of the most beautiful nature, but I do not care a straw for them. The simple flowers of our spring are what I want to see again. (Keats, *Letters* 465)

Awakened by illness to the shapes and colours of his immediate surroundings, the poet muses not just on any "natural beauties" but specifically on those that long experience has made familiar to him, the "simple flowers" of childhood. His experience of nature's simplicity, much like Coleridge's, is of course anything but simple or familiar. The flowers of childhood are seen or rather envisioned as if for the first time. Thoughts of death do more than merely kindle in the poet a yearning for the familiar; they elicit an experience analogous to first encounter, a sort of re-immersion in the everyday without the expectations and attendant effects of familiarity. Significantly, the experience of simple flowers under such conditions of newness transcends mere novelty or prepossession. Like Wordsworth's 'meanest flower,' the simple flowers of Keats's childhood lie beyond the grasp of words and sentiments. Accessible only to the recreative powers of a "superhuman fancy," the unnamed flowers are nothing less than objects of sublime wonder. The nature of that sublimity, as Keats suggests, is associative as much as it is inherent; it rests not only in shapes and colours that defy description but also in the flowers' connection with childhood itself, with "the most thoughtless and happiest moments of our Lives." The flowers exist, as it were, in two moments simultaneously; like Wordsworth's butterfly, they facilitate a return to scenes of childhood joy, to a state of "thoughtless" experience—experience, in other words, that is unalloyed with the stultifying habits of familiarity.

Juxtaposed against this emphasis on novelty or wonder as the source of everyday consolation is a tendency, already intimated in my discussion of the mystic circle of home, to seek in the everyday precisely that constancy of form and dependability of experience by which the displaced subject may be grounded and re-rooted. One might say that the difference between these approaches expresses itself in a turn from simple flowers to familiar soil. Home is perhaps even too general and diffuse a term for such soil. In the particularizing poetics of John Clare, for example, this intimate and ultimate space of consolation is defined as "my old home of homes" (1).[2] The center of a series of concentric circles of familiarity, the "old home of homes" refers to a precisely delineated topographical space beyond which the subject experiences even common natural objects and manifestations as strange and foreign. For Clare, the old home of homes is comprised of his cottage in Helpstone, the adjacent Royce Wood and parts of Helpstone Heath. To move merely four miles from this center to the village of Northborough, where "The Flitting" was composed in 1832, is to be displaced, as Clare suggests, to "[s]trange scenes[,] mere shadows[, . . .] / Vague unpersonifying things" (89–90). For Clare, that which is "strange" and "unpersonifying" is also necessarily incapable of consoling the subject:

> Alone and in a stranger scene,
> Far, far from spots my heart esteems,
> The closen with their ancient green,

> Heath, woods, and pastures, sunny streams.
> The hawthorns here were hung with may,
> But still they seem in deader green,
> The sun een seems to lose its way
> Nor knows the quarter it is in. (49–56)

Rather than distinguishing hawthorns and sunshine as markers of nature's constancy, the poet recognizes them principally (and, indeed, somewhat irrationally) by their difference from the hawthorns and sunshine of Helpstone. Unconsoled by what is to him a less vibrant, less certain topography than that which his "heart esteems," Clare pines for the embrace of familiarity. Unable to find in nature what he seeks, he turns ultimately to books to supply the want of well-known sentiments; yet even books, as he suggests, trifle with the happiness by "follow[ing] fashions new / And throw[ing] all old esteems away" (69–70). The new or unfamiliar is for Clare an insubstantial, barren ground where "flowers never grew" (71); its principal domain is the city and its typical manifestations are "high-flown fangled things" (153) whose "splendour passes for sublime" (156). The old home of homes, by contrast, is a soil from which "the grass eternal springs" (215), its power or energy deriving from its predictability and constancy, its timeless regeneration of familiarity. Clare's perception of this power, interestingly, is reiterated some twenty years later by another (though rather more distant) Romantic writer whose characterization of grass as a "uniform hieroglyphic" whose meaning is "[a]ll goes onward and outward, nothing collapses,"[3] likewise emphasizes the solace of familiar soil.

It is worth noting that the role of illness, so central to Keats's numinous encounter with simple flowers, also and perhaps even more profoundly shapes the yearning for familiar soil. Insofar as the experience of familiarity is bound up with acts of recollection, its effects on the subject include a removal from the present moment, a removal, that is, from the place and condition of illness itself. Familiar soil, as Dorothy Wordsworth reveals in "Thoughts on my Sickbed" (c.1831), is therefore not simply a solace but a site of freedom from pain. Its power, notably, is experienced not all at once but in a series of steps that carry her, like the embowered Coleridge, beyond the confines of the sickbed. The first of these steps is facilitated by Wordsworth's sudden awareness of her present surroundings, meaning not the immediate context of the bed but rather the backdrop of "this sunny spring" (2).[4] By yielding her heart's "echoing string" (4) to spring's "prelusive sounds" (3), Dorothy experiences a re-animation of the memories of "youthful days" (9)—what she describes as her "hidden life" (5). The very antithesis of frailty and prostration, the "hidden life" is characterized by a joyful, lively engagement with natural plenitude:

> With busy eyes I pierced the lane
> In quest of known and unknown things;
> The primrose a lamp on its fortress rock,
> The silent butterfly spreading its wings,
>
> The violet betrayed by its noiseless breath,
> The daffodil dancing in the breeze,
> The carolling thrush on his naked perch,
> Towering above the budding trees. (13–20)

This finely focussed catalogue of everyday life, descried by a busyness not merely of eye but also of nose and ear, for a moment usurps Dorothy's "feeble frame" (6), giving over its cares to the memories of "careless days" (25). These memories and their attendant joy are for Dorothy in fact so intense that they pierce, as she writes, "to my couch of rest" (31) and thus transform the sickbed into a momentary space of solace.

Notably, a still more tangible usurpation by familiar soil is triggered by an unexpected gift of flowers from visiting friends. Not only are they the "first flowers of the year" (34)—symbolic, therefore, of healing and renewal—but they are "[c]ulled from the precincts of our home, / From nooks to memory dear" (35–36). Thus, what Dorothy experiences is a realization or, more precisely, a materialization of memory: real flowers picked from recollected space. The effect of this "[u]nprompted and unbidden" (38) gift, this fortuitous encroachment of home on the space of illness, is not simply to animate her "hidden life," that is, her memories of home, but to bring them more fully to "consciousness" (40). The simple flowers of home thus trigger a miraculous return to the soil from which they grew:

> I felt a power unfelt before,
> Controlling weakness, languor, pain;
> It bore me to the terrace-walk,
> I trod the hills again.
>
> No prisoner in this lonely room,
> I *saw* the green banks of the Wye. . . . (41–46)

This last in a series of steps from recollection to realization to reanimated joy brings Dorothy finally to the re-experience of familiarity. Her emphasis on the directness and authenticity of that experience ("I trod," "I *saw*") is unmistakable. Indeed, for Dorothy the return to familiar soil represents a confluence of the physical, perceptual and visionary. Though she concedes that it is by an act of "memory [that] I was there" (52), her memory of home, in this case the textualized 'home' that is the Wye Valley of "Tintern Abbey," is so vivid and prepossessing that it overwhelms the reality of her life of sickness.[5] The return to familiar soil—the realization of her hidden life—is therefore a momentary return to health, to a condition at least of control, as she suggests, over "weakness, languor, pain." What simple flowers could only intimate the familiar soil of home ensures.

The differences in consolatory emphasis that I have thus far only been teasing out, differences between flowers and soil, between defamiliarizing wondrousness and timeless familiarity, adumbrate a broader distinction in the Romantic engagement and preoccupation with everyday life. This distinction corresponds in significant ways to that articulated in Wordsworth's "Immortality Ode" between the "best philosopher" and "the philosophic mind." The "best philosopher" is Wordsworth's much debated (and by Coleridge much maligned) characterization of the child as a sort of intuitive reader of wondrous presence in the manifestations of everyday life. To the child, as Wordsworth suggests, "every common sight [is] . . . / Apparelled in celestial light, / The glory and the freshness of a dream" (2–5).[6] The emphasis on "freshness" clearly recalls Keats's experience of simple flowers, the only difference being that what the adult likens to the operation of a "superhuman fancy" is for the child, at least according to Wordsworth, an entirely natural mode of perception. Drawing on his own childhood engagement with material reality, Wordsworth describes the experience of "freshness" in the Fenwick Note (1843) on the "Ode":

> . . . I was often unable to think of external things as having external existence, and I communed with all I saw as something not apart from, but inherent in, my own immaterial nature. Many times while going to school have I grasped at the wall or the tree to recall myself from this abyss of idealism to the reality. At that time I was afraid of such processes. In later periods of life I have deplored (as we have all reason to do) a subjugation of an opposite character, and have rejoiced over the remembrances. . . . To that dreamlike vividness and splendour which invest objects of sight in childhood, everyone (I believe, if he would look back) could bear testimony, and I need not dwell upon it here.[7]

For Wordsworth, "dreamlike vividness and splendour" define the true or pure character of everyday objects and it is only the trappings of age—what he glosses in the "Ode" as "earthly freight / And custom" (129–130)—that dull our senses to this reality. What the child recognizes as essence (*natura naturans*) is to the growing boy an "abyss of idealism" and to the adult a dream so distant that it is recalled or re-experienced only rarely and partially, in flashes of childlike vision such as Keats's. Such flashes are not arbitrary but seem to depend on a prior susceptibility to "celestial light," on a removal, that is, of "earthly freight." For Keats, it is the recognition of the imminence of death, an experience at least structurally cognate with the child's perpetual awareness of the "eternal deep" (112), the source and termination of all being, that prompts his perception of wondrous novelty in simple flowers.

What the "best philosopher" inevitably loses with age, the adult may, as Wordsworth suggests, retrieve in part through the development of a "philosophic mind." Though freighted with cares, responsibilities and distractions, all of which obscure not only the "soul's immensity" (109) but also the immensity of everyday life, the adult can, by attending with "primal sympathy" (184) to that which is immediately around him/her, "find / Strength in what remains behind" (183). Much as the poet's consolation derives from his dismissal of "shadowy recollections" (152) in favour of a re-engagement with present reality, with the song of birds and play of lambs, so the adult's compensation for the lost radiance of childhood rests in a return to the present, to the light and joy that yet remain. For Wordsworth, notably, such light and joy are associated with familiarity, with the "*habitual* sway" (194, emphasis added) of our everyday surroundings. Familiarity, as he suggests, serves not to lessen, but instead increases, joy: "I love the brooks which down their channels fret / Even more than when I tripped as lightly as they" (195–196). Having lost that immediate delight which accompanies the child's recognition of nature's inherent "celestial light," the adult must develop a "love" for nature through habitual intercourse with its varied manifestations—everything from "fountains, meadows, hills and groves" (190) to the "meanest flower" (205). Learning to love that which is ostensibly mean, whether in nature or in the human other, is to exercise one's "primal sympathy." Such love also, by extension, makes one amenable to the consolations of mean objects and narrow scenes. The "soothing thoughts" (186) that revolve around such substantial centers are, as Wordsworth contends, an integral constituent of the philosophic mind.

As I have suggested, the unique experiences of material reality that Wordsworth ascribes to the best philosopher and the philosophic mind, the child and the adult respectively, correspond to a broader distinction in the Romantic approach to everyday life as a source of consolation. This distinction, although ostensibly little more than a disparity in perspective between simple flowers and familiar soil, reflects a substantially different understanding of the self's relationship to the everyday. The Keatsean reversion to childhood experience, to the perceptual sensitivity of the best philosopher, in coming to terms with thoughts of death represents a markedly different coping strategy from Dorothy Wordsworth's visionary return home, a return facilitated not simply by an act of memory but by an exercise of control over illness in the present. Simple flowers, simply put, appear to console by displacing the subject from the difficulties and hardships of everyday life, from present experience to that of the past, that of the child. Familiar soil, conversely, incorporates an experience of the present as well as the past; it is a consolation gained not through a temporal displacement but rather by a spatial replacement of the self; its powers of solace inhere not so much in what lies behind as in what remains before, the narrow present scenes that past experience has made both genial and fructifying. One response to the everyday in effect subordinates material reality to what Judith Plotz characterizes as the Romantic "vocation of childhood," while the other foregrounds the actual spaces and objects of everyday life as they are experienced (or more properly, *re*-experienced) in the present. Before exploring the nature of these responses in the literature of the period, I wish to stress that they are conceived here as means of consolation, not Freudian defense mechanisms. I am drawing a distinction, in other words, between two operative coping strategies, not between what in Freud's terms are rigid, unconscious and inherently pathological defensive postures (Snyder and Dinoff 13). The ability to cope, as C.R. Snyder and Beth L. Dinoff point out in a recent analysis of the psychology of coping, "is a precious gift" (14), a way, that is, of keeping oneself awake to hope, to wonder, to the possibilities of everyday life. The different Romantic expressions of consolation are therefore approached as varieties of the same gift—a gift redoubled as it is shared with the reader.

    The Keatsean consolation of returning to the experiences, indeed, to the very perceptions, of childhood, is, as I have suggested, elucidated by Plotz's theorization of childhood as a vocation actively pursued by adult writers. What she defines as "a meaningful work and a meaningful life" (xii) quite clearly transcends even the broadest chronological parameters of childhood. Indeed, the experiences of the best philosopher, associated in Wordsworth's view with a narrow window of years preceding the "inevitable yoke" of duty, custom and role-play, often appear in Romantic texts (even in Wordsworth's) as numinous moments of adult perception. One of the paradoxes, then, that Plotz's work serves to reveal about the Romantic representation of childhood is its tendency to foreground an image of the "absolute child" (Plotz xvi) from whose unchanging purity and perfection adult experience is forever dissevered—an impulse that Geoffrey Hartmann has termed "eudaemonia" (181)—while at the same time using the adult work of writing to recover and relive the idealized life of the child. De Quincey's "Sabbatic vision" on the mail-coach, for example, occurs in spite of what he characterizes as the ruinous effects of the schoolmaster's lore on the child's "sublimer thoughts." Distinguishing the adult's "faithful heart" from his/her "false feigning lips," De Quincey seems to invoke a sort of ineradicable childhood presence, a residue of magical thinking that neither schooling nor age can entirely dispel. In fact, in some extraordinary instances, as De Quincey claims in *Suspiria de Profundis* (1845), that residue is revealed as an unfathomably deep reservoir of memories and experiences, which, when set in motion by "great convulsions,"[8] entirely overruns the subject's perceptual machinery. The example he relates is drawn from the experience of his mother, who, in her youth, fell into a brook and nearly drowned:

> Eventually (but after what lapse of time nobody ever knew) she was saved from death by a farmer who, riding in some distant lane, had seen her rise to the surface—but not until she had descended within the abyss of death, and looked into its secrets as far, perhaps, as ever human eye *can* have looked that had permission to return. At a certain stage of this descent, a blow seemed to strike her, phosphoric radiance sprang forth from her eyeballs, and immediately a mighty theatre expanded within her brain. In a moment, in the twinkling of an eye, every act, every design of her past life lived again—arraying themselves not as a succession but as parts of a coexistence. Such a light fell upon the whole path of her life backwards into the shades of infancy, as the light perhaps which wrapped the destined apostle on his road to Damascus. Yet that light blinded for a season, but hers poured celestial vision upon the brain, so that her consciousness became omnipresent at one moment to every feature in the infinite review.[9]

Forming part of a longer discussion on the brain as palimpsest, this passage elucidates the incorruptible traces of childhood or infant experience, still radiantly vivid, that underlie all present impressions, perceptions and actions. Although De Quincey's mother was at the time of the accident not much more than a child herself, the sudden reanimation of what is described as her "past life" intimates the depth and richness of those experiences ascribed to the best philosopher. They represent, as the author notes, "a mighty theatre"—yet one from whose grandeur the youth and even the adult are clearly not cut off. The grandeur of childhood is preserved in every detail, every act, every design, and is thus potentially accessible to the adult in moments of "celestial vision."

Drawing on his own experience, De Quincey in fact specifies the means by which such access may be gained and the resurrection of childhood memory habitually repeated: "it is repeated and ten thousand times repeated by opium, for those who are its martyrs."[10] Indeed, for De Quincey one of the consolations of addiction is its tendency to return to him his past life in all the vividness and detail of present experience. Opium's powers of resurrection are particularly potent, as he notes, when coupled with music. His description, for example, of Tuesday and Saturday nights at the London Opera House, listening to Giuseppina Grassini, after having downed his glass of "laudanum negus," recalls the "mighty theatre" of his mother's mind:

> a chorus, &c. of elaborate harmony, displayed before me, as in a piece of arras work, the whole of my past life—not as if recalled by an act of memory, but as if present and incarnated in the music: no longer painful to dwell upon: but the detail of its incidents removed, or blended in some hazy abstraction; and its passions exalted, spiritualized, and sublimed. All this was to be had for five shillings.[11]

While this self-induced return to a "sublimed" past is clearly not a response to physical trauma or a coping strategy or, still less, an example of the unsought contentedness that Keats associates with the material existence of everyday life, it does elucidate the ineradicable presence of the best philosopher, the easy slippage, one might say, between adult and child experience. And, in fact, there are rather striking similarities between this exalted experience of the past and Keats's defamiliarizing encounter with the simple flowers of childhood. Indeed, De Quincey's operatic experience of his "past life" is also in a sense an experience of what is *un*familiar to him; his childhood, as he notes, is "no longer painful to dwell upon" because the details have been so arranged or blurred as to leave only a sense of prepossessing wondrousness. This wondrousness is certainly to him, if not an outright consolation, then a means of safely revisiting a childhood marked by "affliction, ostracism, and loss" (Plotz 129).[12] Moreover, as with Keats, the source of that wondrousness is a flower, in De Quincey's case not a flower of childhood (by his own account, he did not taste opium before 1804) but one with which he became quickly and habitually familiar. Flowers, indeed not just opium poppies, appear elsewhere in De Quincey's work as gateways to childhood experience, to a period of preternatural innocence and transcendent vision. Commenting, for example, in the 1856 revisions to the *Confessions* on the role of Christianity as a divining or '*rhabdomantical*'[13] faith that calls up a hidden grandeur of sentiment by seizing upon a corresponding visible grandeur of material form, De Quincey offers the following analysis of the inherent and symbolic fecundity of everyday flowers:

> Flowers, for example, that are so pathetic in their beauty, frail as the clouds, and in their colouring as gorgeous as the heavens, had through thousands of years been the heritage of children—honoured as the jewellery of God only by *them*—when suddenly the voice of Christianity, counter-signing the voice of infancy, raised them to a grandeur transcending the Hebrew throne, although founded by God himself, and pronounced Solomon in all his glory not to be arrayed like one of these. (*Confessions* 173–174)

For De Quincey, flowers are a site for exploring the perceptual and spiritual sensitivity of children; they are, as he notes, "the heritage of children." To honour them as children do is in effect to return to one's own childhood, to see the world, as Keats illustrates, again for the first time.

The tendency to seek in nature's everyday manifestations the consolations of the past is perhaps nowhere more readily evident than in the work of Wordsworth, whom Plotz describes as "the touchstone and origin figure in discussions of Romantic childhood" (45). Not only is his greatest poetic achievement actuated by the desire, as he suggests, to "fetch / Invigorating thoughts from former years" (*Prelude* I.648–649), but his genius has been characterized and distinguished at least historically by the visionary light it sheds on the things of everyday life, recreating them, as it were, with an almost childlike subtlety and freshness of perception. Certainly for Coleridge it is Wordsworth's evocation of novelty and wondrousness that marks his particular power as a poet of everyday life. Commenting on the genesis of the *Lyrical Ballads*, for example, Coleridge attributes to Wordsworth the following depth of vision and design:

> Mr Wordsworth, on the other hand, was to propose to himself as his object to give the charm of novelty to things of every day, and to excite a feeling analogous to the supernatural, by awakening the mind's attention from the lethargy of custom and directing it to the loveliness and the wonders of the world before us; an inexhaustible treasure, but for which, in consequence of the film of familiarity and selfish solicitude, we have eyes yet see not, ears that hear not, and hearts that neither feel nor understand. (*Biographia* 169)

Simple Flowers and Familiar Soil   163

With typical perspicacity, Coleridge seizes upon what is arguably the essence of Wordsworthian poetics: the revisioning of apparent familiarity. Culled from "the poet's own meditative observation," Wordsworth's descriptions of everyday life are, as Coleridge reiterates in Chapter XXII, "fresh and have the dew [still] upon them" (*Biographia* 265). By piercing "the film of familiarity"—a phrase later adopted by Shelley in *A Defense of Poetry*—Wordsworth's work in effect returns to the reader an experience of childlike wonderment. Whether that experience is, as Coleridge seems to suggest, grounded in the vicarious perception of the "inexhaustible treasure" that lies scattered around us, or, as Hazlitt maintains in *The Spirit of the Age*, imposed by "the strength of [Wordsworth's] own aspirations" (254), it is offered by the poet as a consolatory refuge from the blindness and distraction of adult experience.

Evidence of Wordsworth's susceptibility to everyday solace is indeed scattered throughout his work, beginning, as Coleridge notes, in the *Lyrical Ballads*, expounded in the *Prelude*, and elucidated perhaps most profoundly in his Epitaphs and Elegiac Pieces. I would like to focus on three seminal examples or moments in this chronology, each serving to reveal an engagement with quotidian reality behind the "film of familiarity." The first, "A Whirl-blast from behind the hill," is drawn from the *Lyrical Ballads* and evinces, as Susan Levin suggests, a mutually developing vocabulary of experience shared by William and Dorothy (13–14). The event that inspires the poem is briefly recounted in Dorothy's Alfoxden Journal in the entry for March 18, 1798:

> The Coleridges left us. A cold, windy morning. Walked with them half way. On our return, sheltered under hollies, during a hail-shower. The withered leaves danced with the hailstones. William wrote a description of the storm. (*Journals* 10)

William's poetic reflection on the hail-shower echoes his sister's sense of subjective embowerment, of being at once sheltered and transfixed, as well as emphasizing the scene's animistic, indeed, almost performative, energy:

> I sat within an undergrove
> Of tallest hollies, tall and green;
> A fairer bower was never seen.
> From year to year the spacious floor
> With withered leaves is covered o'er,

> You could not lay a hair between:
> And all the year the bower is green.
> But see! where'er the hailstones drop
> The withered leaves all skip and hop,
> There's not a breeze—no breath of air—
> Yet here, and there, and everywhere
> Along the floor, beneath the shade
> By those embowering hollies made,
> The leaves in myriads jump and spring,
> As if with pipes and music rare
> Some Robin Good-fellow were there,
> And all those leaves, that jump and spring,
> Were each a joyous, living thing. (6–23)[14]

Like Dorothy's journal entry, Wordsworth's poem reveals a remarkable sensitivity to the motions of natural otherness. Wordsworth, in fact, chooses to foreground and centralize those motions by erasing his sister from the poetic encounter. Indeed, for Wordsworth the experience is represented as a solitary, undistracted, engagement with nature's everyday wonders. In this instance, the wonder of withered leaves reanimated by the patter of hailstones seems to derive from a disruption of nature's familiar rhythms. As Wordsworth's description indicates, the bower is (to the poet, at least) "[f]rom year to year" the same: it has a "spacious" floor thickly covered over with dead leaves and is green "all the year." The introduction of hail to this familiar environment brings profound and unexpected change—not destruction but apparent life, nature's version of the Valley of Dry Bones. Unable or unwilling simply to reason away the defamiliarization of a hitherto static and predictable scene, the quickening of death itself, Wordsworth invokes the figure of Robin Goodfellow—a less mischievous version of Shakespeare's Puck whom Lucy Newlyn likens rather to Pan (107)—as nature's animating spirit. Not only does this suggestion of supernatural agency recall the poet's reversion to "faery days" in *An Evening Walk* but it is offered in spite of his recognition that the scene is inherently illusory. Indeed, Wordsworth is quite clear about attributing the leaves' motion to the force of the hailstones, yet he allows himself and the reader to entertain the possibility of a spritely presence lurking beneath apparent familiarity, ready at any moment to raise death to joyous life. The effect of the poet's readiness to consider such possibilities, to be swayed by the spectacle of everyday wonder, is, as the concluding stanza suggests, profoundly solacing:

Oh! grant me Heaven a heart at ease,
That I may never cease to find,
Even in appearances like these,
Enough to nourish and to stir my mind! (24–27)

Recalling Coleridge's epiphany in the lime-tree bower, Wordsworth's prayer for an untroubled, childlike "heart at ease" rests in a recognition that the consolations and inspirations of everyday wonder, of "appearances like these," depend not so much on a clarity as on an innocence of perspective that believes in the improbabilities, the inherent magic, of nature's animating forces.

Notwithstanding its epic pretensions, its subsumption of the grand sweep of history within the even grander sweep of what Alan Liu characterizes as "Wordsworth's culminating ideology of self" (388), *The Prelude*, like the *Lyrical Ballads*, is informed by the consolations of narrow scenes and everyday wonder, particularly as they facilitate a return to childhood experience. From the poet's reflections in Book I on "the life / In common things" (I.117–118), to what he describes as an enlargement of his sympathies for "the common range of visible things" (II.182) in Book II, to his recognition in Book III of a "moral life" in "every natural form, rock, fruit or flower, / Even the loose stones that cover the highway" (III.124–125), to his return, in Book VIII, to "Nature's primitive gifts" (VIII.99), and to the elucidation, finally, in Book XI of those "ordinary sight[s]" (XI.309) by which his mind is "nourished and invisibly repaired" (XI.265)—there is at the heart of *The Prelude* a quotidian sensibility, a substantial centre of ordinariness somehow made wondrous and extraordinary. While the scope of the present study does not allow for a detailed examination of the poem in its entirety, I would like to attend to Wordsworth's discussion of the sources of imaginative restoration or solace, specifically those that inhere in the immediate, day-to-day experience of living. While a good deal has been written about what the poet claims are "the hiding-places of [his] power" (XI.336), his numinous childhood memories or "spots of time," comparatively little critical attention has been devoted to the seminal images from Book XII that lie, as it were, plainly in the poet's and the reader's view. These images, notably, are likewise linked to childhood experience. As Wordsworth suggests, they form part of his early education, tutoring him "[t]o look with feelings of fraternal love / Upon those unassuming things that hold / A silent station in this beauteous world" (XII.50–52). The image of the public road, for example, indeed a most unassuming and seemingly unpropitious spectacle, is central to the claims of imaginative recovery in Book XII:

> I love a public road: few sights there are
> That please me more; such object hath had power
> O'er my imagination since the dawn
> Of childhood, when its disappearing line,
> Seen daily afar off, on one bare steep
> Beyond the limits which my feet had trod,
> Was like a guide into eternity,
> At least to things unknown and without bound.
> Even something of the grandeur which invests
> The mariner who sails the roaring sea
> Through storm and darkness, early in my mind
> Surrounded, too, the wanderers of the earth;
> Grandeur as much, and loveliness far more.
> Awed have I been by strolling Bedlamites;
> From many other uncouth vagrants (passed
> In fear) have walked with quicker step; but why
> Take note of this? When I began to enquire,
> To watch and question those I met, and held
> Familiar talk with them, the lonely roads
> Were schools to me in which I daily read
> With most delight the passions of mankind,
> There saw into the depth of human souls,
> Souls that appear to have no depth at all
> To vulgar eyes. (XII.145–168)

The tutelage of the public roadway, as Wordsworth makes clear, is such that it reveals not only the human other (i.e. the strolling Bedlamite) in all the depth and passion of his/her soul but also, and no less importantly, the childhood self. Indeed, the road leads by a series of familiar steps back to "the dawn / Of childhood," to the very source of imaginative vision and captivation. The road's powers of transport rest, as Wordsworth explains, in its evocation of infinity: "its disappearing line . . . / Was like a guide into eternity." To borrow words from the "Ode," the roadway "cometh from afar."[15] It is both a sign and a realization of "things unknown and without bound," a thread that winds its way to and from the sublime. This association is in fact already intimated in Book XI, in the second spot of time, where Wordsworth recalls waiting for his father's horses above two intersecting roads between Ambleside and Hawkshead, peering, as he notes, into the "indisputable shapes" (XI.382) of mist that advanced along their disappearing lines. The roadway is in this instance a liminal space, leading from the certitude of arrival to a home of unanticipated departure, a home of death and sorrow. For the adult poet, significantly, the road becomes in after-years a source of consolation, an integral part of those "spectacles and sounds to which / I often would repair, and thence would drink, / As at a fountain" (XI.383–385). The road in effect keeps alive the memories of childlike waiting, memories that to the poet initially appeared a "chastisement" (XI.370) but were ultimately incorporated into a deeper lesson of corrected desires. Book XII clearly builds upon this notion of the road as a site of tutelage, solace and repair. By returning the poet to the dawn of childhood, the public road in turn revives the aesthetic experiences of road walking, the prepossessing sense of "grandeur," "loveliness" and even awe, as well as the lesson that "Education" alone cannot teach, the extension, namely, of one's sympathies to all humanity, no matter how "uncouth" or lowly. While the tutelage of the roadway for the boy-poet centers primarily on the bond between self and other, on the recognition, if you will, of living always already in community, for the adult, the lessons of a simple line stretching into eternity are no less profound. Indeed, because the roadway returns Wordsworth to his imaginative roots, to the infinite itself, and recovers in midst of that return the lessons of childhood, specifically of a sympathetic imagination, the public roadway is prized as an invaluable source of solace. "[T]here I found," as Wordsworth concludes, "Hope to my hope, and to my pleasure peace / And steadiness, and healing and repose / To every angry passion" (XII.179–181, emphasis added).

The solace of everyday life, particularly as it facilitates a return along plainly discernible lines to the visionary experiences of the past, is perhaps nowhere more vividly emphasized than in Wordsworth's Epitaphs and Elegiac Pieces, particularly those dedicated to his brother John, who perished at sea in 1805. Having already alluded in my discussion of Romantic literary floriculture to Wordsworth's consolatory reflections on the daisy as a site of shared fraternal love and a means, as he suggests, of "repair[ing] / My heart with gladness" (46–47),[16] I would like to consider his reliance on another solacing flower in "Elegiac Verses, In Memory of my Brother, John Wordsworth" (1842). Significantly, the flower in this instance is an unnamed species that commentators have in fact identified not as a flower at all but as moss campion (*Silene acaulis*). Wordsworth's turn from the daisy, which he describes in "To the Same Flower" as the "unassuming Common-place / Of Nature" (5–6), to an unnamed but presumably no less common plant seems on one hand to reiterate his brother's humble, inconspicuous character while also on the other hand intimating the hidden depth and inscrutability of the apparently ordinary. As he suggests, the "unknown Flower" (16)—the essence of all ordinariness that still somehow eludes our grasp—is an apt and "[a]ffecting type of him I mourn" (17).[17] This notion of an ultimately elusive and mysterious familiarity also pervades the poet's recollections of walking with his brother along the mountain track between Grasmere and Grisedale Hawes, where the poem was composed:

> Here did we stop; and here looked round
> While each into himself descends,
> For that last thought of parting Friends
> That is not to be found.
> Hidden was Grasmere Vale from sight,
> Our home and his, his heart's delight,
> His quiet heart's selected home.
> But time before him melts away,
> And he hath feeling of a day
> Of blessedness to come. (21–30)

This memory of the two brothers' last moments together is notable for its lapse into silence, its very retreat from shared experience. Searching for the fitting words to express what is common to them both—their deep affection for one another—the brothers descend "each into himself" and thus move invariably beyond the pale of words, beyond familiarity itself. For Wordsworth, however, it is precisely this unfamiliar silence which allows him, by filling it with the imagined thoughts of his brother, to fashion his own consolation.

The nature of that consolation is a prophetic vision of "blessedness to come"—a time, one must presume, of gathering again in familiar surroundings, of transcending the barriers of distance and even death, a time of homecoming. With John's death, the imputed wish for reunion becomes the poet's remaining hope. And in waiting for the realization of that hope Wordsworth has, as he notes, an additional fount of solace:

> From many a humble source, to pains
> Like these, there comes a mild release;
> Even here I feel it, even this Plant
> Is in its beauty ministrant
> To comfort and to peace. (46–50)

Whereas the daisy recalls John to the poet's mind because it was above all other flowers beloved by him, the unknown flower serves to reflect his enduring presence still more directly by its unassuming beauty and its communication of "comfort" and "peace." Both a reminder of what was and a visible symbol of that which yet remains and is to come, the unknown flower, this "type" of John himself, brings by its mere presence "a mild release" from pain. The unknown thus becomes a companionable form and one, moreover, capable of at last filling the silence of the brothers' last moments together. For in imagining John's reaction to the flower, Wordsworth in effect replays their parting:

> He would have loved thy modest grace,
> Meek Flower! To Him I would have said,
> "It grows upon its native bed
> Beside our Parting-place;
> There, cleaving to the ground, it lies
> With multitude of purple eyes,
> Spangling a cushion green like moss;
> But we will see it, joyful tide!
> Some day, to see it in its pride,
> The mountains we will cross." (51–60)

Finding the words he could not find before, the poet returns to the past and offers a companionate thought to his brother's apprehension of "blessedness to come." In this instance, blessedness consists not merely of a reunion but of a return expressly to the place of departure, to the very mound of moss and purple blossoms that has transfixed the poet. The two brothers will in fact return, as Wordsworth claims, not so much to see one another as "to see *it* in its pride" (emphasis added).

Notably, the poem's concluding stanza reintroduces an elegiac tone by emphasizing the transience of such healing moments, the transience in fact of hope itself. As though recalled from the absorbing visions of fraternal communion to the reality of aloneness, Wordsworth surrenders the fleeting hope of simple flowers in bloom to the cold and enduring truth of stones:

> Here let a monumental Stone
> Stand sacred as a Shrine;
> And to the few who pass this way,
> Traveller or Shepherd, let it say,
> Long as these mighty rocks endure,—
> Oh do not Thou too fondly brood,
> Although deserving of all good,
> On any earthly hope, however pure! (63–70)

The consolations of simple flowers, of a wondrous return to an imagined past, are for Wordsworth necessarily brief. Here indeed is one of the few occasions in his body of work where recollection is seen to carry risks as well as pleasures. Although he does not trouble himself to elucidate the hazards of brooding "too fondly" on the past (whether real or imagined), one may assume that they have something to do with a consequent unfitness for the present, an unpreparedness for the reality of grief and aloneness. Hence his turn to the "monumental Stone" which, unlike the unnamed flower, speaks of enduring absence, not presence. In the presence of his grief Wordsworth cannot count on consolation. It is indeed only by turning from the present to the past that he finds "release." A reliance on simple flowers, as I suggested in the opening, is predicated on a displacement of the self to a time of untroubled experience, a state of childlike vision. Yet such displacement, as Wordsworth proves, cannot be continued indefinitely. All sufferers must at last return to the present and confront the grief that yet remains. For Wordsworth that return is profoundly unconsoling; it necessitates grim resolutions, a hardening of the self against "earthly hope," a rock-like determination to hold loosely the things of this world.

Having thus, as it were, arrived at the consolatory limitations of simple flowers, I would like to consider the role of familiar soil as a source of strength and solace in the literature of the period. As I have suggested above, familiar soil is inextricably bound up with the spaces and experiences of home. Such soil is not, however, simply reducible to a physical habitation or a particular environment called 'home'; it is both greater than home in that it transcends the mere expression of space and also smaller in that it may be localized to a room or to a corner of a garden or even a path in the woods. Familiar soil is above all a refuge from the distractions and divisions, the turmoil and din, of public life; it is an intensely personal or private experience of (a) space that is always already there. Leigh Hunt, for example, characterizes home in "Our Cottage" (1836) in terms unapologetically isolationist:

> No news comes here; no scandal; no routine
> Of morning visit; not a postman's knock—
> That double thrust of the long staff of care.
> We are as distant from the world, in spirit
> If not in place, as though in Crusoe's isle,
> And please ourselves with being ignorant
> Even of the country some five miles beyond. (9–15)[18]

Not unlike Clare's "old home of homes," Hunt's cottage (an imaginary home conceived while the poet was living in a relatively quiet corner of Chelsea) is such an exceedingly localized and intimate expression of home that the surrounding countryside is comparatively strange and the larger world beyond, utterly alien and irrelevant. What marks the difference between the privacy of familiar soil and the public sphere of "news" and "scandal" is, as Hunt notes, less a measurable distance of miles than a "spirit" of refuge and retreat, a willing ignorance of all that is not conducive to peace within the "cottage nest" (60).

The emphasis on peace is indeed central to what Gary Kelly describes as a broad nineteenth-century shift in social sympathy from the world of business and politics to that of the home and family. As he suggests in a recent edition of the works of Felicia Hemans, "in the aftermath of the French Revolution and Napoleonic Wars this idea of [familial] community was often contrasted with what was seen as an irredeemably conflicted public and political sphere" (106).[19] Home and domestic concerns did not so much resolve these conflicts as offer a means, a space, of retreating from them. And that space of retreat, as Marilyn Butler observes in *Romantics, Rebels and Reactionaries*, was conspicuously "humble, modest, [and] quietist" (183) in its aspirations. While Felicia Hemans is arguably the foremost (and indisputably the most popular) poet of this "new era of introversion" (Butler 182), the increasing emphasis on home is in fact already evident, as Kelly suggests, in the late eighteenth century, in works produced in the immediate aftermath of the French Revolution. The yearning for familiar soil is, for example, a central theme in Charlotte Smith's *The Emigrants* (1793). Indeed, what distinguishes the poem's speaker (herself an outcast) from the French exiles "thrown / [. . .] on England's coast" (II.11–12)[20] is her still untarnished belief in the inviolate refuge of home:

> And o'er our vallies, cloath'd with springing corn,
> No hostile hoof shall trample, nor fierce flames
> Wither the wood's young verdure, ere it form
> Gradual the laughing May's luxuriant shade;
> For, by the rude sea guarded, we are safe,
> And feel not evils such as with deep sighs
> The Emigrants deplore, as they recal
> The Summer past, when Nature seem'd to lose
> Her course in wild distemperature, and aid,
> With seasons all revers'd, destructive War. (206–215)

What is of course significant about this passage is the apparent absence of any sense of personal or intimate connection to familiar soil. The "guarded" space of home is generally and publicly conceived; it is England as a whole, a patchwork of unnamed valleys and woods. Notwithstanding its intimations of rest and retreat, *The Emigrants* remains a resolutely public and political text. Indeed, even the closing appeal to "Reason, Liberty, and Peace" (II.444) is based on a conception of this triumvirate as "*public* virtue[s]" (439, emphasis added). The peace, in other words, of home and hearth is for Smith secondary to that of the nation.

Other writers, meanwhile, worn out and wearied by the turmoil of public life, favoured not so much a reconciliation of its aims with those of the family as an outright severing of these realms. Poetry in fact often served as a site for dramatizing the ongoing conflict between public and private interests. Anne Grant's "A Familiar Epistle to a Friend" (1795) offers a particularly striking account of the initial struggles and eventual consolations of drawing oneself back from the world. Although Grant is writing in an essentially outmoded Augustan form whose prominence gave way in the Romantic period to lyric poetry, the verse epistle's roots in the domestic, familial and everyday make it an ideal vehicle for exploring the consolations of familiarity. Indeed, the most obvious consolation is the epistle's presupposition of community. As William C. Dowling observes, epistolary poetry "constitute[s] itself as a mode of simultaneous address, a double register within which it is possible to speak to one audience directly while always addressing another by implication" (12). Grant, notably, exploits this "double register" for two ostensibly conflicted purposes: she alternately turns private grief into public lament and withdraws from public lament to private consolation. What further complicates the poet's vacillation between these discursive positions is her tendency to undercut expressions of grief and lament with a playful, at times even a satiric tone that suggests a weariness as much with the rhetoric of housewifely plaint as with the actual grievances that inspire it. Like Barbauld, in other words, who simultaneously elucidates and exaggerates the hardships of the housewife's lot in "Washing Day" by framing them in mock-epic terms, Grant foregrounds the folly of presenting the domestic sphere in either purely sentimental or comic terms, choosing instead to stray continually between these positions and thus locate the 'truth' of domesticity, of its actual hardships and consolations, in a third term, a sort of mediate position that accommodates the sentimental and comic without being reduced to either one. While this third term, as I will suggest, is expressed most clearly in the poem's conclusion, in the resolution, that is, of public and private interests, its articulation depends on a prior initiation into the rhetoric first of domestic satire and then of sentimentality.

Addressing herself to a childhood friend in response to what is cursorily alluded to as a nostalgic epistle on bygone days, Grant begins the poem by adopting a tone of indignant lament that, although rooted in personal or private experience, plainly exceeds by its epic pretensions the slenderness of that context:

> Dear Beatrice, with pleasure I read your kind letter;
> On the subject, methinks, there could scarce be a better:
> How vivid the scenes it recalled to my view,
> And how lively it wakened remembrance anew!
> Yet our souls are so crusted with housewifely moss,
> That Fancy's bright furnace yields nothing but dross:
> Surrounded with balling, and squalling, and prattle,
> With handmaids unhandy, and gossiping tattle,
> Cut fingers to bandage, and stockings to darn,
> And labyrinths endless of ill-managed yarn,
> Through whose windings Daedalean bewildered we wander,
> Like draggle-tailed nymphs of the mazy Meander,
> Till at length, like the hero of Macedon, tired
> Of the slow perseverance untwisting required,
> We brandish our scissors, resolved on the spot,
> Since we cannot unravel, to cut through the knot. (1–16)[21]

Dispensing quickly with the pleasantries of familiar address, Grant proceeds to characterize all domestic life that falls within "[her] view" as an anathema to wonder and consolation. Far from being a refuge for the harried soul, home and its familiar rounds of responsibility, here glossed as "housewifely moss," are likened to an encumbering crust that dulls and delimits the operations of a once lively fancy. Hemmed in on all sides by din and duty, "balling and squalling," the generalized housewife experiences space as a jumble of "windings" and dead ends, the escape from which can only be effected by severing the 'knot' of marriage itself, an act, or rather, a resolution that here takes on heroic dimensions. As in Pope's *The Rape of the Lock*, the brandishing of scissors signals an intensification of the terms and tone of domestic struggle and brings the poem's opening to a moment of comic climax. The anticipated "snip" is not, however, heard. On the contrary, in shifting the point of attack from housewifery to marriage itself, Grant begins to tinge the comic generalities of public address with the bitter details of personal experience.

This tendency is most clearly evident in her reflections on the singular drudgery that is the life of the vicar's wife. Although addressed to all the vicars' wives of England, Grant's account of the "labour incessant" (25) and the "self-same minute occupation" (27) that gradually starve imagination ("Invention") is plainly grounded in personal experience[22] and serves, moreover, to elicit personal recollections:

> What a change of the scene and the actors appears?
> 'Tis now but a dozen and odd of short years,
> Since when we, and the season, and fancy were young,
> On Tarfe's flowery banks our gay whimsies we sung,
> Regardless of profit, and hopeless of fame,
> Yet heedless of censure and fearless of blame,
> We traversed the vale, or we haunted the grove,
> As free as the birds that were chanting above;
> Where the fair face of Nature was bright with a smile,
> Enraptured in silence we gazed for a while;
> Then as clear and as artless resounded our lays,
> As the sky or the stream we endeavoured to praise. . . . (35–46)

The unmistakable references to the length of Grant's own marriage ("a dozen and odd of short years" at the time of the poem's publication) and the topography of her parental home (the Tarfe is a river that runs into Loch Ness at Fort Augustus) mark an increasingly personal narrative of longing, one that verges in fact on the sentimental. Although the poet retains the plural pronoun, its implied antecedent is not the collective vicars' wives of England but rather Beatrice and herself, a pair of childhood friends separated by the duties of marriage. The time she evokes—"when we, and the season, and fancy were young"—is a period of preternatural intimacy and innocence, a space of consoling familiarity. Indeed, the "Tarfe's flowery banks," much more so than her residence in Laggan, epitomize familiar soil. It is there, as she notes, that she was both physically and imaginatively "free" to roam and revel, to indulge "sublime meditation" (54) and "the workings of fancy" (55). With marriage, however, and the attendant exchange of familiar for unfamiliar soil, and leisure for unending toil, life becomes both physically and creatively stultifying:

> The cottage so humble, or sanctified dome,
> For the revels of fancy afforded no room;
> And the lyre and the garland, were forced to give place
> To duties domestic and records of grace. (69–72)

What Grant foregrounds here are the differences between mere domestic space and familiar soil. Echoing Bachelard's notion that the chief benefit of home is that it "shelters daydreaming [and . . .] allows one to dream in peace," Grant juxtaposes the erstwhile spaces of youthful dreaming with those of present housewifely bondage—the cottage and the church.

In an unexpected move of resistance and resilience, the poet does not, however, simply resign herself to a sentimental yearning for the familiar soil of the past. Indeed, what is so significant about the poem as a narrative of coping and consolation is its insistence on present amelioration. Unlike Wordsworth's recollections that only bring into stark relief the comparative impossibilities of the present, Grant's childhood memories of familiar soil inspire a resumption of old familiar habits—in particular, the composition of verse:

> But when slowly and surely the cold hand of time
> Had stole my complexion, and withered my prime,
> Resolved for a while to respire at my ease,
> In Clydesdale I courted the soft western breeze;
> Whose fresh breathing whispers my languor could soothe,
> With visions of fancy, and dreams of my youth.
> While slowly retracing my dear native Clyde,
> And reviewing my visage, so changed, in its tide,
> As sad and reluctant I strove to retire,
> To my grasp was presented my trusty old lyre—
> I snatched it, I strummed it, and thrummed it again. . . . (107–117)

The process of self-consolation is for Grant two-fold, beginning with a return to familiar soil ("my dear native Clyde") and culminating in a recovery of the familiar practices, if not the years, of youth. While the moment of poetic inspiration is decidedly muted and is in fact presented as an assertion rather of chance than will, Grant's response to the gift of the lyre—"I snatched it, I strummed it"—registers the twice-iterated agency of a reawakened self. This rekindling of her "poetical fire" (101) prompts Grant to consider not only the personal effects of writing, such as the "soothing [of] pain" (140), but also the public role of the written word. Desirous, as she notes, of not "warbl[ing] in vain" (144), Grant weighs the "sweet Peace that delights in the shade" (148) against the "noisy applause [and] tinsel parade" (147) of public recognition. Yet rather than imagining the effects of fame on herself, she instructs her readers by the examples of more popular women writers of her day such as Anna Seward, Anne Hunter and Helen Maria Williams. The costs of their fame, as she notes, include not only the slight misdirections of "vanity" (155) and "caprice" (156), but also more the serious displacements from the habitual and familiar rounds of domestic life:

> Creation's proud Master observed with a sneer,
> That like comets eccentric forsaking their sphere,
> Their brightness so gazed at, would never produce,
> Or pleasure, or profit, or comfort, or use.
> . . . .
> The duties and joys of the mother and wife,
> The nameless soft comforts of calm private life,
> Fell victims together at Vanity's shrine,
> For who could endure to exist and not shine! (157–167)

Retracing Johnson's trajectory of fame from *The Vanity of Human Wishes*,[23] Grant satirizes the female pursuit of literary renown as an aberrant ("eccentric") divergence from natural spheres of motion, a ripple, if you will, in the fabric of the universe. The benefits of momentary "brightness" are offset, as she notes, by the loss of one's purpose and usefulness as well as the "soft comforts of calm private life." Fleeting public renown, in other words, comes at the expense of one's more lasting and substantial private life; the warmth of familiarity is traded for the lustre of fame. Williams suffers the thrust of Grant's attack in part because her fame impels her beyond the borders of England and of home. Once "[t]he delight of her friends, of her country the pride" (175), Williams is castigated for trading such security for the "new pandemonium" (183) of France. The consequences of that choice, as Grant observes, include a severe contraction of the spaces and freedoms of home: "Now with equals in misery hid in some hole, / Her body a prison confining her soul" (186–187).

Thus admonished by the pitfalls of public fame and resolved finally to seek the more substantial consolations of home, Grant concludes the poem with an impassioned defence of domestic life and familiar soil, one that notably eschews the excesses of comic and sentimental rhetoric:

> No longer pursue those fond lovers of fame,
> Nor envy the honours and trophies they claim;
> No further excursions to speculate roam,
> But fix our attention and pleasure at home:
> Why regret when celebrity proves such a curse,
> The cares of the mother and toils of the nurse:

> While the nurse finds delight in sweet infancy's smiles,
> And hope the fond mother's long trouble beguiles.
> 'But why these quick feelings, or why this nice ear,
> Or musical accents, if no one must hear?
> Why blossoms of fancy all scattered to waste,
> The glow sympathetic, or pleasures of taste?'
> Ask why in the mountains the floweret should blow,
> Which none but the hermit is destined to know?
> Why the wild woods re-echo with melody clear,
> Which none but the hunter is destined to hear?
> When often enjoyed and but seldom they're shown,
> Our riches and pleasures are truly our own. (190–206)

In this dramatic reversal of the poem's opening sentiments, Grant not only expounds the private consolations of domesticity (such as infant smiles and maternal hopes), but urges a general cessation of "excursions to speculate," a rubric that seems to include everything from philosophical to political to aesthetic travels. The net of her directives is clearly cast wide enough to implicate an audience far more numerous than her epistle's lone addressee. Indeed, the remonstrances she anticipates seem cobbled together from a broad chorus of voices desirous for fame. In answering their concerns about the "blossoms of fancy all scattered to waste," Grant offers the consolation of pleasing at the very least oneself—a consolation of admittedly meagre scope but one tested and refined by her own experience. Rather than "[d]epend[ing] for joy on the praise of the crowd" (212), she recommends poetry as a source of private joy, a joy that is "genuine and free from alloy" (209) because it originates within the poet and may be habitually rekindled. This joy is of course also "genuine" because it is part and parcel of daily life. Indeed, the value of home-spun poetic joy lies in its capacity to "solace [one's] labours, and lighten [one's] cares" (208). Domestically-produced poetry thus mitigates care while also in effect perpetuating both the spaces and labours of familiarity. As I have suggested, these spaces and labours are for Grant substantial and dependable, particularly when compared with the shifting ground and ephemeral trophies of public life. The permanence of home serves in fact to prefigure an eternal space of consolation, what Grant in the poem's clearest evocation of wondrousness calls "the evergreen plain" (232). This soil is at once transcendent in that it exists "beyond earth" (227) and also familiar in that it is perfumed by the blossoms of youthful fancy—blossoms, as Grant notes, "[t]hat cheered my fond heart till they died on my breast" (228). By waking these blossoms "to life and new fragrance again" (230), the evergreen plain, a sort of fabulous expansion of the Tarfe's flowery banks, offers a space of unending creativity and consolation, a home after home. What the slender solace of poetry cannot effect in this life, a return namely to the spaces of youthful freedom and friendship, the evergreen plain promises in the next.

The model of domesticity that Grant adumbrates in the 1790s is, as I have suggested, refined and more fully realized by Felicia Hemans, whose popularity, as Kelly argues, owes to her success in addressing the interests and values of a predominantly middle-class nineteenth-century reading public (15). Chief among those interests was the establishment and maintenance of a secure and stable domestic sphere—a somewhat more localized version of what we today distinguish as "homeland security." Building upon irenic poems by women (such as Charlotte Smith) "that deplore the domestic cost of war and especially its cost to women, conventionally the custodians and nurturers of the domestic sphere" (Kelly 20), Hemans's early verse articulates a consolatory and isolationist middle-class ideology of home.[24] This ideology is most comprehensively set forth in *The Domestic Affections and Other Poems* (1812), a collection published while the poet was herself entering a new domestic situation through her marriage to Captain Hemans. The collection's titular poem, though it begins from a position of perfunctory uncertainty about the source of life's "tranquil joys" (1),[25] quickly dispels these doubts and focuses in on the object of its inquiry:

> Nursed on the lap of solitude and shade,
> The violet smiles, embosomed in the glade;
> There sheds her spirit on the lonely gale,
> Gem of seclusion! treasure of the vale!
> Thus, far from life's tumultuous road,
> Domestic bliss has fixed her calm abode. (19–24)

Hemans's notion of "[d]omestic bliss" is most obviously and inextricably bound up with retirement and seclusion. Choosing, like Grant, the example of the "embosomed" flower as her model of home, Hemans sets it far beyond the reach of "life's tumultuous road." The security of home is in fact unassailable even for the elements of nature. "Stern winter," for example, "bursting from the polar clime" (52) cannot encroach upon or disturb the domestic scene, whose "heaven is still serene, / [Its] star, unclouded, and [its] myrtle green" (59–60).

Again, it is important to note that Hemans's understanding of domesticity or home is grounded not exclusively in its physical manifestations but also in its affective associations. Home is as much a *feeling of home* as a specific place; it is an internalisation as well as an external manifestation of familiar soil. And this internalisation, as Hemans points out, enables one, when displaced and overwhelmed by life, to fashion a return merely by reflection:

> Thus, when oppressed with rude tumultuous cares,
> To thee, sweet home, the fainting mind repairs,
> Still to thy breast, a wearied pilgrim flies,
> Her ark of refuge from uncertain skies.
> Bower of repose! when torn from all we love,
> Through toil we struggle, or through distance rove;
> To *thee* we turn, still faithful from afar,
> Thee, our bright vista! thee, our magnetic star!
> And from the martial field, the troubled sea,
> Unfettered thought still roves to bliss and thee! (73–82)

Although defined initially as a refuge from generalized "cares" and "toil," home, as the passage's concluding couplet suggests, is also and perhaps most importantly an asylum from the theatre of war. This asylum may, as Hemans notes, be reached in thought, as when the weary soldier "sinks in slumbers" (130) on the field of combat and there "[m]eets the warm teardrop, and the long embrace; / While the sweet welcome vibrates through his heart" (134–135). Hemans also, however, articulates a fuller experience of home, one that is linked to the physical reality of familiar soil:

> And oh! for him, the child of rude alarms,
> Reared by stern danger in the school of arms;
> How sweet to change the war-song's pealing note,
> For woodland sounds, in summer air that float,
> Through vales of peace, o'er mountain wilds to roam,
> And breathe his native gales that whisper "Home!" (147–152)

Whereas the internalisation of home serves only to lighten the burden of a displaced existence in a landscape of death, the actual return to "native" scenes enables the soldier to re-establish a communion with life itself; once home, he is free to "breathe."

As a space of generalized solace, home in Hemans's view is a refuge not only for humanity's "deserted and forlorn" (191)—her list includes soldiers, wanderers, the shipwrecked, emigrants and the sick—but also for those whose business, at least traditionally conceived, consists in the regular transcendence of domesticity, namely figures of "genius" such as the poet.

Hemans's description of the poet, prefigured by that of the "aspiring eagle" (166) which, after "[d]art[ing] o'er the clouds, exulting to admire, / Meridian glory" (167–168), "speeds to joys more calmly / 'Midst the dear inmates of his lonely nest" (173–174), emphasizes the importance, indeed the inevitability, of returning home:

> Thus Genius, mounting on his bright career,
> Through the wide regions of the mental sphere;
> And proudly waving, in his gifted hand,
> O'er Fancy's worlds, Invention's plastic wand;
> Fearless and firm, with lightning-eye surveys
> The clearest heaven of intellectual rays;
> Yet on his course though loftiest hopes attend,
> And kindling raptures aid him to ascend;
> (While in his mind, with high-born grandeur fraught,
> Dilate the noblest energies of thought;)
> Still, from the bliss, ethereal and refined,
> Which crowns the soarings of triumphant mind,
> At length he flies, to that serene retreat,
> Where calm and pure, the mild affections meet,
> Embosomed there, to feel and to impart,
> The softer pleasures of the social heart. (175–190)

What Hemans delineates here is in effect a corrective to traditional notions of poetic genius. Indeed, the poet's return to the "serene retreat" of home is a necessary counterpart or addendum to "the soarings of triumphant mind" which serve, as Hemans notes, to remove the subject from familiar soil and social intercourse. Recalling Mellor's model of the masculine sublime, the experience of solitary genius, if not softened by the pleasures of community, tends to self-apotheosis: a proud waving of Invention's wand. While Hemans does not disparage such pursuits, her understanding of genius clearly transcends them. True or complete genius must, in her view, attend with no less firmness and devotion to the development of "mild affections" and a "social heart." Simply to "feel" is not enough; genius must also "*impart*" (emphasis added). Insofar as familiar soil facilitates the communication of affection by grounding one in community, it is as much the province of genius as "clearest heaven."

Not only does Hemans make room for genius at the hearth but she imbues the space of home with a wondrousness, a "bliss, ethereal and refined," that rivals loftiest heaven. As the poem's conclusion intimates, the source of that wonder is familiarity itself. Construed here as a presence or spirit that remains even after loss, familiarity is capable of ministering palpably to those forsaken or bereaved:

> Ye gentle spirits of departed friends!
> If e'er on earth your buoyant wing descends;
> If with benignant care, ye linger near,
> To guard the objects in existence dear;
> If hovering o'er, ethereal band! ye view
> The tender sorrows, to *your* memory true;
> . . . .
> Oh! then, amidst that holy calm, be near,
> Breathe your light whisper softly in her ear!
> With secret spells her wounded mind compose;
> And chase the faithful tear—for you that flows;
> Be near! when moonlight spreads the charm you loved,
> O'er scenes where once your *earthly* footstep roved;
> Then, while she wanders o'er the sparkling dew,
> Through glens, and wood-paths, once endeared by you,
> And fondly lingers, in your favourite bowers,
> And pauses oft, recalling former hours;
> Then wave your pinion o'er each well-known vale,
> Float in the moonbeam, sigh upon the gale!
> Bid your wild symphonies remotely swell,
> Borne by the summer-wind, from grot and dell;
> And touch your viewless harps, and soothe her soul,
> With soft enchantments and divine control! (372–397)

What begins as a speculative consideration of the possibility of being attended in sorrow by the spirits of the departed culminates in a vision, in fact, almost an invocation, of consolatory hauntedness. The nature of that consolation seems to inhere, as Hemans suggests, in the intersection of being and place, spirit and familiar soil. Familiarity is in effect an expression of undying presence. To return, therefore, to "favourite bowers" is to return not merely to memory but to present encounter; to return is to haunt and to be haunted in the now. One of the paradoxes or mysteries of familiar soil is that it allows the bereaved and departed to meet and yet also to miss each other. Whereas the bereaved returns to familiar soil, as Hemans notes, to recall "former hours" and thus, despite physical presence, to be absent in thought, the departed, the essence of thought or spirit, manifests him/herself physically through the animation of nature. Each, as it were, reaches for the other with half-presence and discovers half-absence. Hemans's model of consolation seems in fact to imply that the near-success (or near-futility) of such encounters ensures a habitual return by the bereaved and departed to familiar soil. Acts of return, perhaps more appropriately termed acts of commemoration, are hopeful callings into presence, means of perpetuating the consolations of familiarity.

What I have distinguished as discrete coping strategies or means of consolation, namely, the experience of simple flowers and familiar soil, are each, as it were, predicated on acts of return, the difference being that the expression of return is primarily temporal in one case and spatial in the other. These are not, however, mutually exclusive experiences of everyday reality. Indeed, each partakes at some level of the other. The wondrous return to childhood is, for example, notwithstanding the sense of prepossessing novelty, a repetition of what has gone before; it is in effect an experience of haunting déjà-vu, a recollection and rearticulation of a bygone but not departed self. In like manner, the experience of familiarity, as Hemans reveals, is not, despite our sense of returning to what we know so well, devoid of wonder or surprise (even if the full range of that wonder is not always readily perceptible). Hemans, indeed, allows us to conceive of familiar soil as something that may, behind the scenes, be inherently mysterious or other-worldly; the very places that habitual experience has made dear may, as she proposes, be invested and animated by an unrecognisable otherness. Where the everyday is concerned, the novel is never entirely new, nor the familiar entirely known.

The full force of this realization and its consolatory potential are perhaps nowhere more vividly registered than in Book VII of *The Prelude*, where Wordsworth, articulating what is in essence a synthesis of the consolations of wondrous novelty and dependable familiarity, describes an encounter with a blind beggar on the streets of London. It is with this spot of time, so central to the poetics of everyday life, everyday consolation, and everyday sublimity, that I would like to close:

> O Friend! one feeling was there which belonged
> To this great city, by exclusive right;
> How often, in the overflowing streets,
> Have I gone forwards with the crowd, and said
> Unto myself, 'The face of every one
> That passes by me is a mystery!'
> Thus have I looked, nor ceased to look, oppressed
> By thoughts of what and whither, when and how,
> Until the shapes before my eyes became

>   A second-sight procession, such as glides
>   Over still mountains, or appears in dreams;
>   And all the ballast of familiar life,
>   The present, and the past; hope, fear; all stays,
>   All laws of acting, thinking, speaking man
>   Went from me, neither knowing me, nor known.
>   And once, far-travelled in such mood, beyond
>   The reach of common indications, lost
>   Amid the moving pageant, 'twas my chance
>   Abruptly to be smitten with the view
>   Of a blind Beggar, who, with upright face,
>   Stood, propped against a wall, upon his chest
>   Wearing a written paper, to explain
>   The story of the man, and who he was.
>   My mind did at this spectacle turn round
>   As with the might of waters, and it seemed
>   To me that in this label was a type,
>   Or emblem, of the utmost that we know,
>   Both of ourselves and of the universe;
>   And, on the shape of the unmoving man,
>   His fixèd face and sightless eyes, I looked,
>   As if admonished from another world. (VII.592–622)

Positioned both spatially and, I would argue, thematically at the center of the 1805–6 *Prelude*, this passage evinces Wordsworth's particular talent for revealing in terms at once numinous and matter-of-fact the "inexhaustible treasure" (to borrow Coleridge's phrase) of everyday life. A spot of time all its own, Wordsworth's encounter with the beggar represents a movement beyond words, a descent to the primordial rudiments of knowledge and knowing, to "types" and "emblems"—what in another of the poet's well-known descents are glossed as "[t]he types and symbols of Eternity" (VI.571). Yet here the geographical context is not alpine but urban; here the power of nature is not expressed in immensity or vastness but is drawn instead into the simple lines of a human face and the accompanying narrative of self.

At first glance this passage appears to offer little in the way of consolation, in part because it reinforces Wordsworth's prevailing sense of isolation in the city. The epiphany that precedes the poet's encounter with the beggar—"The face of every one / That passes by me is a mystery!"—is indeed the stuff of despair. Not only do London's inhabitants live, as Wordsworth discovers early in his stay, among their neighbours as "[s]trangers, and knowing not each other's names" (VII.120), but the very possibility of communion is thwarted by an even deeper and indeed unbridgeable chasm between self and other: the ineffability of the human face. For one inclined to search "[f]or good in the familiar face of life" (XII.67), the sudden realization of impenetrable mystery in the human face (which, notwithstanding its innumerable variations, is arguably the most familiar of all faces) may rightly be expected to bring grief, not solace. Wordsworth seems to suggest as much when he numbers the loss of "the ballast of familiar life" among the consequences of entering a sea of inscrutable faces. While the appearance of what he describes as a "second-sight procession" of humanity is aesthetically stimulating, its emotional effect entails an erasure of subjectivity. Wordsworth becomes for a moment "lost / Amid the moving pageant," a dreamlike cipher "far-travelled" beyond even his own recognition.

It is here, however, at his furthest reach from self and other, that he describes being startled back to reality, "smitten," as he says, "with the view / Of a blind Beggar." The Beggar, specifically his "*upright face*" (emphasis added), returns the poet to the world. What appears on one hand as a further intensification or deepening of the mystery of the face—in this case a face that can see neither itself nor its elemental autobiography and thus appears to lack, as David Simpson notes, any social identity at all (53)—is also on the other hand a bell that tolls the poet in Keatsean fashion back to himself and, moreover, to humanity. Forlorn in the moving pageant, Wordsworth finds himself suddenly in company, face to face. The gravity of the encounter is apprehended both abruptly and dimly. In a motion of awe that recalls the boy-poet suddenly wheeling around his stolen boat on the Patterdale and returning to shore, the adult-poet's mind "turn[s] round" at the sight of the Beggar "with the might of waters" and arrives at an epiphany that seems to underline the intractable mystery of the face while also, at the same moment, mitigating the despair of that truth. What Wordsworth realizes is that the human face, in this case an unknown face but one nevertheless typologically familiar, contains the sum, "the utmost," of what we know or can know. This most immediate of wonders, in other words, both satisfies and exceeds all our knowing. At once strange and yet always already familiar, the face contains the utmost that we know "[b]oth of ourselves and of the universe." The (story of the) face, in short, is a microcosm of the universe—vast, transcendent, inherently sublime.

Perhaps most important to the encounter itself, to this silent meeting of the lost and the blind, is the impression that Wordsworth carries with him of being "admonished." An echo of the chastisement that he associates with the second spot of time, this admonition "from another world" seems directed not only at the misplaced pride of human knowledge but also, and perhaps more importantly, at its focus. The poet (and by extension, the reader) is cautioned not only against thinking more of the scope of his knowledge than he ought but also about the misapplication or misdirection of that knowledge. And the knowledge that pertains to the face-to-face encounter between self and other is, as I would like to suggest, primarily ethical in nature. It is knowledge or, more properly, tutelage similar in kind to what the poet associates with the public roadway: the tutelage of the other rooted in imaginative sympathy. For Wordsworth, such sympathy is an expression of that "unconscious love and reverence / Of human nature" (VIII.413–414) that proceeds from a prior tutelage in the love of nature itself. In the post-metaphysical philosophy of writers like Emmanuel Levinas, it is an expression of one's ethical responsibility for the other. As Levinas suggests in *Ethics and Infinity*, the mere appearance of the human face is sufficient to call forth the full range of one's sympathies and powers of action:

> The first word of the face is the "Thou shalt not kill." It is an order. There is a commandment in the appearance of the face, as if a master spoke to me. However, at the same time, the face of the Other is destitute; it is the poor for whom I can do all and to whom I owe all. And me, whoever I may be, but as a "first person," I am he who finds the resources to respond to the call. (89)

The blind Beggar's face, in other words, is not simply a code written in timeless symbols but an expression of immediate denuded destitution: it is a face of need. And while it is not clear if or how the poet heeds the call of the face—such details tend to find expression not in William's but in Dorothy's work—his momentary transfixion is at least suggestive of having *heard* the call. Indeed, the poet's sense of admonitory presence may have rather less to do with a perception of unanticipated depth or other-worldliness than with a sudden realization that beneath the generalized epistemological "type" is a story of individual human need—beneath the upright face is a bowed spirit. From being lost in the crowd, the poet is called into relationship with the other and from the consolation of community he is brought, still further, to responsibility. Perhaps this is inevitable. Perhaps the gift of consolation is always already attended by the responsibility to share.

Conclusion
The Modern Remains of "Visionary Dreariness"

It happens every so often that our scholarly preoccupations not only intersect with but directly enhance our interactions with the world at large, and that those interactions in turn inform and refine the course of study that originally provoked them. The present project is an example of such a refinement, what I would characterize more precisely as a cleansing of the doors of perception. Indeed one cannot, I think, examine the literature of everyday life without becoming by degrees more sensibly aware of and alive to one's own habitual surroundings and motions. The emphasis on 'degrees' is important here because perceptual cleansing is never the result of a single motion, a clean sweep; we begin to see rather in part, one spot at a time. In support of this notion I submit from personal experience an admittedly unspectacular but nevertheless memorable moment, one that serves, moreover, as a preliminary corrective to Weiskel's dismissive commentary on the effects of daffodils on the modern.[1] The experience followed and was, I think, quite clearly informed by an intensive re-reading of Dorothy Wordsworth's Alfoxden and Grasmere Journals in the spring of 2001. I recall being particularly struck by Wordsworth's description of winter trees in the entry for May 14, 1802:

> The woods looked miserable, the coppices green as grass which looked quite unnatural and they seemed half shrivelled up as if they shrunk from the air. O thought I! what a beautiful thing God has made winter to be by stripping the trees and letting us see their shapes and forms. What a freedom does it seem to give to the storms! (*Journals* 125)

A few days after revolving in my mind this curious immersion in miserable beauty, I happened to be striding across Dalhousie's upper campus on a colourless March morning, eyes turned down, collar against the wind, when, while passing under a tree whose presence I had perhaps never even registered before, a bird-call from above stopped me. Something about its clarity, its precise arrival in the lapse of my own thoughts, arrested all progress. I looked up and saw above me not a bird but a tangle of slick-grey branches flowing in all directions like spilled quicksilver. I do not know how long I stood transfixed while bodies continued to press by me but I do know that I have never seen a tree like it before or since.

Perhaps our own perception needs at times the tutelage of another's seeing; and here I mean our critical as well as our sensory perception. For without such tutelage we risk dismissing the transcendent effects of the everyday not only on our experience of the present but also on that of the past. Indeed, the slippage between Weiskel's claim that our modern aesthetic consciousness is unimpressed by daffodils and the perpetuation of what Karina Williamson calls a "debased Romanticism" in which ordinary experience is stripped of aesthetic value is deceptively swift and easy. As Margaret Ezell suggests in the specific context of reading feminist literary history, "our understanding of the past is shaped by the largely unconscious acceptance and inculcation of present-day ideologies in our narratives of history" (15). Like McGann, in other words, Ezell cautions against establishing an unhistorical symmetry between the critic and the work (or period) in question. The problem, as Ezell and McGann make clear, is not with the idea that there are symmetries between past and present experience but rather with a critically unsound reliance on ideology to determine and perpetuate them. Where the experience of everyday life is concerned—an experience arguably more resistant to the shifting trends of age, politics and culture (not to mention ideology)—there are, I would suggest, obvious and prevailing symmetries between the past and the present. For example, notwithstanding certain modulations in context and frequency, not to mention the material differences that may govern such activities, we continue to walk, to read, to cook, to wash, to play, et cetera. We continue, moreover, in the midst of these habitual activities to regard and reflect upon the world around us. Often we turn up our collar against the dreariness of everyday life but occasionally we still manage to catch glimpses of the visionary in its midst: occasionally we still look up at trees as if for the first time. And even if we have never done so, that experience is by no means beyond our seasoned, habituated consciousness. According to Coleridge, it is to be gained if not directly then at least vicariously through the experience of "genius," for genius, if we recall his description from the *Biographia*, "produces the strongest impressions of novelty while it rescues the most admitted truths from the impotence caused by the very circumstances of their universal admission" (49). Genius, in other words, schools the reader in *re*perceiving familiarity. To frame this idea more generally, our acquaintance with the past readies our doors of perception for cleansing.

I would in fact suggest that where the quotidian sublime is concerned, it is not only the Romantic past but also our more recent literary history that schools us in the finer arts of perception (suggesting again the experiential continuities of everyday life). In framing this position, I will be drawing upon a recent essay by Seamus Perry (entitled "Ordinary Consolation and Its Modern Fate") that questions the modernity of Coleridge's "long imaginative investment [. . .] in the idea of consolation" (479). Perry, as I have already indicated in my discussion of the *consolatio*, characterizes the modern response to the possibility of solace, specifically a solace grounded in "ordinariness" (481), as a vacillation between despair and disgust. As evidence he marshals a list of mock- or anti-elegiac elegies such as Swinburne's "Ave Atque Vale," Larkin's "Aubade," John Betjeman's "I.M. Walter Ramsden," and Geoffrey Hill's "In Memory of Jane Fraser"—each foregrounding not simply a want of faith in the bastions of religion but a sort of disabused cynicism that comes from living in a context of perceived apathy or thoughtlessness, where neither nature nor the human other is seen as a willing facilitator of one's survival, let alone one's happiness. Yet rather than simply perpetuating Weiskel's critical indifference to the wonders of everyday life, Perry stops short of proclaiming an effective end to consolation. Instead, he turns from Swinburne to Seamus Heaney and from Betjeman to Julian Barnes to reveal the lingering, if somewhat muted, influence of Coleridgean consolation. To this admittedly preliminary list one could also add other names; indeed, it is possible, I think, to trace strains of a wondrous and consolatory engagement with everyday life right through the literature of the later nineteenth century into that of the modern period. It is of course beyond the reach of the present study to propose a definitive history of quotidian sublimity, one that traces not only the continuities in our experience of numinous ordinariness but also the subtle and at times profound variations (at least some of which are attributable to the shift from rural to urban domestic settings; to globalization and the consequent proliferation of cross-cultural communities and contexts; to industrialization, mechanization, automation and computerization, and their effects on our daily interactions with the environment and with one another; and, to technological innovations that allow us to see not only a world in a grain of sand but grains of sand on other worlds). Nevertheless, I would like to offer a sample of moments from post-Romantic writings that reflect the continued operation of an aesthetic of everyday wonder. The prevalence or representativeness of these moments I do not undertake to explore, except to suggest that, as in the Romantic period, they occur alongside (and in spite of) the sort of inconsolable and world-weary disdain for commonness that Perry mentions.

The first two examples are drawn from well-known works of the mid-nineteenth century and have still plainly upon their roots the soil of Romanticism's particulate engagement with everyday life. Particularity is indeed the guiding aesthetic principle behind the first of these texts, Thoreau's *Walden*, whose rigorously empirical naturalism recalls the work of Clare (of course one of the ironies of this comparison is that Clare's removal to Northampton Asylum in 1841 following his escape from High Beech coincides almost to the year with Thoreau's removal to Walden Pond to begin living a freer life). The following description of pickerel—fish being to Thoreau what birds are to Clare—appears in "The Pond in Winter":

> Ah, the pickerel of Walden! when I see them lying on the ice, or in the well which the fisherman cuts in the ice, making a little hole to admit the water, I am always surprised by their rare beauty, as if they were fabulous fishes, they are so foreign to the streets, even to the woods, foreign as Arabia to our Concord life. They possess a quite dazzling and transcendent beauty which separates them by a wide interval from the cadaverous cod and haddock whose fame is trumpeted in our streets. They are not green like the pines, nor gray like the stones, nor blue like the sky; but they have, to my eyes, if possible, yet rarer colors, like flowers and precious stones, as if they were the pearls, the animalized *nuclei* or crystals of the Walden water. They, of course, are Walden all over and all through; are themselves small Waldens in the animal kingdom, Waldenses. It is surprising that they are caught here,—that in this deep and capacious spring, far beneath the rattling teams and chaises and tinkling sleighs that travel the Walden road, this great gold and emerald fish swims. (268)

What this passage most obviously shares with Clare's work is an authorial viewpoint that is almost literally immersed in and consequently entranced by the details of material reality—details that shimmer unnoticed under the very ruts and rhythms of everyday life. There is, in other words, an evocation here of unknown familiarity, of something hidden in plain view. Although Thoreau has seen pickerel before, he is, as he notes, "*always surprised* by their rare beauty, as if they were fabulous fishes" (emphasis added). Familiarity does not subdue wonder; the "fabulous" always usurps the known. It is notable, moreover, that what begins as a description of "rare beauty" turns rather quickly to an encounter with transcendence. Thoreau indeed cannot define what he sees. Even the repeated approach through metaphor fails because the fish are *not* like anything else; they are incomparable, inscrutable, the stuff solely of imagination—"as if they were [. . .] the animalized nuclei or crystals of the Walden water." Like Coleridge's, Thoreau's imagination is particularizing in nature: it sees by seeing through. The consequences of the author's in-sight include a further intensification or deepening of the numinous encounter. For when conceived as the very nuclei of the pond, the pickerel take on an even more rarified character; they become, as it were, the essence of Walden Pond, neither simply fish nor water but an infusion somehow of both. In this instance at least, Thoreau's empiricism is visionary in nature. Indeed, his scientific analogy serves to swim the pond with sublime presence—a presence that is at once irreducibly local and familiar but also "foreign as Arabia."

In order to elucidate the range and variety of encounters with everyday reality in post-Romantic writing, I would like to offer as a counterbalance to the foregoing example of defamiliarization a contemporaneous moment of consoling familiarity from George Eliot's *The Mill on the Floss*. Occurring early in the novel, at the end of a chapter detailing the yet untarnished world of Tom and Maggie's childhood, the 'spot' in question marks the appearance of the narrator herself in the midst of her tale, strolling, as it were, in nostalgic sympathy with the Tullivers:

> The wood I walk in on this mild May day, with the young yellow-brown foliage of the oaks between me and the blue sky, the white starflowers and the blue-eyed speedwell and the ground ivy at my feet—what grove of tropic palms, what strange ferns or splendid broad-petalled blossoms, could ever thrill such deep and delicate fibres within me as this home-scene? These familiar flowers, these furrowed and grassy fields, each with a sort of personality given to it by the capricious hedgerows—such things as these are the mother tongue of our imagination, the language that is laden with all the subtle inextricable associations the fleeting hours of our childhood left behind them. Our delight in the sunshine on the deep-bladed grass to-day, might be no more than the faint perception of wearied souls, if it were not for the sunshine and the grass in the far-off years which still live in us, and transform our perception into love. (37–38)

Prefaced by a rhetorical question whose answer it only underlines—"What novelty is worth that sweet monotony where everything is known, and *loved* because it is known?" (37)—this passage registers a Wordsworthian attachment to familiarity. And by 'Wordsworthian' I mean to evoke both William's and Dorothy's engagement with familiarity, the one tending to the consolations (imaginative and experiential) of the past, and the other, more often, to a solacing immersion in the present. Eliot seems in fact to conflate these experiences by suggesting that familiarity is at its core a re-experience of the past in the present; familiarity, as she puts it, is past perception transformed into present "love." One cannot, therefore, return to well-known scenes without returning still further to "the fleeting hours of our childhood." That said, it is only in the present, only in a moment built upon and saturated by prior perception, that we experience the love—and consequently the consolation—of familiar scenes. Consolation for Eliot's narrator consists therefore not in a simple re-experience of the "fleeting scenes" of the past (as is the case for William) but rather in a distillation of those scenes in the present, a reduction, if you will, to an essence of love. It is monotony that makes us love and love that makes monotony "sweet."

While the foregoing examples from Thoreau and Eliot manifest, as I have said, a still recognizably Romantic predisposition to the natural world, an abiding trust, that is, in nature as a repository of untarnished innocence and imaginative possibility, such trust is not essential to the experience of everyday wonder. Indeed, the following episodes from works of the later nineteenth century reveal an engagement with everyday life from distinctly un-Romantic subject positions or perspectives. In the first example, a passage drawn from the conclusion of Thomas Hardy's *The Mayor of Casterbridge* (1886), that perspective is already nascently modern in that it comprehends an ever widening and deepening vortex of bleakness, cynicism and futility. Hardy's text is indeed haunted at its core by the question that Michael Henchard, the novel's self-made and self-proclaimed "outcast" (355), asks of his daughter Elizabeth-Jane after suffering the public humiliation of the 'Skimmington ride': "Are miracles still worked, do ye think . . . ?" (332). Notwithstanding Elizabeth's unconsoling response, her life as Hardy describes it in the novel's closing paragraphs offers evidence of an at least lingering susceptibility to the miracles of everyday life:

> As the lively and sparkling emotions of her early married life cohered into an equable serenity, the finer movements of her nature found scope in discovering to the narrow-lived ones around her the secret (as she had once learnt it) of making limited opportunities endurable; which she deemed to consist in the cunning enlargement, by a species of microscopic treatment, of those minute forms of satisfaction that offer themselves to everybody not in positive pain; which, thus handled, have much of the same effect upon wider life as wider interests cursorily embraced. (368)

Articulated in a series of refinements and diminutions ("finer," "narrow-lived," "limited," "microscopic," "minute"), Elizabeth's meagre consolation is significant because it enables her to withstand the bitter lesson of her youth, namely "that happiness was but the occasional episode in a general drama of pain" (369). Her focus on "those minute forms of satisfaction that offer themselves to everybody"—a sort of democratization of solace—does not so much alter life's "general drama of pain" as make it sufferable. This is clearly not the Wordsworthian consolation of returning through nature to one's childhood and thereby removing oneself, however briefly, from pain; if anything, this passage recalls the strategy of consolation outlined by Anne Grant, a strategy devoted to present amelioration. Then again, Hardy draws a much harder line than Grant by refusing to offer the someday-solace of an "evergreen-plain." Consolation is here simply understood as the ability to endure present pain and to make that endurance "endurable," that is, to make it last. Moreover, whereas the Romantic (particularly the Coleridgean) view tends to emphasize nature's role in facilitating consolation by actively usurping our senses and thus turning our gaze outward, the process that Hardy articulates is rather more dependent on individual action or what he terms "cunning." In whatever the limited opportunities of everyday life consist, their consolatory potential rests in the subject's ability to manipulate them—to enlarge, accentuate, prolong—so as to enhance their "inspiring effect." The hoped-for end of such labour is nothing more or less than a life of "equable serenity."

The second example, a poem by Gerard Manley Hopkins entitled "Ashboughs" (1887), is likewise un-Romantic but for different reasons. Rather than foregrounding the need to enhance nature's limited consolations with human "cunning," Hopkins's work locates solace in the divine presence that nature incarnates. Thus where Hardy is philosophically (pre)modern, Hopkins is pre-Romantic. This is of course not to suggest that an awareness of the "general drama of pain" is absent from Hopkins's work. "Ashboughs" is in fact intimately related to pain; not only was it composed during Hopkins's isolating and emotionally withering stay in Dublin but it appears as a fair copy above drafts of "To seem the stranger" and "I wake and feel," two of the so-called Sonnets of Desolation which critics have numbered "among the most splendid poems of suffering in our language" (Houghton and Stange 692). In this context of profound despair, "Ashboughs" represents an unexpectedly efficacious consolation:

> Not of all my eyes see, wandering on the world,
> Is anything a milk to the mind so, so sighs deep
> Poetry to it, as a tree whose boughs break in the sky.

> Say it is ashboughs: whether on a December day and furled
> Fast or they in clammyish lashtender combs creep
> Apart wide and new-nestle at heaven most high.
> They touch heaven, tabour on it; how their talons sweep
> The smouldering enormous winter welkin! May
> Mells blue and snowwhite through them, a fringe and fray
> Of greenery: it is old earth's groping towards the steep
>   Heaven whom she childs us by.[2]

For the poet at least, ashboughs are not merely one of those minute forms of everyday satisfaction that must be swelled into significance; they represent, instead, the very culmination—the *summum bonum*—of perceptible solace. Unrivalled by anything discernible in an expansive survey of the world, this tangle of branches, this "milk to the mind," appears to owe its consolatory powers to its intimation of transcendence, its unending approach, that is, to "heaven most high." Indeed, for Hopkins the boughs' significance has to do rather with their inclination than their form or essence; or, to put it another way, essence is here reducible to inclination; the boughs are defined by their gesture to something beyond themselves, something unutterably vast. Thus, instead of lingering over the "shapes and forms" of leafless trees as Dorothy Wordsworth does, Hopkins seizes on the patches of "blue and snowwhite" visible between the branches. These glimpses of sky, notably, represent an engagement with a "Heaven" that is not only vast but also benevolent and life-giving. The masculine Heaven whom female earth "childs us by" is quite clearly a manifestation of divine presence. To direct one's gaze up the boughs of a tree is therefore, in Hopkins's ecotheology, a process tending invariably to God. And as the poet suggests, any tree will do: "Say it is ashboughs."

The capacity of everyday life to sustain such diverse experiences of wonder and solace is likewise evident in the literature of the twentieth century where, as Perry suggests, the recovery of the world (and by extension, the other within the world) is effected by an appeal "not to something without the world, but, mysteriously, to the world itself which is the very world of all of us" (485). What Perry articulates here is in effect a mediate position between Hardy's emphasis on the role of human cunning and Hopkins's deference to the animating presence of God—a position that brings one in what I think is a strikingly ironic turn back to the Romantic investment in everyday life typified by writers like Coleridge, Clare and Dorothy Wordsworth. Indeed, the two spots with which I will close recover that Romantic fascination with ordinariness which reveals itself in the experience of seeing deeply into things so as to see them anew.

The first appears in James Agee's *Let Us Now Praise Famous Men* (1941), the textual account of three Alabama share-cropping families in the late 1930s, commissioned by *Fortune* magazine and supplemented by a series of now famous photographs by Walker Evans. The book, if one may call it such, is an early example of embedded journalism; more than that, however, it is an aesthetic (and emotional) investment in the minute material reality of another's everyday life, a life in this case of unrelenting labour and poverty. Although the stuff of life is in every way stamped and scarred by these twin burdens, Agee's gaze manages by a sort of sympathetic scrupulosity to effect a redemptive relationship with all that it touches. The chapter on 'Clothing,' for example, contains the following description of overalls (pronounced, as Agee notes, "overhauls"):

> The changes that age, use, weather, work upon these. . . . The structures sag, and take on the look, some of use; some, the pencil pockets, the pretty atrophies of what is never used; the edges of the thigh pockets become stretched and lie open, fluted, like the gills of a fish. The bright seams lose their whiteness and are lines and ridges. The whole fabric is shrunken to size, which was bought large. The whole shape, texture, color, finally substance, are all changed. The shape, particularly along the urgent frontage of the thighs, so that the whole structure of the knee and musculature of the thigh is sculptured there; each man's garment wearing the shape and beauty of his induplicable body. The texture and the color change in union, by sweat, sun, laundering, between the steady pressures of its use and age: both, at length, into realms of fine softness and marvel of draping and velvet plays of light which chamois and silk can only suggest, not touch; and into a region and scale of blues, subtle, delicious, and deft beyond what I have ever seen elsewhere approached except in rare skies, the smoky light some days are filmed with, and some of the blues of Cézanne: one could watch and touch even one such garment, study it, with the eyes, the fingers, and the subtlest lips, almost illimitably long, and never fully learn it; and I saw no two which did not hold some world of exquisiteness of its own. (267)

With a scrupulosity reminiscent of Dorothy Wordsworth's description of the patched and threadbare attire of the old sailor in the Grasmere Journals, Agee 'over-hauls' our expectations of descriptive journalism by sketching not merely an article of clothing, an arrangement of fabric, seams and stitches, but something that verges on the transcendent, something that evokes the hidden grandeur of the person to whom they belong. The overalls are indeed inextricably linked to subjectivity; individualized like a fingerprint, like skin, they are inseparable from the human labourer who wears his body into them with sweat even as they are worn from without by heat and dust (and later, by laundering). This passage in fact recalls a description of nest-building by Jules Michelet that Bachelard includes in *The Poetics of Space*. Reflecting on the fact that the nest is shaped by the bird's body, "pressed on countless times by [its] breast, its heart, surely with difficulty in breathing, perhaps even, with palpitations" (qtd. in Bachelard 101), Michelet distills the process of home-making to a series of small acts of suffering that end finally in shelter and comfort. Garment-making, as Agee describes it, is likewise rooted in suffering and directed to the production of shelter and comfort for the body. Such comfort, characterized by the wearing away of new, stiff fabric into "realms of fine softness," may indeed be one of the only tangible consolations of the tenant farmer's labour. For the observer, however, there is the additional aesthetic consolation of wonder. Indeed, as Agee suggests in the preceding paragraph, overalls are "marvels of nature" (267).[3] Their marvellousness, notably, derives from a two-fold process of particularization: the refinement of colour and texture by "the steady pressures of use and age," and the scrupulous analysis by the observer's eyes, fingers and lips to determine the detail or depth of that refinement. As Agee makes clear, the observer's task (not unlike the labourer's) is "illimitably long" and ultimately unavailing because the marvel of overalls is never to be fully known. Their exquisiteness of colour is as rare, as studied, as "some of the blues of Cézanne," suggesting a sort of unwitting genius on the part of the labourer that the observer cannot pierce or resolve. Indeed, one of the effects of Agee's scrutiny, one of its sympathetic byproducts, is that it reverses the roles of artist and reader/viewer. Although the farmer has no use for the overalls' pencil pocket because he cannot write or figure, his clothes carry the imprints of an eloquence that Agee's words cannot in all their profusion rival or unravel.

The final spot comes from the pages of Annie Dillard's *Pilgrim at Tinker Creek* (1974), a work whose naturalist ethos recalls Aldo Leopold's *A Sand County Almanac* and of course Thoreau's *Walden*, but whose roots lie, I think, still deeper in the Romantic period. The following passage, for example, so characteristic of Dillard's non-interventionist approach to natural otherness, bears striking similarities to Dorothy Wordsworth's watchful communion with the swallows on her window ledge. While standing by the window of her cottage in Tinker Creek, Virginia, idly watching the distant water "lurch over the dam and round the shaded bend of the cliff" (215), Dillard is distracted by a more immediate spectacle:

The Modern Remains of "Visionary Dreariness" 197

> All at once something wonderful happened, although at first it seemed perfectly ordinary. A female goldfinch suddenly hove into view. She lighted weightlessly on the head of a bankside purple thistle and began emptying the seedcase, sowing the air with down.
>
> The lighted frame of my window filled. The down rose and spread in all directions, wafting over the dam's waterfall and wavering between the tulip trunks and into the meadow. It vaulted towards the orchard in a puff; it hovered over the ripening pawpaw fruit and staggered up the steep-faced terrace. It jerked, floated, rolled, veered, swayed. The thistledown faltered toward the cottage and gusted clear to the motorbike woods; it rose and entered the shaggy arms of pecans. At last it strayed like snow, blind and sweet, into the pool of the creek upstream, and into the race of the creek over rocks down. It shuddered onto the tips of growing grasses, where it poised, light, still wracked by errant quivers. I was holding my breath. Is this where we live, I thought, in this place at this moment, with the air so light and wild? (215–216)

It is difficult to know if the "perfectly ordinary" is here usurped by the "wonderful" or if they arrive, as it were, in sudden simultaneity, always already inflected one by the other. Indeed, even before the air is sown with thistledown, Dillard appears to be holding her breath, riveted by the finch's approach, by its improbable translation of heaving energy into weightless landing. With that flourish of movement, the creek and dam are for a moment entirely obscured, waiting, as it were, to be reanimated by the bird's prolific labour. And it is that labour, the emptying of the seedcase, which fills not only the window frame but Dillard's eye, utterly captivating her as Dorothy is captivated by the swallows' twittering, their swimming round and round. Ceaseless, circular motion is indeed at the heart of both of these moments of quotidian sublimity. In Dillard's example, that circularity is expressed in waves of thistledown rippling out from an epicentre of "perfectly ordinary" movement to transform the countryside, from cottage to woods to creek, into a marvel of quivering energy. Not only are the physical surfaces of nature animated but the very wind itself in all its swirling subtlety is made for a moment perceptible, its innumerable courses clarified by the eddying down. Dillard's astonishment, what in the analytic of the sublime is theorized as an attempt to represent external vastness internally, is fittingly expressed by the act of holding her breath, a sort of bodily analogy of the mind turning over the vastness of the wind. The question that frames her astonishment—"Is this where we live [. . .] in this place at this moment?"—ripples out, like the down itself, from a personal context into the generalized realm of everyday life. Dillard's question serves in effect as an invitation to us as readers to be likewise astonished by the places and moments of our present reality, to await the arrival of perfectly wonderful ordinariness.

The foregoing examples from the nineteenth and twentieth centuries serve, I think, to accentuate the symmetries between our past and present experience of everyday life, whether that experience is written or lived; they allow us, in short, to understand that the ripples of wonder that inundate our present consciousness come from afar. This is not to suggest that our experiences of wonder are derivative or that they can only ever be gained by a prior tutelage in the perceptions of 'genius' (what I would characterize more precisely as "seeing as other"), but rather that everyday life is dependably wondrous, that its sources of imaginative vision and consolation are not only ubiquitous but in some sense timeless—eternal as the springing grass. This, then, is one reason for resisting Weiskel's aesthetic marginalization of ordinariness. Yet there is also another, one more immediate and compelling, one that lies as deep within us as everyday life itself. In order to tease it out, I will return to Perry's essay, specifically to the paragraph at which his thesis turns itself abruptly and indeed somewhat unexpectedly against the impossibility of modern consolation:

> I began by saying that consolation may seem an exemplarily pre-modern kind of ambition: to find it already lurking within reality, though habitually disguised by self-absorption, does not sound very like the modern world-view I set out at the start. And I suppose the other-worldly resources of classical solace are indeed largely lost; but perhaps we move a little fast if we accept the demise of ordinariness's consolation as an essentially modern characteristic—although its survival may require the sanctions of tentativeness or self-deprecation or the rueful recognition of incongruity. (482)

The note of caution Perry sounds, albeit complicated by caveats, is one that rests not so much on the promise of countervailing evidence to the demise of ordinary consolation (although, as I have suggested, he does offer brief examples from Heaney and Barnes to that effect) as on a sort of innate hesitation to drop the curtain on his own thesis. We move, as he says, "a little fast" if we relegate the ordinary to a position of powerlessness and meaninglessness in our lives. Despite conceding that "[i]t is very difficult to say much about this [i.e. the wonder of common things] without sounding empty-headed," Perry reminds us (and arguably himself) that "it seems worth the attempt" (484). There is value, in other words, simply in considering the possibility that what we know of common things is not all that common things are. Here then is the empty-headed-sounding core of Perry's argument, namely that the consolations of ordinariness, however they are individually conceived or experienced, depend on our willingness to re-examine the ordinary, to re-read the details of its expression. And yet even if we can train ourselves, as Agee suggests, to study those details "illimitably long," we must be prepared to encounter a residue of marvellousness that eludes the grasp of logic and language. The ordinary, like the sublime itself in other words, at some level transcends signification; its value or impact is felt but never entirely susceptible to explanation. Our experience of ordinariness is so entwined with our fundamental experience of living that it sits, as it were, too deep within consciousness to be easily or completely educed. That idea, that conviction of lurking, unfathomable depth, lies I think at the root of Perry's hesitation to resign modernity to a post-consolatory experience of everyday life.

If the difficulty in sounding everyday life is suggestive of its depth, that depth, I would argue, may be defined principally as the depth of otherness. Indeed, in order to see the everyday anew, one must break the habit, as Perry puts it, of "self-absorption." More than anything, familiarity is induced by looking too much within; its "film" hangs not upon the natural world but upon our own doors of perception, dimming and distorting what lies beyond them. Freshness of perception, conversely, is characterized by an engagement with the natural world as other; seeing anew begins by gazing without. Thus, if the nineteenth-century experience of quotidian sublimity represents a counterpoint to the Kantian emphasis on self-apotheosizing transcendence, its role in the modern period may be conceived as an antidote to the kind of solipsism that Perry attributes to the increasing "disenchantment of nature" (479). Of course as Wordsworth's encounter with the blind beggar reveals, the effects of gazing without may also transcend a mere revitalization of the bonds between self and nature. To attend anew and with self-effacing care to that which is always already around us distils not only an ecological but also an *ethical* consciousness. Indeed, part of the everyday landscape to which our habits of solipsism tend to inure us is the face of the human other, a face of need no less than of wonder. To learn to gaze without is thus to find oneself always in community—always consolable and always responsible.

Notes

NOTES TO THE INTRODUCTION

1. Marjorie Hope Nicolson's *Mountain Gloom and Mountain Glory: The Development of the Aesthetics of the Infinite* (Ithaca, New York: Cornell University Press, 1959) initiated a critical reassessment of Burnet's treatise as a possible precursor of the Romantic sublime.
2. "Auguries of Innocence," *The Poetical Works of William Blake*, ed. John Sampson (Oxford: Clarendon, 1905) 288.
3. "Ode: Intimations of Immortality from Recollections of Early Childhood," *The Poetical Works of William Wordsworth*, ed. William Knight, vol. 4 (Edinburgh: William Paterson, 1882) 51.
4. A trend both reflected and supported by the publication of several new anthologies of Romantic poetry and prose, among them Jennifer Breen's editions of *Women Romantic Poets: 1785–1832* (London: J.M. Dent & Sons, 1992) and *Women Romantics 1785–1832: Writing in Prose* (London: J.M. Dent, 1996); Anne K. Mellor and Richard M. Matlack's *British Literature 1780–1830* (Fort Worth: Harcourt Brace, 1996); Duncan Wu's *Romantic Women Poets: An Anthology* (Oxford: Blackwell, 1997); Paula R. Feldman's *British Women Poets of the Romantic Era: An Anthology* (Baltimore: Johns Hopkins University Press, 1997); and Andrew Ashfield's *Romantic Women Poets, 1770–1838: An Anthology* 2 vols. (Manchester and New York: Manchester University Press, 1995, 1997).
5. Critics like Meena Alexander, conversely, claim that Romantic women writers voluntarily "withdrew from a vision that seemed to reach, without mediation to divinity." See *Women and Romanticism* (Savage, Maryland: Barnes & Noble, 1989) 167.
6. William Wordsworth, *The Prelude, 1805–6*, Ed. J.C. Maxwell (Penguin Books, 1971) XI, 478–480.
7. Wordsworth, *Poetical Works* V, 20.

8. Dorothy Wordsworth, "Floating Island at Hawkshead: An Incident in the Schemes of Nature" *Romanticism: An Anthology*, ed. Duncan Wu (Oxford: Blackwell, 1994) 501–2.
9. *The Prose of John Clare*, eds. J.W. and Anne Tibble (London: Routledge & Kegan Paul, 1951) 252.
10. John Keats, *The Letters of John Keats*, eds. Maurice B. Forman and Harry B. Forman, 2nd ed. (Oxford University Press, 1935) 69.
11. Where such attempts have been made, the "everyday" is typically defined by what it is *not*. Ludwig Wittgenstein, for example, as suddenly aborts his discussion of "the feeling of 'familiarity'" as he begins it, concluding that "[i]t is easier to get at a feeling of unfamiliarity or unnaturalness." See *Philosophical Investigations*, trans. G.E.M. Anscombe (Oxford: Blackwell, 1963) 156. Stanley Cavell, in like manner, attributes the "relative neglect [of the everyday] in contemporary intellectual life" to that fact that "we have become, by degrees, estranged from the world, the everyday, and thus experience it [only] as oddity." See *In Quest of the Ordinary: Lines of Skepticism and Romanticism* (University of Chicago Press, 1988) 153, 166.
12. 'The familiar is not the known.' Quoted in Henri Lefebvre's *Critique of Everyday Life*, trans. John Moore, 2nd ed. (London: Verso, 1991) 15.
13. The proposed second and third volumes were tentatively entitled *Fondements d'une sociologie de la quotidienneté* and *De la modernité au modernisme (Pour une métaphilosophie du quotidien)*.
14. "Lines Written in the Album at Elbingerode, in the Hartz Forest," *The Collected Works of Samuel Taylor Coleridge: Poetical Works*, ed. J.C.C. Mays, vol. 16.2.1 (Princeton University Press, 2002) 712.

NOTES TO CHAPTER ONE

1. Coleridge, *Collected Works* 16.2.1, 711–713.
2. Robert Southey, *The Poems of Robert Southey*, ed. Maurice H. Fitzgerald (London: Oxford University Press, 1909) 406.
3. In Kathleen Coburn, ed., *Inquiring Spirit: A New Presentation of Coleridge from His Published and Unpublished Writings* (Toronto: University of Toronto Press, 1979) 233.
4. This poem, from MS, is a variation of "On the Poet's Eye."
5. Coleridge, *Collected Works* 16.3.2, 824.
6. William Blake, *The Marriage of Heaven and Hell, Blake's Poetry and Designs*, eds. Mary Lynn Johnson and John E. Grant (New York and London: W.W. Norton &Co., 1979) 93.
7. See for example Wordsworth's Preface to the *Lyrical Ballads* where he argues, that "the human mind is capable of being excited without the application of gross and violent stimulants" (*Prose Works* I, 128).

8. *The Works of Anna Lætitia Barbauld*, vol. I (London: Longman, Hurst, Rees, Orme, Brown and Green, 1825) 209.
9. William Wordsworth, *Home at Grasmere* (MS. B), ed. Beth Darlington (Ithaca, NY: Cornell University Press, 1977) 38–40.
10. William Cowper, *The Task* (London: The Scolar Press Ltd., 1973) 93.
11. *The Complete Poetical Works of Burns* (Boston: Houghton Mifflin Company, 1897) 28.
12. Breen, *Women Romantic Poets* 43.

NOTES TO CHAPTER TWO

1. Samuel Taylor Coleridge, "Lecture Notes and Other Fragments," *Shakespearean Criticism*, ed. Thomas Middleton Raysor, vol. 1 (London: J.M. Dent & Sons Ltd, 1960) 198.
2. Alexander Pope, *An Essay on Criticism, The Poetical Works of Alexander Pope, with Memoir, Critical Dissertation and Explanatory Notes,* ed. George Gilfillan, vol. 2 (Edinburgh: James Nichol, 1856) 37.
3. Blake's work thus gives expression to what Bate characterizes in guarded terms as Romanticism's "occasional hope, inferable if unformulated, of disclosing *the naturalistic and almost independent 'truth' of the particular*" (emphasis added). See *From Classic to Romantic: Premises of Taste in Eighteenth-Century England* (New York: Harper & Row, 1961) 184.
4. William Blake, *Milton*, eds. E.R.D. Maclagan and A.G.B. Russell (London: A.H. Bullen, 1907) 29.
5. Burns, *Complete Poetical Works* 38.
6. Lonsdale 318.
7. One may also add to this sub-group poems like Blake's "Ah, Sun-Flower" and "The Lilly" from *Songs of Experience*.
8. In *Romantic Women Poets: An Anthology*, ed. Duncan Wu (Oxford: Blackwell, 1997) 254.
9. Lonsdale 458–459.
10. Wordsworth, *Poetical Works* III, 43.
11. Lawrence Buell likewise contends that such readings should emphasize the environment's interest and value independent of its human affiliations. See *The Environmental Imagination: Thoreau, Nature Writing, and the Formation of American Culture* (Cambridge, MA: Belknap-Harvard University Press, 1995).
12. In *Selected Poems and Prose*, eds. Eric Robinson and Geoffrey Summerfield (Oxford University Press, 1966) 184–185.
13. Barbauld, *Works* I, 55.
14. *John Clare: Poems Chiefly from Manuscript* (London: Richard Cobden-Sanderson, 1920) 197.

15. Susan Levin, for example, argues that the governing narrative in the *Grasmere Journals* is that of William's marriage to Mary Hutchinson, and that the story of the swallows, consequently, reflects "[Dorothy's] fears about what Mary's presence will do to her harmonious nest." See *Dorothy Wordsworth & Romanticism* (Rutgers State University, 1987) 28.
16. Dorothy Wordsworth, *Journals of Dorothy Wordsworth*, ed., Mary Moorman 2nd ed. (Oxford University Press, 1971) 137.
17. *The Lyrical Ballads, 1798–1805* (London: Methuen & Co., 1903) 173.
18. In Eric Robinson and Geoffrey Summerfield, eds., *Clare: Selected Poems and Prose* (Oxford University Press, 1966) 147–148. (I have here adopted the editors' practice of presenting Clare's work without correcting for spelling, grammar and punctuation.)
19. John Clare, *Birds Nest: Poems by John Clare*, ed. Anne Tibble (Mid Northumberland Arts Group, 1973) 20.
20. Clare, *Birds Nest* 63.
21. Clare, *Birds Nest* 45.
22. John Clare, *The Rural Muse* (London: Whittaker & Co., 1835) 31.
23. Clare, *Birds Nest* 39.
24. Clare, *Birds Nest* 25.
25. Clare, *Poems and Prose* 124.
26. Wordsworth, *Poetical Works* II, 254.
27. Wordsworth, *Poetical Works* II, 266–267.
28. Barbauld, *Works* I, 280.
29. Burns, *Complete Poetical Works* 43.
30. Clare, *Prose of John Clare* 199.
31. An interesting echo of Samuel Johnson's deference to the "common reader" as the final adjudicator of all literary merit. See "Life of Gray" in Donald Greene ed., *Samuel Johnson* (Oxford University Press, 1990) 768.
32. Clare, *Prose of John Clare* 194.
33. Clare, *Poems Chiefly from Manuscript* 86.
34. Clare, *Poems and Prose* 118–119.
35. In the *Natural History Letters*, for example, he distinguishes between a knowledge of "the manners & habits of Insects" and a knowledge of "the names they go bye," in other words, between branches of entomology based on direct observation and on reading or memorization, respectively. See *Prose of John Clare* 193.

NOTES TO CHAPTER THREE

1. In *Poems Chiefly Written in Retirement, With Memoirs of the Life of the Author* (London: W.H. Parker, 1801) 129. The "public turmoil" to which Thelwall refers included violent attacks against him, most recently at

Stockport, which forced him to withdraw from radical politics in the summer of 1797.
2. One of the ironies, as Michael Scrivener notes, is that Thelwall's visit to Alfoxden in fact resulted in the Wordsworths losing their lease to Alfoxden cottage and being forced to leave their home in 1798. See *Seditious Allegories: John Thelwall & Jacobin Writing* (Pennsylvania State University Press, 2001) 222.
3. This idea is reiterated in "On leaving the Bottoms of Glocestershire," written a few weeks later, wherein the poet distinguishes the "pious inutility" of the hermit's life from the "holier Industry" of cottagers whose honest labour does not preclude hospitality.
4. Barbauld, *Works* I, 202.
5. See Brown's description of Keswick Vale in his *Letter to Lord Lyttleton* (1767), Gray's journal of his Lakes tour in 1769, Hutchinson's *Excursion to the Lakes in Westmoreland and Cumberland* (1774), West's *Guide to the Lakes* (1778), Gilpin's *Observations* on the Lakes (1786) and Clarke's *Survey of the Lakes* (1787).
6. Wordsworth, *Poetical Works* I, 6.
7. A small, oval mirror carried by picturesque tourists who would hang it by the upper part of its case in order to frame ideal vistas or prospects; its operation depended, ironically, on the subject turning his/her back on the natural scene itself.
8. Anne D. Wallace characterizes these respective modes of pedestrianism as "deliberate excursive walking" and "walking as restrictive daily necessity." See *Walking, Literature, and English Culture: The Origins and Uses of Peripatetic in the Nineteenth Century* (Oxford, Clarendon Press, 1993) 166, 169.
9. Wu 499–500.
10. In *Leigh Hunt as Poet and Essayist*, ed., Charles Kent (London and New York: Frederick Warne and Co., 1889) 321.
11. Coleridge, *Collected Works* 16.1.1, 453.
12. The literal meaning of Viktor Shklovsky's term '*ostraneiye*,' generally glossed as defamiliarization. See "Art as Technique," *Literary Aesthetics: A Reader*, eds., Alan Singer and Allen Dunn (Blackwell Publishers, 2000) 224–229.
13. Wordsworth, *Poetical Works* I, 269.
14. Wordsworth, *Poetical Works* I, 269.
15. Wordsworth, *Poetical Works* V, 69.
16. From an extract entitled "The Affliction of Childhood." In *Romanticism: An Anthology*, ed. Duncan Wu (Oxford: Blackwell, 1995) 690.
17. *The Poetical Works and Other Writings of John Keats*, ed. H. Buxton Forman, vol. I (London: Reeves & Turner, 1889) 79.
18. Coleridge, *Collected Works* 16.1.1, 351.
19. Coleridge, *Collected Works* 16.1.1, 455.

NOTES TO CHAPTER FOUR

1. Notably, this passage from Job also expresses the distinctive *sermo humilis* or "lowliness" of the Biblical style through which, as Erich Auerbach argues, "the highest mysteries of the faith may be set forth." As a sort of parallel to the Incarnation, the *sermo humilis* attests rhetorically to "the holy sublimity [that] . . . is rooted in everyday life." See *Literary Language & Its Public in Late Latin Antiquity and in the Middle Ages*, trans. Ralph Manheim (Princeton University Press, 1965) 37, 65.
2. "The Flitting," *Poems Chiefly from Manuscript* 159.
3. Walt Whitman, "Song of Myself," *The Works of Walt Whitman* (Wordsworth Editions Ltd., 1995) 31, 32.
4. Wu 502.
5. This idea is reiterated in "Lines written (rather say begun) on the morning of Sunday April 6th, the third approach of Spring-time since my illness began" (c.1832) which Dorothy concludes with the consolation that "No prisoner am I on this couch / My mind is free to roam."
6. Wordsworth, *Poetical Works* IV, 48.
7. Wordsworth, *Poetical Works* IV, 47.
8. Wu 692.
9. Wu 693.
10. Wu 693.
11. Thomas De Quincey, *Confessions of an English Opium-Eater*, ed. Alethea Hayter (Penguin Books, 1986) 79.
12. Before De Quincey was eight years old, he lost his father and two of his beloved sisters. The death of nine-year-old Elizabeth to hydrocephalus is recalled in "The Affliction of Childhood" in *Suspiria de Profundis*. It is notable, moreover, that the deaths particularly of children had on De Quincey, even in adulthood, haunting and profoundly debilitating effects. When Catherine Wordsworth died in 1812 at the age of three, De Quincey slept nightly on her grave for a period of several months and claims to have seen her spectre. See Grevel Lindop, *The Opium-Eater: A Life of Thomas De Quincey* (New York: Taplinger, 1981) 202.
13. The noun he uses is "*rhabdomancy*," meaning "rod-magic" or divination in general.
14. *Lyrical Ballads* 322.
15. Wordsworth, *Poetical Works* IV, 50.
16. From "To the Same Flower" (1807), the second of three daisy poems. See Wordsworth, *Poetical Works* II, 317.
17. Wordsworth, *Poetical Works* III, 48.
18. See *Leigh Hunt as Poet and Essayist*, ed. Charles Kent (London and New York: Frederick Warne and Co., 1889) 45.

19. One may note a concomitant shift in the tone and subject matter of nineteenth-century pictorial art from the public and grand to what Robert Rosenblum characterizes as "the ordinary, the workaday, the comfortable" (172). German and Scandinavian countries adopted the term 'Biedermeier' to describe the burgeoning aesthetic investment in domestic life. As Rosenblum notes, 'Gemütlichkeit,' meaning a sort of warm and congenial coziness, began to pervade the canvases of genre, portrait and landscape painters alike. See Robert Rosenblum and H.W. Janson, eds. *19th-Century Art* (Englewood Cliffs, New Jersey: Prentice-Hall, 1984) 172–175.
20. *The Emigrants, A Poem in Two Books* (London: Printed for T. Dadell, 1793) 40.
21. Anne Grant, *Poems on Various Subjects*, (Edinburgh: J. Moir, 1803) 236–237.
22. Having married Reverend James Grant, a military chapain, in 1779, and moved with him from her home at Fort Augustus to the parish of Laggan in Inverness, Anne bore him twelve children, of whom four died. When her husband died in 1801, Anne lost their manse and was forced to raise the eight children by herself, all the while paying back her husband's accumulated debts through the publication of her poetry. See Wu, *Romantic Women Poets* 142–143.
23. "They mount, they shine, evaporate, and fall" (75). See *Samuel Johnson*, ed. Donald Greene (Oxford University Press, 1990) 14.
24. Hemans's later verse, notably, although it maintains the emphasis on domestic consolation, tends increasingly to conflate private and public spheres by linking the strength and security of the individual home to nationhood. In such works as "The Homes of England," for example, the home becomes a microcosm for the larger project of nation building. One of the notable ironies of Hemans's development of a politics of domesticity, as Susan Wolfson argues, is that where the conflation of these spheres leads to an appropriation of the private by the public, the result, typified in *Records of Women*, is a "failure of domestic ideals to sustain and fulfil women's lives." See "'Domestic Affections' and 'the spear of Minerva': Felicia Hemans and the Dilemma of Gender," *Re-Visioning Romanticism: British Women Writers, 1776–1837*, eds. Carol Shiner Wilson and Joel Haefner (University of Pennsylvania Press, 1994) 145.
25. Felicia Hemans, "The Domestic Affections," *The Poetical Works of Mrs. Hemans* (London: Frederick Warne and Co., 1800) 30.

NOTES TO THE CONCLUSION

1. See above, pages 21–22.
2. *Poems of Gerard Manley Hopkins*, ed. Robert Bridges (London: Humphrey Milford, 1918) 74.

3. An idea, notably, that also recalls Thomas Carlyle's *Sartor Resartus*, where it is proposed that "[our] daily life is girt with Wonder, and based on Wonder, and [our] very blankets *and breeches* are Miracles" (emphasis added). See *A Carlyle Reader: Selections from the Writings of Thomas Carlyle*, ed. G.B. Tennyson (Cambridge University Press, 1984) 311.

Bibliography

Abrams, M.H. *Natural Supernaturalism: Tradition and Revolution in Romantic Literature.* New York and London: W.W. Norton & Co., 1971.
———. *The Mirror and the Lamp: Romantic Theory and the Critical Tradition.* London: Oxford University Press, 1953.
Addison, Joseph. *The Spectator* No.412. *Eighteenth-Century English Literature.* Eds. Geoffrey Tillotson, Paul Fussell, Jr. and Marshall Waingrow. Harcourt Brace Jovanovich College Publishers, 1969. 335–337.
Agee, James and Walker Evans. *Let Us Now Praise Famous Men.* Ed. John Hersey. Boston, MA: Houghton Mifflin Co., 1988.
Alexander, Meena. *Women in Romanticism.* Savage, Maryland: Barnes & Noble, 1989.
Ardener, Shirley, ed. *Women and Space: Ground Rules and Social Maps.* Oxford: Berg Publishers, 1993.
Ashfield, Andrew and Peter de Bolla, eds. *The Sublime: A Reader in British Eighteenth-Century Aesthetic Theory.* Cambridge University Press, 1996.
Aubin, Robert A. *Topographic Poetry in Eighteenth-Century England.* New York: Modern Language Association, 1936.
Auerbach, Erich. *Literary Language and Its Public in Late Latin Antiquity and in the Middle Ages.* Trans. Ralph Manheim. Princeton University Press, 1965.
Bachelard, Gaston. *The Poetics of Space.* Trans. Maria Jolas. Boston: Beacon Press, 1969.
Baillie, John. *Essay on the Sublime.* New York: Kraus Reprint Corporation, 1967.
Barbauld, Anna Letitia. *The Works of Anna Lætitia Barbauld.* 2 vols. London: Longman, Hurst, Rees, Orme, Brown and Green, 1825.
Bate, Jonathan. *Romantic Ecology: Wordsworth and the Environmental Tradition.* London and New York: Routledge, 1991.
Bate, Walter Jackson. *From Classic to Romantic: Premises of Taste in Eighteenth-Century England.* New York: Harper & Row, 1961.
Blair, Hugh. *Lectures on Rhetoric and Belles Lettres.* Ed. Harold F. Harding. Vol. 1. Southern Illinois University Press, 1965.

Blake, William. "Marginalia: On *The Works of Joshua Reynolds.*" *Blake's Poetry and Designs*. Eds. Mary Lynn Johnson and John E. Grant. New York: W.W. Norton and Company, 1979. 438–444.

———. *Milton*. Eds. E.R.D. Maclagan and A.G.B. Russell. London: A.H. Bullen, 1907.

———. *The Marriage of Heaven and Hell. Blake's Poetry and Designs*. Eds. Mary Lynn Johnson and John E. Grant. New York: W.W. Norton and Company, 1979. 81–102.

———. *The Poetical Works of William Blake*. Ed. John Sampson. Oxford: Clarendon, 1905.

Bold, Alan. *A Burns Companion*. New York, NY: St. Martin's Press, 1991.

Bourdieu, Pierre. *Outline of a Theory of Practice*. Trans. Richard Nice. Cambridge University Press, 1977.

———. *The Field of Cultural Production: Essays on Art and Literature*. Ed. Randal Johnson. Columbia University Press, 1993.

Brain, Tracy. "'Or shall I bring you the sound of poisons?': Silent Spring and Sylvia Plath." *Writing the Environment: Ecocriticism and Literature*. Eds. Richard Kerridge and Neil Sammells. London and New York: Zed Books Ltd., 1998.

Breen, Jennifer, ed. *Women Romantic Poets 1785–1832 An Anthology*. London: J.M.Dent & Sons, 1992.

Brooks, Linda Marie. *The Menace of the Sublime to the Individual Self*. Lewiston, New York: The Edwin Mellen Press, 1996.

Brownlow, Timothy. *John Clare and Picturesque Landscape*. Oxford: Clarendon Press, 1983.

Buell, Lawrence. *The Environmental Imagination: Thoreau, Nature Writing, and the Formation of American Culture*. Cambridge, MA: Belknap-Harvard University Press, 1995.

Burke, Edmund. *A Philosophical Enquiry into the Origin of Our Ideas of the Sublime and the Beautiful*. Ed. J.T. Boulton. London, 1958.

Burns, Robert. *The Complete Poetical Works of Burns*. Boston: Houghton Mifflin Company, 1897.

Butler, Marilyn. *Romantics, Rebels and Reactionaries: English Literature and its Background 1760–1830*. Oxford University Press, 1981.

Cardinal, Roger. "Romantic Travel." *Rewriting the Self: Histories from the Renaissance to the Present*. Ed. Roy Porter. London and New York: Routledge, 1997. 135–155.

Carlyle, Thomas. *A Carlyle Reader: Selections form the Writings of Thomas Carlyle*. Ed. G.B. Tennyson. Cambridge University Press, 1984.

Cavell, Stanley. *In Quest of the Ordinary: Lines of Skepticism and Romanticism*. University of Chicago Press, 1988.

Certeau, Michel de. *The Practice of Everyday Life*. Trans. Steven F. Rendall. Berkeley: University of California Press, 1984.

Christ, Carol T. *The Finer Optic: The Aesthetic of Particularity in Victorian Poetry.* New Haven and London: Yale University Press, 1975.
Clare, John. *Birds Nest: Poems by John Clare.* Ed. Anne Tibble. Mid Northumberland Arts Group, 1973.
———. *John Clare: Poems Chiefly from Manuscript.* London: Richard Cobden-Sanderson, 1920.
———. *Poems of John Clare's Madness.* Ed. Geoffrey Grigson. London: Routledge & Kegan Paul, 1949.
———. *Selected Poems and Prose.* Eds. Eric Robinson and Geoffrey Summerfield. Oxford University Press, 1966.
———. *The Prose of John Clare.* Eds. J.W. and Anne Tibble. London: Routledge & Kegan Paul, 1951.
———. *The Rural Muse.* London: Whittaker & Co., 1835.
Clarke, Bruce. "Wordsworth's Departed Swans: Sublimation and Sublimity in *Home at Grasmere*." *Studies in Romanticism* 19.3 (1980): 355–374.
Coburn, Kathleen, ed. *Inquiring Spirit: A New Presentation of Coleridge from His Published and Unpublished Prose Writings.* Toronto: University of Toronto Press, 1979.
Coleridge, Samuel Taylor. *Biographia Literaria, Or Biographical Sketches of my Literary Life and Opinions.* London: J.M. Dent & Sons Ltd., 1965.
———. *The Collected Works of Samuel Taylor Coleridge: Poetical Works.* Ed. J.C.C. Mays. vol. 16. Princeton University Press, 2002.
———. *Shakespearean Criticism.* Ed. Thomas Middleton Raysor. 2 vols. London: J.M. Dent & Sons Ltd., 1960.
Cowper, William. *The Task.* London: The Scolar Press Ltd., 1973.
Curran, Stuart. "The I Altered." *Romanticism and Feminism.* Ed. Anne K. Mellor. Indiana University Press, 1988. 185–207.
Deguy, Michel. "The Discourse of Exaltation: Contribution to a Rereading of Pseudo-Longinus." *Of the Sublime: Presence in Question.* Trans. Jeffrey S. Librett. Albany, NY: State University of New York Press, 1993. 5–24.
De Luca, Vincent Arthur. *Thomas De Quincey: The Prose of Vision.* Toronto: University of Toronto Press, 1980.
———. *Words of Eternity: Blake and the Poetics of the Sublime.* Princeton University Press, 1991.
De Quincey, Thomas. *Confessions of an English Opium-Eater.* Ed. Alethea Hayter. Penguin Books, 1986.
———. *The English Mail-Coach* and Other Essays. London: J.M. Dent & Sons Ltd., 1961.
Dillard, Annie. *Pilgrim at Tinker Creek.* New York: Harper's Magazine Press, 1974.
Dowling, William C. *The Epistolary Moment: The Poetics of the Eighteenth-Century Verse Epistle.* Princeton University Press, 1991.
Eliot, George. *The Mill on the Floss.* Ed. Gordon S. Haight. Boston, MA: Houghton Mifflin Company, 1961.

Elledge, Scott. "The Background and Development in English Criticism of the Theories of Generality and Particularity." *PMLA* 62 (1947):147–182.
Ehnenn, Jill. "Writing Against, Writing Through: Subjectivity, Vocation, and Authorship in the Work of Dorothy Wordsworth." *South Atlantic Review* 64.1 (1999): 72–90.
Ezell, Margaret J. *Writing Women's Literary History*. Baltimore: Johns Hopkins University Press, 1993.
Fay, Elizabeth A. *A Feminist Introduction to Romanticism*. Oxford: Blackwell, 1998.
———. "Wordsworthian Lives: The Commonplace of Extraordinary Emotion." *Wordsworth Circle* 28.2 (1997): 87–91.
Ferguson, Frances. *Solitude and the Sublime: Romanticism and the Aesthetics of Individuation*. New York: Routledge, 1992.
Freeman, Barbara Claire. *The Feminine Sublime: Gender and Excess in Women's Fiction*. University of California Press, 1995.
Gerard, Alexander. *An Essay on Taste*. Ed. Walter J. Hipple. Scholars' Facsimiles & Reprints, 1963.
Gilpin, William. *Three Essays: on Picturesque Beauty; on Picturesque Travel; and on Sketching Landscape*. London, 1792.
Goodridge, John. *Rural Life in Eighteenth-Century Poetry*. Cambridge University Press, 1995.
Grant, Anne. *Poems on Various Subjects*. Edinburgh: J. Moir, 1803.
Gregg, Robert C. *Consolation Philosophy*. The Philadelphia Patristic Foundation, Ltd., 1975.
Gregory, Horace, ed. *The Triumph of Life: Poems of Consolation for the English-Speaking World*. New York: The Viking Press, 1943.
Haefner, Joel. "The Romantic Scene(s) of Writing." *Re-Visioning Romanticism: British Women Writers, 1776–1837*. Eds. Carol Shiner Wilson and Joel Haefner. University of Pennsylvania Press, 1994. 256–273.
Hardy, Thomas. *The Mayor of Casterbridge*. Ed. Norman Page. Broadview Press, 1997.
Hartmann, Geoffrey. "Wordsworth and Goethe in Literary History." *The Fate of Reading*. Chicago and London: University of Chicago Press, 1975. 179–200.
Hazlitt, William. *Table Talk; or, Original Essays. The Collected Works of William Hazlitt*. Eds. A.R. Waller and Arnold Glover. Vol. 6. London: J.M. Dent & Co., 1903. 5–330.
———. *The Spirit of the Age, 1825*. Menston, Yorkshire: Scolar Press Ltd., 1971.
Hemans, Felicia. *The Domestic Affections 1812*. New York: Woodstock Books, 1995.
———. *The Poetical Works of Mrs. Hemans*. London: Frederick Warne and Co., 1800.
Hertz, Neil. "The Notion of Blockage in the Literature of the Sublime." *Romanticism*. Ed. Cynthia Chase. London: Longman, 1993. 78–97.
Homans, Margaret. *Women Writers and Poetic Identity: Dorothy Wordsworth, Emily Brontë, and Emily Dickinson*. Princeton University Press, 1980.

Home, Henry. *Elements of Criticism*. Ed. Abraham Mills. New York: Huntington and Savage, 1846.
Hopkins, Gerard Manley. *Poems of Gerard Manley Hopkins*. Ed. Robert Bridges. London: Humphrey Milford, 1918.
Houghton, Walter E. and G. Robert Stange, eds. *Victorian Poetry and Poetics*. 2nd ed. Boston, MA: Houghton Mifflin Company, 1968.
Hunt, Leigh. *Leigh Hunt as Poet and Essayist*. Ed. Charles Kent. London and New York: Frederick Warne and Co., 1889.
Jarvis, Robin. *Romantic Writing and Pedestrian Travel*. London: MacMillan, 1997.
Johnson, Samuel. "Life of Thomson." *Samuel Johnson*. Ed. Donald Greene. Oxford University Press, 1990. 753–754.
———. Preface. *The Plays of William Shakespeare*. *Samuel Johnson*. Ed. Donald Greene. Oxford University Press, 1990. 419–456.
———. *Rambler* No.36. *Samuel Johnson*. Ed. Donald Greene. Oxford University Press, 1990. 190–193.
Jones, Christine Kenyon. "'Minute Obeisances': Beasts, Birds and Wordsworth's Ecological Credentials." *Romanticism* 4.1 (1998): 74–89.
Jones, John. *The Egotistical Sublime: A History of Wordsworth's Imagination*. London: Chatto & Windus, 1954.
Kant, Immanuel. *Critique of Aesthetic Judgment*. Trans. James Creed Meredith. Oxford: Clarendon, 1911.
Keats, John. *The Letters of John Keats*. Eds. Maurice B. Forman and Harry B. Forman. 2nd ed. Oxford University Press, 1935.
———. *The Poetical Works and Other Writings of John Keats*. Ed. H. Buxton Forman. 4 vols. London: Reeves & Turner, 1889.
Keith, W.J. *The Poetry of Nature: Rural Perspectives in Poetry from Wordsworth to the Present*. Toronto: University of Toronto Press, 1980.
Kelley, Theresa M. "Wordsworth, Kant, and the Romantic Sublime." *Philological Quarterly* 63.1 (1984):130–140.
Kelly, Gary, ed. *Felicia Hemans: Selected Poems, Prose, and Letters*. Broadview, 2002.
Land, Stephen K. *From Signs to Propositions: The Concept of Form in Eighteenth-Century Semantic Theory*. London: Longman, 1974.
Landry, Donna. *The Invention of the Countryside: Hunting, Walking and Ecology in English Literature, 1671–1831*. Palgrave, 2001.
Langbauer, Laurie. "Cultural Studies and the Politics of the Everyday." *Diacritics* 22.1 (1992): 47–65.
Lefebvre, Henri. *Critique of Everyday Life*. Trans. John Moore. 2nd ed. London: Verso, 1991.
Leighton, Angela. *Shelley and the Sublime: An Interpretation of the Major Poems*. Cambridge UP, 1984.
Levin, Susan M. *Dorothy Wordsworth & Romanticism*. New Brunswick: Rutgers, 1987.
Levinas, Emmanuel. *Ethics and Infinity*. Trans. Richard A. Cohen. Duquesne University Press, 1985.

Lindop, Grevel. *The Opium-Eater: A Life of Thomas De Quincey.* New York: Taplinger, 1981.
Liu, Alan. "On the Autobiographical Present: Dorothy Wordsworth's *Grasmere Journals.*" *Criticism* 26.2 (1984): 115–137.
———. *Wordsworth: The Sense of History.* Stanford, CA: Stanford University Press, 1989.
Longinus. *The Works of Dionysius Longinus On the Sublime.* Trans. W. Rhys Roberts. 2nd Ed. Cambridge UP, 1907.
Lonsdale, Roger, ed. *Eighteenth-Century Women Poets.* Oxford University Press, 1990.
Man, Paul de. "The Intentional Structure." *Wordsworth: A Collection of Critical Essays.* Ed. M.H. Abrams. Englewood Cliffs: Prentice-Hall, 1972. 133–144.
Mazel, David, ed. *A Century of Early Ecocriticism.* Athens and London: The University of Georgia Press, 2001.
McCormick, Anita Hemphill. "'I Shall Be Beloved—I Want No More': Dorothy Wordsworth's Rhetoric and the Appeal to Feeling in *The Grasmere Journals.*" *Philological Quarterly* 69.4 (1990): 471–493.
McGann, Jerome, J. *The Romantic Ideology, A Critical Investigation.* University of Chicago Press, 1983.
Mellor, Anne K. "Coleridge's 'This Lime-Tree Bower my Prison' and the Categories of English Landscape." *Studies in Romanticism* 18 (1979): 253–270.
———. "Immortality or Monstrosity? Reflections on the Sublime in Romantic Literature and Art." *The Romantic Imagination: Literature and Art in England and Germany.* Eds. Frederick Burwick and Jurgen Klein. Rodopi, 1996. 225–239.
———. *Romanticism and Gender.* New York and London: Routledge, 1993.
Mellor, Anne K. and Richard M. Matlack. *British Literature 1780–1830.* Fort Worth: Harcourt Brace, 1996.
Mitford, Mary Russell. *Our Village.* London: J.M. Dent & Sons Ltd., 1928.
Modiano, Raimonda. *Coleridge and the Concept of Nature.* Florida State University Press, 1985.
———. "The Kantian Seduction: Wordsworth on the Sublime." *Deutsche Romantik and English Romanticism.* Eds. Theodore G. Gish and Sandra G. Frieden. Munich: Fink, 1984. 17–26.
Monk, Samuel H. *The Sublime, A Study of Critical Theories in XVIII-Century England.* University of Michigan Press, 1960.
Nancy, Jean-Luc. "The Sublime Offering." *Of the Sublime: Presence in Question.* Trans. Jeffrey S. Librett. Albany, NY: State University of New York Press, 1993. 25–53.
Newlyn, Lucy. *Coleridge, Wordsworth and the Language of Allusion.* Oxford University Press, 1986.
Nicolson, Marjorie Hope. *Mountain Gloom and Mountain Glory: The Development of the Aesthetics of the Infinite.* Ithaca, New York: Cornell University Press, 1959.
Noyes, Russell, ed. "Introductory Survey: Major Aspects of English Romanticism." *English Romantic Poetry and Prose.* New York: Oxford UP, 1956. xix-xxxvi.

Owen, W.J.B. "A Sense of the Infinite." *The Wordsworth Circle* 21.1 (1990): 18–27.
Perry, Seamus. "Ordinary Consolation and its Modern Fate." *European Romantic Review* 14.4 (2003): 479–486.
Plotz, Judith. *Romanticism and the Vocation of Childhood*. New York: Palgrave, 2001.
Pope, Alexander. *The Poetical Works of Alexander Pope, with Memoir, Critical Dissertation and Explanatory Notes*. Ed. George Gilfillan. 2vols. Edinburgh: James Nichol, 1856.
Reynolds, Joshua. *The Discourses of Joshua Reynolds*. London: James Carpenter, 1842.
Rosenblum, Robert and H.W. Janson, eds. *19th-Century Art*. Englewood Cliffs, New Jersey: Prentice-Hall, 1984.
Ross, Kristin. "Streetwise: The French Invention of Everyday Life." *Parallax: A Journal of Metadiscursive Theory and Cultural Practices* 2 (1996): 67–75.
Ruskin, John. *Modern Painters*. Ed. David Barrie. New York: Alfred A. Knopf, 1987.
Rzepka, Charles J. *Sacramental Commodities: Gift, Text, and the Sublime in De Quincey*. Amherst, MA: University of Massachusetts Press, 1995.
Scrivener, Michael. *Seditious Allegories: John Thelwall & Jacobin Writing*. Pennsylvania State University Press, 2001.
Shklovsky, Viktor. "Art as Technique." *Literary Aesthetics: A Reader*. Eds. Alan Singer and Allen Dunn. Blackwell Publishers, 2000. 223–229.
Silverman, Hugh J. and Gary E. Aylesworth, eds. *The Textual Sublime: Deconstruction and its Differences*. New York: State University of New York Press, 1990.
Simpson, David. *Wordsworth and the Figurings of the Real*. Humanities Press Inc., 1982.
Smith, Charlotte. *The Emigrants, A Poem in Two Books*. London: Printed for T. Cadell, 1793.
Snyder, C.R. and Beth L. Dinoff. "Coping: Where Have You Been?" *Coping: The Psychology Of What Works*. Ed. C.R. Snyder. Oxford University Press, 1999.
Snyder, Franklyn Bliss. *The Life of Robert Burns*. New York, 1932.
Southey, Robert. *Poems of Robert Southey*. Ed. Maurice H. Fitzgerald. London: Oxford University Press, 1909.
Storey, Mark. *The Poetry of John Clare: A Critical Introduction*. New York: St Martin's Press, 1974.
Strickland, Edward. "John Clare and the Sublime." *Criticism: A Quarterly for Literature and the Arts* 29.2 (1987): 141–161.
Sychrava, Juliet. *Schiller to Derrida: Idealism in Aesthetics*. Cambridge University Press, 1989.
Thelwall, John. *Poems Chiefly Written in Retirement, With Memoirs of the Life of the Author*. London: W.H. Parker, 1801.
Thoreau, Henry David. *Journals*. Eds. John C. Broderick, Elizabeth Hall Witherell, William L. Howarth, Robert Sattlemeyer and Thomas Blanding. 8 vols. Princeton University Press, 1981.
———. *Walden and Other Writings*. Ed. Brooks Atkinson. New York: Modern Library Paperback Edition, 2000.

Wallace, Anne D. *Walking, Literature, and English Culture: The Origins and Uses of Peripatetic in the Nineteenth Century*. Oxford: Clarendon Press, 1993.

Weiskel, Thomas. *The Romantic Sublime: Studies in the Structure and Psychology of Transcendence*. Baltimore and London: Johns Hopkins University Press, 1976.

Whitman, Walt. "Song of Myself," *The Works of Walt Whitman*. Wordsworth Editions Ltd., 1995. 26–85.

Williamson, Karina. "The Tenth Muse: Women Writers and the Poetry of Common Life." *Early Romantics: Perspectives in British Poetry from Pope to Wordsworth*. Ed. Thomas Woodman. New York: St. Martin's, 1998. 185–199.

Wilson, Carol Shiner. "Lost Needles, Tangled Threads: Stitchery, Domesticity, and the Artistic Enterprise in Barbauld, Edgeworth, Taylor, and Lamb." *Re-Visioning Romanticism: British Women Writers, 1776–1837*. Eds. Carol Shiner Wilson and Joel Haefner. University of Pennsylvania Press, 1994. 167–190.

Wittgenstein, Ludwig. *Philosophical Investigations*. Trans. G.E.M. Anscombe. Oxford: Blackwell, 1963.

Wolfson, Susan J. "'Domestic Affections' and 'the spear of Minerva': Felicia Hemans and the Dilemma of Gender." *Re-Visioning Romanticism: British Women Writers, 1776–1837*. Eds. Carol Shiner Wilson and Joel Haefner. University of Pennsylvania Press, 1994. 128–166.

Wollstonecraft, Mary. *A Vindication of the Rights of Men*. Intro. Eleanor Louise Nicholes. Scholars' Facsimiles & Reprints, 1960.

Woof, Pamela. "Dorothy Wordsworth's *Grasmere Journals*: Readings in a Familiar Text." *The Wordsworth Circle* 20.1 (1989): 37–42.

———. "The Alfoxden Journal and its Mysteries." *Wordsworth Circle* 26.3 (1995): 125–133.

Wordsworth, Dorothy. *Journals of Dorothy Wordsworth*. Ed. Mary Moorman, 2nd ed. Oxford UP, 1971.

Wordsworth, William. *Home at Grasmere*. Ed. Beth Darlington. Ithaca, NY: Cornell University Press, 1977.

———. *The Poetical Works of William Wordsworth*. Ed. William Knight. 10 vols. Edinburgh: William Paterson, 1882.

———. *The Prelude*. Ed. J.C. Maxwell. Penguin Books Ltd., 1971.

———. *The Prose Works of William Wordsworth*. Eds. W.J.B. Owen and Jane Worthington Smyser. Vol. II. Oxford: Clarendon, 1974.

Wordsworth, William and Samuel Taylor Coleridge. *The Lyrical Ballads, 1798–1805*. London: Methuen & Co., 1903.

Wu, Duncan, ed. *Romantic Women Poets: An Anthology*. Oxford: Blackwell, 1997.

———. *Romanticism: An Anthology*. Oxford: Blackwell, 1995.

Index

A
Abrams, M. H., 4, 6
   The Mirror and the Lamp, 67s
   Natural Supernaturalism, 4, 6
   on wonders of everyday life, 4, 52, 61
Addison, Joseph, 1, 33
   The Spectator, 33–34
aesthetics
   Burkean, 4, 5, 36–40
   of coach travel, 114, 138–139
   Enlightenment, 36
   generalization, disdain for, 73
   of grandeur, 40, 53, 74
   history of, 1, 33
   Kantian, 4, 23–24, 40–44
   Longinian, 33, 37
   Romantic, 3, 7, 53, 65
   sublime, 7, 23–24, 33–34
   of walking, 118–119
Agee, James
   Let Us Now Praise Famous Men, 195–196, 199
"The Ants" (Clare), 106–107
"Apologia Pro Vita Sua" (Coleridge), 31
Ardener, Shirley, 45
"Ashboughs" (Hopkins), 193–194
Ashfield, Andrew, 1, 33, 36
"Aubade" (Larkin), 189
Aubin, Robert A.
   Topographical Poetry in Eighteenth-Century England, 120
Augustan writers, 33, 66, 172
Austen, Jane, 7

aut prodesse aut delectare (Horace), 67
"Ave Atque Vale" (Swinburne), 189

B
Bachelard, Gaston, 20, 79, 84–85, 87, 89, 98, 108, 175
   The Poetics of Space, 85, 196
Bailey, Benjamin, 153
Baillie, Joanna, 1, 15, 20, 53
   Fugitive Verses, 56
   "A Winter's Day," 56–62
Baillie, John, 1, 34–36
   An Essay on the Sublime, 34–36
Barbauld, Anna Letitia, 15, 20, 65
   "The Caterpillar," 99, 101–103
   "An Inventory of the Furniture in Dr. Priestley's Study," 81–83
   "To Mr. [S. T.] C[olerid]ge," 44–45
   "Washing Day," 115–118, 172
Barnes, Julian, 189
Bate, Jonathan
   Romantic Ecology, 97
Bate, Walter Jackson
   From Classic to Romantic, 68
the beautiful, 38, 39, 138, 139
Bekenntnis (Hegel), 17, 109
Betjeman, John
   "I. M. Walter Ramsden," 189
'the big six,' 6
Biographia Literaria (Coleridge), 20–21, 27–28, 31, 162, 163, 188
Birds Nest (Clare), 90–98
Blackwood's Magazine, 53–54

Blair, Hugh
   Lectures on Rhetoric and Belles Letters, 40
Blake, William, 6, 65, 139
   The Marriage of Heaven and Hell, 31
   renouncing of Reynolds's *Discourse*, 72–74, 75, 76
   'Self Annihilation' notion, 119
   world in a grain of sand, 3, 15, 74, 131, 189
Boethius
   The Consolation of Philosophy, 151
Boileau, 1
Bold, Alan, 103–104
Book of Revelation, 4
Bourdieu, Pierre
   Outline of a Theory of Practice, 17
Brain, Tracy, 78
Brontë, Emily, 16
Brooks, Linda Marie, 23, 27
Brown, John, 120
Brownlow, Timothy, 99
Burke, Edmund, 1, 4, 42, 108
   on coach travel, 138
   Enlightenment theory of taste, 36–37
   on minuteness, 37–40
   A Philosophical Enquiry into the Origins of Our Ideas of the Sublime and the Beautiful, 5, 18, 36–39, 68
   sublime, Burkean, 8, 15–16
Burnet, Thomas
   Sacred Theory of the Earth, 2
Burney, Fanny, 7
Burns, Robert, 15, 16, 20, 65
   The Cotter's Saturday Night," 53, 54–55, 60
   "To a Louse," 99, 103–105
   "To a Mountain Daisy," 76
Butler, Marilyn
   Romantics, Rebels and Reactionaries, 171
"To a Butterfly" (Wordsworth, W.), 99–101
Byron, Lord, 6

C

Cambridge Platonists, 2
Cappadocian Christian writers, 151
Cardinal, Roger, 3
Castle of Otranto (Walpole), 18

"The Caterpillar" (Barbauld), 99, 101–103
childhood
   experiences of every day life, 146, 153–154, 157–159, 161, 165
   and flowers, 153–154, 157, 158, 159, 161
   grandeur, 160
   memories, 77, 155–156, 160–161, 165, 167, 175
   Romantic, 162
Christ, Carol, 70, 76, 77
Cicero
   Tuscular Disputations, 151
Clare, John, 15, 16, 20, 65, 85, 190, 194
   "The Ants," 106–107
   Birds Nest, 90–98
   "The Daisy," 76
   'Dewdrops,' 13–14, 17
   "Farm Breakfast," 83–84
   "The Flitting," 154–155
   Natural History Letters, 99, 105, 106
   Nature Notes, 99, 105, 107
   Northampton Asylum Notebooks, 13
   "The Ragwort," 76, 78–79
   The Village Minstrel, 106
   "The Water Lilies," 76
   "The Wild Flower Nosgay," 76
Clarke, Bruce, 49
Clarke, James, 120
   Survey of the Lakes, 122
"Coaches and Their Horses" (Hunt), 137–138
Coleridge, Samuel Taylor, 15, 16, 194
   "Apologia Pro Vita Sua," 31
   Barbauld's "To Mr. [S. T.] C[olerid]ge," 44–45
   Biographia Literaria, 20–21, 27–28, 31, 162, 163, 188
   Brocken and, 24, 25, 26–27, 28
   Cumbria mountains, and journal writings of travels in, 28–31
   'The Eolian Harp,' 46
   'Frost at Midnight,' 46, 132
   Hazlitt's assessment of, 4
   "Lines Written in the Album at Elbingerode, in the Hartz Forest," 24–25
   on nature, general and essential as interpenetration, 65

Index

self-intuition, defined, 31–32
on Shakespeare's characters, 66–68
Thelwall's garden debates, 114–115, 117
"This-Lime Tree Bower My Prison," 144–150, 153
on Wordsworth's descriptions of everyday, 162–163
common observation, 105–106
community
  facilitation of, 146, 149
  familial, 8, 21, 44, 60–61, 62, 171, 172
  fellowship and, 149–150
  founding of, 147, 149
  genius and, 180
  home (nest) and, 85, 87, 97–98, 115
  imaginative, 21, 146
  of joy, 58, 147, 149
  and self, 144
  women as care givers and keepers of, 47, 57
  worship and, 61
The Companion (Hunt), 131
Concept of Nature (Modiano), 31, 43, 144
Confessions of an English Opium-Eater (De Quincey), 161–162
consolatio, 151–152, 189
Consolatio ad Apollonium (Plutarch), 151
consolation
  of addiction, 161
  of discovery, 152
  of familiar soil, 20, 151–185
  modern, 198
  philosophical writing on, 151–152
  of simple flowers, 151–185
  wonder and, 151–154
  Wordsworthian, 191–193
The Consolation of Philosophy (Boethius), 151
Consolation Philosophy (Gregg), 152
"The Cotter's Saturday Night" (Burns), 53, 54–55, 60
Cowper, William
  The Task, 53
Crantor
  On Grief, 151
Critique of Aesthetic Judgment (Kant), 5, 40, 42

Critique of Everyday Life (Lefebvre), 17–18
Cumbria, mountains of, 28
Curran, Stuart
  "terra incognita," 16, 18

D

"The Daisy" (Clare), 76
"To the Daisy" (Wordsworth, W.), 76, 77, 78
de Bolla, Peter, 1, 33, 36
de Certeau, Michel, 17–20, 131, 134, 137, 140
  on pedestrianism, 112–114, 118, 129, 143–144
  The Practice of Everyday Life, 18, 111
defamiliarization, 14, 164, 191
A Defense of Poetry (Shelley), 163
Deguy, Michel, 2
de Luca, Vincent, 73, 138–139
Dennis, John, 1
dephlogisticated air (oxygen), 81
De Quincey, Thomas, 15, 20
  Confessions of an English Opium-Eater, 161–162
  The English Mail-Coach, 138–142, 160
  on flowers, symbolic fecundity of, 162
  operatic experience of, 160–161
  Suspiria De Profundis, 141, 160–161
'Dewdrops' (Clare), 13–14, 17
Dillard, Annie
  Pilgrim at Tinker Creek, 196–198
Dinoff, Beth L., 159
Discourses (Reynolds), 70–73, 74, 75
The Domestic Affections and Other Poems (Hemans), 178–182
domestic literature, 46–47
Dowling, William C., 172

E

ego, 4, 5, 79, 153
The Egotistical Sublime (Jones), 4
Ehnenn, Jill, 85
"Elegiac Verses, In Memory of my Brother, John Wordsworth" (Wordsworth, W.), 167–170
Elements of Criticism (Home), 40
Eliot, George
  The Mill on the Floss, 191–192

Elliot, Obadiah, 137
The Emigrants (Smith), 171–172
Enfield, William, 56
The English Mail-Coach (De Quincey), 138–142, 160
Enlightenment, 1, 33, 36, 68, 108
environmental reading, 78
'The Eolian Harp' (Coleridge), 46
Erkenntnis (Hegel), 17, 109, 133
An Essay on Criticism (Pope), 69–70
An Essay on Taste (Gerard), 39–40
An Essay on the Sublime (Baillie), 34–36
Ethics and Infinity (Levinas), 185
eudaemonia, 159–160
Evans, Walker, 195
An Evening Walk (Wordsworth, W.), 120–125, 164
everyday life; *see also* experiences, of everyday life; wonders, of everyday life
   activities of, 17–19, 112–115, 118, 131, 132, 134, 188
   consolations, 44, 45, 152–153, 165, 172
   coping with, 158–159
   creativity in, 20, 113–115
   objects in, 20–21, 33–38, 42, 49
   perfectly ordinary and, 197
   Romantic vocation of childhood and, 159–160
   shining qualities of, 108–109
   spaces or settings, 18–19
   sublimity of, 11–17, 32, 151
   theorizations of, 17–18
   transcendent effects of, 188
   visionary dreariness of, 10, 11, 13, 15, 17, 58, 75, 188
The Excursion (Wordsworth, W.), 137
experiences, of everyday life
   of childhood, 146, 159, 161, 165
   of domesticity, 19–20, 45–47, 46
   of everyday reality, 182
   of home, 170
   of the landscape, 150
   of material reality, 158
   of relationship, 47
   of road walking, 167
   of sublimity, 39–40
   of supernature, 46
   of visionary power, 142
Ezell, Margaret, 188

F

Falconar, Harriet
   "The Snowdrop," 76, 77
   "The Violet," 76
"A Familiar Epistle to a Friend" (Grant), 172–178
familiarity, 33–34, 49, 79, 151–158, 191–192
   defamiliarization, 14, 164, 191
   film of, 162–163
   joy and, 158
   regeneration of, 155–157
   wonder of everyday life and, 151–153
   yearning for, in times of war, 171–172
familiar soil, 20, 151–185
"Farm Breakfast" (Clare), 83–84
Fay, Elizabeth
   A Feminist Introduction to Romanticism, 7
felicitous space, defined, 79
The Feminine Sublime (Freeman), 7
A Feminist Introduction to Romanticism (Fay), 7
Ferrier, Susan, 8
The Field of Cultural Production (Johnson), 17
flammable air (hydrogen), 81
"The Flitting" (Clare), 154–155
"Floating Island at Hawkshead" (Wordsworth, D.), 12–13, 17
Fortune magazine, 195
Freeman, Barbara, 7–8, 10
   The Feminine Sublime (Freeman), 7
French Revolution, 171
From Classic to Romantic (Bate), 68
'Frost at Midnight' (Coleridge), 46, 132
Fugitive Verses (Baillie), 56

G

genius, 72, 74, 75, 179–181, 188–189
Gerard, Alexander
   An Essay on Taste, 39–40
Gilpin, William, 120
grandeur

Index

aesthetics of, 40, 53, 74
of childhood, 160
enthusiasm of, 34–35
expressions of, variety and contrast in, 75
natural, 4, 24, 29, 31, 33, 40, 50
rhetoric of, 41
of sentiment, 162
simplicity of, 68
Grant, Anne, 15, 20, 193
"A Familiar Epistle to a Friend," 172–178
Grassini, Giuseppina, 161
Gray, Thomas, 120
Gregg, Robert C.
Consolation Philosophy, 152

H

Hardy, Thomas, 194
The Mayor of Casterbridge, 192–193
Hartmann, Geoffrey, 159
Hazlitt, William, 15, 20, 65
Coleridge, assessment of, 4
on genius, 75–76
"On Going a Journey," 129–131
renouncing of Reynolds's *Discourse,* 74–75
The Spirit of the Age, 163
Table Talk, 74, 75, 76, 129
Heaney, Seamus, 189
Hegel, G. W. F.
Bekenntnis, 17, 109
Erkenntnis, 17, 109, 133
Hemans, Felicia, 15, 20, 171
The Domestic Affections and Other Poems, 178–182
Hertz, Neil, 30
Hill, Geoffrey
"In Memory of Jane Fraser," 189
home, 24–26; *see also* space, and home
Baillie's "A Winter's Day," 56–62
Burn's The Cotter's Saturday Night," 53, 54–55, 60
call to return, 45
displacement from, 25, 43, 143, 147, 151
domesticity, 19, 20, 45, 46, 47, 85, 91, 173–178
family circle, 61–62
and house, 87
"mystic circle," 26, 53, 55, 62, 85, 98, 112, 114, 154
as sanctuary, 46, 55, 59, 87
sublime retirement in, 52
Wordsworth on, in *Home at Grasmere,* 47–53
Home, Henry
Elements of Criticism, 40
Home at Grasmere (Wordsworth, W.), 47–53, 127–128, 136
homelessness, 88
homemaking, 85, 87, 88–89, 91, 196
Hood, Thomas
"The Song of the Shirt," 117
Hopkins, Gerard Manley
"Ashboughs," 193–194
Sonnets of Desolation, 193
Horace
aut prodesse aut delectare, 67
Horace, Gregory
The Triumph of Life, 152
Household Gods
Hunt, Leigh, 15, 20
"Coaches and Their Horses," 137–138
The Companion, 131
"Our Cottage," 170–171
"Walks Home By Night," 131–134
Hunter, Anne, 175
Hutchinson, William, 120
Hymn to the Penates (Southey), 25–26, 46, 47

I

"I. M. Walter Ramsden" (Betjeman), 189
ideal excellence, 70
"In Memory of Jane Fraser" (Hill), 189
intimate immensity, 63, 90, 98
expression of, 79
Romanticism, engagement with, 20, 83–84, 99
of space, 20, 63, 79–84, 90, 98–99
unfathomable familiarity, 79
"An Inventory of the Furniture in Dr. Priestley's Study" (Barbauld), 81–83
Irigaray, Luce, 7

J

Jacobins, 81
Jarvis, Robin, 113–114, 119, 120, 121, 124–125, 129
Johnson, Randal
  The Field of Cultural Production, 17
Johnson, Samuel
  Lives of the Poets, 69
  Preface, *The Plays of William Shakespeare*, 66, 69
  Rambler No.36, 68, 69
  Rasselas, 68–69
  on Shakespeare's characters, 66–67
  The Vanity of Human Wishes, 25, 176
Jones, Christine Kenyon, 101
Jones, John, 6
  The Egotistical Sublime (Jones), 4
The Journals of Dorothy Wordsworth (Wordsworth, D.)
  Alfoxden, 125–126, 163, 187
  Grasmere, 85–90, 125–127, 187, 195

K

Kant, Immanuel, 1, 29–30, 77, 108
  aesthetics of, 4, 23–24, 40–44
  Critique of Aesthetic Judgment, 5–6, 40, 42
Keats, John, 4, 16, 20
  "On First Looking Into Chapman's Homer," 143
  on wonders of everyday life, and flowers of childhood, 153–154, 157, 158, 159, 161, 162
Kelley, Gary, 171
Kelley, Theresa M., 6

L

Lakeland travel writers, 120
Lamb, Charles, 144, 146–147, 149–150
Land, Stephen, 3
Landry, Donna, 149
Langbauer, Laurie, 16–17
Larkin, Philip
  "Aubade," 189
Lectures on Rhetoric and Belles Letters (Blair), 40
Lefebvre, Henri
  Critique of Everyday Life, 17–18
Leighton, Angela, 1–2
Leopold, Aldo
  A Sand County Almanac, 196
Let Us Now Praise Famous Men (Agee), 195–196
Levin, Susan, 47, 163
Levinas, Emmanuel
  Ethics and Infinity, 185
Lewis, Matthew, 18
"Lines Written a Few Miles Above Tintern Abbey" (Wordsworth, W.), 86, 137
"Lines Written in the Album at Elbingerode, in the Hartz Forest" (Coleridge), 24–25
Liu, Alan, 90, 120, 165
Lives of the Poets (Thomson), 69
Longinus, 1, 35, 36, 42, 45
  Peri Hupsous, 32–33
  smallness and transparency, 33, 37
"To a Louse" (Burns), 99, 103–105
Lovejoy, Arthur, 8
Lyrical Ballads (Wordsworth, W.), 59–60, 162, 163, 165

M

The Marriage of Heaven and Hell (Blake), 31
The Mayor of Casterbridge (Hardy), 192–193
Mazel, David, 78
McCormick, Anita, 88
McGann, Jerome, 3, 21–22, 188
Mellor, Anne K.
  masculine sublime, model of, 7, 8–9, 10, 15–16, 77, 146, 180
  Romanticism and Gender, 8
memory, spatial creativity of, 144–150
Michelet, Jules, 196
The Mirror and the Lamp, 67
The Mirror and the Lamp (Abrams), 67
Mitford, Mary Russell, 15, 20, 65, 79–80
  Our Village, 80
Modern Painters (Ruskin), 93
Modiano, Raimonda, 20, 147
  Concept of Nature, 31, 43, 144
Monk, Samuel, 1, 2
Monthly Magazine, 115

Index

Monthly Review, 56
"To a Mountain Daisy" (Burns), 76
"To Mr. [S. T.] C[olerid]ge" (Barbauld), 44–45

N

Nancy, Jean-luc, 1
Napoleonic Wars, 171
Natural History Letters (Clare), 99, 105, 106
natural immensity, 24, 30, 31, 35–36, 43
Natural Supernaturalism (Abrams), 4, 6
nature
  common motion in, 86
  generalized *(natura naturata)*, 65, 66, 68
  insect views, 99–109
  natural essence *(natura naturans)*, 65, 158
  nests, 85–98
  picturesque approach to, and walking, 120–125
  Reynolds on ideal excellence and genius, 70–73
  subordination of, to the human, 77
  wandering in, 120–124, 128–129
Nature Notes (Clare), 99, 105, 107
Northampton Asylum Notebooks (Clare), 13

O

"Ode to the Poppy" (O'Neill), 76, 77
"Ode" (Wordsworth, M.), 8, 157–158, 166
O'Neill, Henrietta
  "Ode to the Poppy," 76, 77
"On First Looking Into Chapman's Homer" (Keats), 143
"On Going a Journey" (Hazlitt), 129–131
On Grief (Crantor), 151
ordinariness
  consolation of, 148, 153, 189, 198–199
  depth of, 167–168
  disdain for, 32–33, 45, 190
  and extraordinary, intersections of, 81
  mysteries of, and science, 82
  as poetic stultification, 128
  Romantic fascination with, 194
  Weiskel's aesthetic marginalization of, 189, 198

wonder of, 62, 165, 198
"Ordinary Consolation and Its Modern Fate" (Seamus), 189
otherness, 100–106
  divine, 5
  formal, 4, 79
  in motion, 137, 142
  natural, 100, 135–136, 164, 196
  and self, bond between, 21, 44, 150, 167, 184–185
  of space and being, 129
  sublimated, 6, 7, 14
"Our Cottage" (Hunt), 170–171
Our Village (Russell), 80
Outline of a Theory of Practice (Bourdieu), 17
Owenson, Sydney, 8

P

particularity, 20, 68–73
  general form of, 70, 72, 73
  intimate immensity and, 62
  minuteness and, 71
pedestrianism, 112–114, 118–119, 124, 129, 132, 134, 143
Peri Hupsous (Longinus), 2, 32–33
Perry, Seamus, 152, 190, 194
  "Ordinary Consolation and Its Modern Fate," 189, 198–199
Phaedo (Plato), 151
Philosophical Enquiry, 138
A Philosophical Enquiry into the Origins of Our Ideas of the Sublime and the Beautiful (Burke), 5, 18, 36–39, 68
the picturesque, 120, 121, 122, 123, 124
Pilgrim at Tinker Creek (Dillard), 196–198
Plato
  Phaedo, 151
The Plays of William Shakespeare (Shakespeare), 66, 69
Plotz, Judith, 159, 162
Plutarch
  Consolatio ad Apollonium, 151
poetics
  of everyday life, 182
  focus, refinement of, 65
  of genius, 20–21, 28, 31, 180

of imagination, 4, 78
of insight, 31, 76
of pedestrianism, 124
of self, 6, 9
of sensitivity to the numinous, 107
stultification, 128
of vision, 31, 54
The Poetics of Space (Bachelard), 85, 196
"The Pond in Winter" (Thoreau), 190–191
Pope, Alexander
   An Essay on Criticism, 69–70
   The Rape of the Lock, 173
The Practice of Everyday Life (de Certeau), 18, 111
The Prelude (Wordsworth, W.), 100
   blind beggar, and face-to-face encounter of self and other, 182–185
   everyday life, solace of, 15, 163, 165–167
   everyday life sublimity, 9–11
   Gondo Ravine passage, 4
   home, space and function of, 51
   ice-skating, 114, 134–137
   imaginative recovery, 165–166
   Lakeland travel writers and, 120
   Mount Snowdon passage, 4, 11
   portraits of mendicants, 59–60
   Romantic childhood and, 162
"The Primrose of the Rock" (Wordsworth, W.), 76

R
Radcliffe, Ann, 7, 18
"The Ragwort" (Clare), 76, 78–79
Rambler No.36 (Johnson), 68, 69
The Rape of the Lock (Pope), 173
Rasselas (Johnson), 68–69
'The Recluse' (Wordsworth, W.), 11, 47
Reynolds, Joshua
   Discourses, 70–73, 74, 75
Rice, James, 153
Robinson, Eric, 90
Robinson, Mary
   "The Snowdrop," 76, 77
robust consciousness, 132–133
Romantic Ecology (Bate), 97
Romanticism
   debased, 16, 188
   displaced and reconstituted theology of nature and imagination, 152
   English, history of, 23
   in everyday life, 189–192
   feminine, 7–8, 46–47
   intimate immensity, engagement with, 20, 83–84, 99
   of self, 3, 23
   sentimental primitivism associated with, 45
   sublime, 2, 3–4, 6, 21
Romanticism and Gender (Mellor), 8
Romantics, Rebels and Reactionaries (Butler), 171
The Romantic Sublime (Weiskel), 4, 6, 15
Ross, Kristin, 112
Ruskin, John
   Modern Painters, 93

S
Sacred Theory of the Earth (Burnet), 2
"To the Same Flower" (Wordsworth, W.), 76, 78, 167
A Sand County Almanac (Leopold), 196
Scafell's summit, 28–31
Scott, Walter
   "The Violet," 76
self
   childlike, 21, 130
   and community, 144
   displacement of, 26, 159, 170
   and nature, 21, 144, 147, 199
   and other, bond between, 21, 44, 150, 167, 184–185
   representational factors, breakdown of, 25
   romantic, 3, 4, 9, 23
self-aggrandizement, 4, 8, 10, 16, 119
self-apotheosis, 3–4, 29, 79, 119, 180, 199
self-consolation, 175, 177
self-expression, 62, 87, 135
self-forgetting, 119
self-intuition, defined, 31–32
Seward, Anna, 175
   "Sonnet: To the Poppy," 76–77
Shakespeare, William, 66–68

The Plays of William Shakespeare, 66, 69
The Tempest, 66
Shelley, Percy Bysshe, 6, 139
  A Defense of Poetry, 163
simple flowers, 20, 151–185
Simpson, David, 184
"To the Small Celandine" (Wordsworth, W.), 76
smallness, 33, 37–39
Smith, Charlotte
  The Emigrants, 171–172
"The Snowdrop" (Falconar), 76, 77
"The Snowdrop" (Robinson), 76, 77
"To a Snowdrop" (Wordsworth, W.), 76
Snyder, C. R., 159
solitary objects, 76–79
"The Song of the Shirt" (Hood), 117
"Sonnet: To the Poppy" (Seward), 76
Sonnets of Desolation (Hopkins), 193
"Sonnet to the Strawberry" (Williams), 76, 77
soul, 34–35
Southey, Robert
  home as a 'mystic circle," 26, 53, 55
  Hymn to the Penates, 25–26, 46, 47
space, and home, 45, 48, 49–51, 61
  comprehensive compartmentalization of, 80
  domestic, 19, 20, 53, 62, 79–84, 90, 92–96, 175
  felicitous, 20, 53, 79, 87, 88
  intimate immensity of, 20, 63, 79–84, 90, 98–99
  labour, role in, 114–118
  lines of texts of history and power, 81–82
  material reality, 111, 134, 157–159, 190, 195
  nests, 85–98
  recollected, 20, 143–144, 147, 150, 156
  for rest and retreat, 171–172, 178–182
  security, invasion of, 90–98
The Spectator (Addison), 33–34
The Spirit of the Age (Hazlitt), 163
Storey, Mark, 65
subjectivity, 6, 67, 184, 196
sublime
  aesthetic, 7, 23–24, 33–34

astonishment, 37
Baillie's essay on, 34–36
blockage, 30
Burkean, 8, 15–16
Coleridgean, 30
concept of, 2–3, 4–5
dynamic, 5, 30, 41, 42
egotistical, 4, 5, 79, 153
in everyday life, 11–17, 32, 151
fashionableness of, 1
feminine, 7–8, 46–47
Kantian, 1, 7–8, 40
Keatsean, 7
labouring movements, 114–118
Longinian, 2–3
masculine, 7, 8–11, 15–16, 77, 146, 180
mathematical, 5, 41
mountaintop, 6, 10, 23–32, 43, 47, 53, 108
quotidian, 11, 15, 17, 19, 23, 43, 46, 53, 62, 79, 108, 189, 197, 199
Romantic, 2, 3–4, 6, 21
wonder, 13, 152, 154
Wordsworthian, 4, 7, 9–12
Summerfield, Geoffrey, 90
supernature, 4–5, 23, 30–31, 39, 42–43, 46, 53
Survey of the Lakes (Clarke), 122
Suspiria De Profundis (De Quincy), 141, 160–161
Swinburne, Charles
  "Ave Atque Vale," 189
symmetry
  between critic and the work, 22, 188
  between past and present, 188, 198

T

Table Talk (Hazlitt), 74, 75, 76, 129
The Task (Cowper), 53
taste, Enlightenment theory of, 36–37
The Tempest (Shakespeare), 66
The Indicator, 137
Thelwall, John, 15, 20, 114–115, 117, 118
"This-Lime Tree Bower My Prison" (Coleridge), 144–150, 153
Thomson, James
  Lives of the Poets, 69

Thoreau, Henry David, 99
'insect view,' 99
Journals, 99
   "The Pond in Winter," 190–191
   Walden, 190, 196
Tibble, Anne, 90
Topographical Poetry in Eighteenth-Century England (Aubin), 120
transcendentalism
   encounter, 4, 16, 40, 42–43, 122
   in everyday life, effects of, 188
   experience, 3, 4, 7–9, 43
   Kantian, 20, 40, 41, 44
   otherness, 6
   power within, 5
   visions, 46, 161
transcendentalist, 20, 40
transportation, modes of; *see also* walking
   coach, 114, 137, 138–142
   ice-skating, 114, 134–137
   incarceration and, 112, 114
   pedestrianism and, 112–114, 118–119, 124, 129, 132, 134, 143
travel, *see* transportation, modes of
Tusculan Disputations (Cicero), 151

U
Unitarian movement, 81

V
The Vanity of Human Wishes (Johnson), 25, 176
The Village Minstrel (Clare), 106
A Vindication of the Rights of Man (Wollstonecraft), 39
"The Violet" (Falconar), 76
"The Violet" (Scott), 76, 77

W
Walden (Thoreau), 190
walking
   aesthetics of, 118–119
   creative power of, 118, 119
   paradox of, 134
   picturesque approach to nature and, 120–124
   radical, 113–114
   regular perambulation, 124–126, 129–134
   self-forgetting and, 119
   wandering and rambling, 120–129
"Walks Home By Night" (Hunt), 131–134
Walpole, Horace
   Castle of Otranto, 18
"Washing Day" (Barbauld), 115–118, 172
"The Water Lilies" (Clare), 76
Weiskel, Thomas, 23, 79, 189, 198
   on daffodils, effect on the modern, 21–22, 187, 188
   The Romantic Sublime, 4, 6, 15
West, Thomas, 120
"A Whirl Blast From Behind the Hill" (Wordsworth, W.), 163–165
"The Wild Flower Nosgay" (Clare), 76
Williams, Helen Maria, 8
   "Sonnet to the Strawberry," 76, 77
Williams, Helen Maria, 175
Williamson, Karina, 16, 19, 46, 188
Wilson, Carol Shiner, 46–47
Wilson, John
   Blackwood's Magazine commentary, 53–54
"A Winter's Day" (Baillie), 56–62
Wolfson, Susan J., 45–46
Wollstonecraft, Mary
   A Vindication of the Rights of Man, 39
wonders, of everyday life
   Abrams on, 4, 52, 61
   consolation of, 151–154
   experiences and, 22, 194, 198
   in familiarity, 151–153
   flowers of childhood and, 153–154, 157–159, 161, 162
   in ordinariness, 62, 165, 198
   sublime, 13, 152, 154
Woof, Pamela, 87
Wordsworth, Dorothy, 15, 20, 47, 65, 194; *see also The Journals of Dorothy Wordsworth*
   "Floating Island at Hawkshead," 12–13, 17
   "Thoughts on my Sickbed," 155–157
Wordsworth, William, 15, 20, 65; *see also The Prelude*

Index

"To a Butterfly," 99–101
"Elegiac Verses, In Memory of my Brother, John Wordsworth," 167–170
Epitaphs of, 163, 167
An Evening Walk, 120–125, 164
everyday, descriptions of, 162–163
The Excursion, 137
Home at Grasmere, 47–53, 127–128, 136
"Lines Written a Few Miles Above Tintern Abbey," 86, 137
Lucy poems, 13

Lyrical Ballad, 59–60, 162, 163, 165
"Ode," 8, 157–158, 166
"The Primrose of the Rock," 76
'The Recluse,' 11, 47
"To the Same Flower," 76, 78, 167
"To the Small Celandine," 76
sublime, Wordsworthian, 4, 7, 9–15
"To a Snowdrop," 76
"To the Daisy," 76, 77, 78
"A Whirl Blast From Behind the Hill," 163–165
Wu, Duncan, 25

For Product Safety Concerns and Information please contact our EU
representative GPSR@taylorandfrancis.com
Taylor & Francis Verlag GmbH, Kaufingerstraße 24, 80331 München, Germany

www.ingramcontent.com/pod-product-compliance
Lightning Source LLC
Chambersburg PA
CBHW071353290426
44108CB00014B/1526